Praise for Doris E. Dempsey's classrc strategies, from around the nation:

This woman is dynamite! As a 30+ year teacher of everything from alternative classes to *ELA [English Language Acquisition] math, rural and inner-city, I know what it takes to survive and be successful as a teacher. This woman is right-on. Everyone should have this seminar.* **–Middle School Language Arts Teacher**

So many concrete, good methods to use. Doris really knows kids and what we can expect (or not!) from our students. **–3rd grade Private School Teacher**

You have given me HOPE after being a student teacher watching a shaming example day after day. Thank you. **–Elementary Art Teacher**

I was held captive by the instructor, content, and presentation. What an informative afternoon. I plan to begin to immediately rethink my teaching and parenting style and use the tools learned today. I can't wait to go home to my teenage son (soon to be 16), and tell him who he is and raise his self-concept, because lately I haven't been doing that. He will be shocked!!! **–6th grade Science Teacher**

Wow! I have learned so much! You have made me really excited to start the school year. I feel powerful! Thanks! **–6th Grade Math Teacher**

Information was vital. The presentation was timely. Not only was the overall philosophy clear, direction to utilize classroom management targeted workable solutions. The best, ever! **–Middle School Principal**

Enlightening. Fantastic. I did not want her to stop instructing! She is totally awesome! **–Middle School Special Education Paraprofessional**

It would be a disservice to our community and staff to not internalize your experiences for the greater being of our community. We are all good teachers, you can make us better. Thank you. **–High School P.E./Health Teacher**

OUTRAGEOUS—one of the most helpful I've been able to attend in 28 years.
–Middle School Music Teacher

Having taught since 1975, I've been to many in-services and presentations, most of which were not useful. Doris has ideas that I took back to class and used, easily, and they made a difference—thank you! **–High School Art Teacher**

Outstanding information. Why didn't I have a class like this in college? Doris is very informed and talented at presenting. This is very helpful.
–Private High School Teacher

Absolutely appropriate for all ages and for all teachers.
–Middle School Band Teacher

Doris Dempsey is a ray of sunshine and positive energy for the teaching profession. Her lectures are so forceful that you are not aware you have sat for hours. An absolutely wonderful experience.
–7th Grade Math Teacher

Doris is like a preacher for teachers! Inspiring and motivating. I like the catch phrases e.g. "I understand", "Bring the light!"
–Early Childhood Education Teacher

Wish I'd had her in 1960. It took me a long time to figure it out.
–6th grade Private School Teacher

Someone is finally addressing the issue of humanity—kindness, love, and acceptance. It was wonderful!
–Elementary Special Education Teacher

Everything you said was so true. I recognized several mistakes I've been making and learned how to fix them. Thank you.
–5th grade Teacher

Doris' positive attitude is infectious and was a great reminder of 'how to be' with students. I saw some of my bad habits used as examples and that made me want to quickly remove them from my 'bag of tricks.'
–8th grade Science Teacher

Great! Why don't they teach this stuff at school!
–6th–8th grade Computers Teacher

Very dynamic presentation. Solid, clear information. Great humor. Thank you so much! Doris had an example and direct solution to every classroom problem or concern.
–8th grade Special Education Teacher

CLASSROOM DISCIPLINE MADE EASY A SYSTEM THAT WORKS FOR THE INNER CITY OR *ANY* CITY

Second Edition, Revised and Expanded

by

DORIS E. DEMPSEY

DECK PUBLISHING, DENVER, COLORADO

Published by:
Deck Publishing
P.O. Box 390024
Denver, CO 80239
Orders Ph/Fax 303-574-0785

Library of Congress Cataloging-in-Publication Data

Dempsey, Doris E.
Classroom Discipline Made Easy: A System That Works For The Inner City Or *Any* City/ Doris E. Dempsey 2nd Edition, Revised and Expanded
Includes Appendix

Library of Congress Control Number: 2006901397
ISBN
0-9654015-2-9
978-0-9654015-2-4
1. Student Behavior Management
2. Classroom Discipline Pre-School, K-12, Elementary – High School, University— Handbooks, Manuals, Textbooks
3. Title
Printed in the United States of America

To God, the only true author,
my mother who is my example and hero,
and
my sons, Chris and Ken, who have been
a source of continuous joy in my life.

CONTENTS

Introduction

**"School Days, School Days
Good Old Golden Rule Days"**

School days just don't seem to be what they used to be... and they're not. So there. So what! There's no time for all of this bemoaning the end of the 50's or whenevers. We're here now, and the students are here. Let's get on with it. The good news is that we're all still human beings, not some alien life forms or gross mutations of the people of the 50s needing to be studied and ultimately altered.

Ready for more good news? Students are still good people who really *want* to learn and to be under the "protective custody" of good and fair disciplinarians. The statistics continuing to confront and startle teachers, parents, and just plain citizens, are not as they seem. Take a moment to visualize just one school—any type, anywhere. Is it a school of 300, 3000, or some number of students in between? Now multiply that sum by the number of schools in your district, state, country. What an enormous aggregate of students are in this great land. When one thinks of the many young people being taught each and every day, the news reports of juvenile delinquents don't seem as horrendous. The simple truth, right in front of our eyes, is that good children and young adults far, far, far outnumber the bad. Their reputation has somehow gotten tarnished, and many well-meaning citizens have joined voices to predict society's demise under the leadership of the next generation. However, if you take a moment to silence the voices and *notice* what is actually occurring, you will see young people going about the business of being children and teens in ways not too dissimilar from those of the past. Further, if we will but focus on the positive, we'll begin to see all of the beautiful and remarkable things being accomplished by the majority of today's youth.

We, as teachers, will be faced with normal, healthy and, yes, sometimes mischievous young minds. That's what we love. That's what we crave. That's why we became teachers! Now let's forget about feeling frightened and threatened, and get on with the business of learning how to help these young people develop into self–actualized, productive students. Ready, Set, SMILE!

Chapter One

RUNNING START

Though most teachers entering the profession do so either wondering what in the world to do if students choose to misbehave, or with a firm plan of action for dealing with the "evil doers," the simple and comforting truth is that PREVENTION IS THE KEY TO EFFECTIVE CLASSROOM DISCIPLINE.

To be sure, there are not enough consequences on this remarkable planet to impel or coerce students or anyone else, for that matter, into being model citizens and paragons of virtue. Just consider, for a moment, the consequences for *adult* misbehavior: warnings, fines, incarceration, loss of property or privilege. Yet, we have scores of adults misbehaving daily. What's my point? **Prevention is the key.** Teachers must create a management system and savvy classroom climate which make students **not want to misbehave**, and affords no *opportunity for* misbehavior. If you abide in this frame of mind, and avoid the pitfalls of negative thinking by refusing to submerge yourself in the quicksand of allowing thoughts, what you hear, and your conversation to vilify today's students, you will be able to develop routines and procedures that will keep your students on the straight and narrow, because as quiet as it's kept, that's *exactly* where they wish to be. Let's begin with the very first step in this prevention process, one that is absolutely essential.

Tell Them Who They Are

As an English teacher, I relished the ideas and language found in certain pieces of classic literature. One of the great authors, in my opinion, is Goethe. So, it is with his words that I commence our journey along the path of preventing student misbehavior.

**" Treat a man as he is, and he will remain as he is.
Treat a man as he can and should be,
and he will become as he can and should be."**

What part does this old and sage advice play in helping teachers to create a disciplined environment for students? We must tell them who they are. I repeat: we **must tell them who they are**. Our students need to *hear* that they are just who we wish them to be. They need to be told that they are students, scholars, good listeners, polite, good sharers, interested in reading and learning, good thinkers, cooperative, fun to be around, fun to teach, willing to try new things, hard workers, and so on. In so doing, we must be truthful, genuine, and consistent, but definitely not patronizing. How can this be accomplished? If you think about it, we tell them who they are with everything we say or do. The problem is that most of the time the message is negative. *" Where's your pencil? Did you know you were coming to school today?" "If you act like 3rd graders, I'll treat you like 3rd graders." "I'm going to teach those who want to learn and are paying attention." "I can't turn my back for one minute without you getting out of your seats!" "I'll just wait for you to decide that you want to cooperate and learn."* These are all statements that I've heard real teachers say over and over again to their students. Of course, those making the statements believe themselves to be agents of motivation. Many are of the mindset that if students are made to experience shame, guilt, or some other form of debasing emotion, those same students will realize the error of their ways, shrink in humility, and "straighten up and fly right," as my grandmother used to say. IT DOESN'T WORK. **Students BECOME who you think they are**. If you think that they're unruly, impolite, uncooperative, or difficult to teach, they will just show you unruly, impolite and uncooperative, in spades! Conversely, if you believe them to be bright, fun, interested, and good learners, *that's* the face they'll show you. I believe that human beings *need* to feel good about themselves in order to thrive.

Upon noticing that one of my students who was never absent from class, was missing one day, I asked his classmates, "Where is Brad?" "He got suspended, Miss Dempsey," was the answer. As I literally gasped in disbelief, one young lady responded, "He's really not that nice, Miss Dempsey. He's just good to you because you think he's nice." Again, I repeat, treat a man as he can and should be, and he will become as he can and should be.

Each day we have a gazillion opportunities to set our students up for success so that we can tell them who they are in the positive. That's what it requires, you see. If you have to step outside of the room during a lesson, take a moment to inform your students in a respectful manner, and to give them a brief, independent activity to do, based upon what you were teaching. Quickly move among your learners to guide even reluctant students toward the task, using encouraging language. Thus, they will be "legally" occupied, and on task while you are detained. Then, when you reenter the classroom, you can tell them what wonderful students they are and how much you appreciate them. Likewise, if a student walks into the room without materials, it's just as easy to say, *"I see that you forgot your book. Please get one from the shelf to use for today, so that you can participate in the lesson with us."* By using these words, you're relaying the message that you believe this student *cares* about learning and *wishes* to participate. This would be said with kindness and graciousness—two commodities, which when genuinely employed, go so much further toward developing a student who will eventually be prepared for class, than the use of sarcastic or punitive jargon such as, " Did you know you had class today? I'm tired of you coming to class without your book. Maybe you should just sit there and get an F!" Sound harsh? These very words, or something similar is said by far too many well-meaning educators, on a daily basis. What's the result? A well-behaved student? I think not. The result is a student who feels denigrated, angry, or sullen, at best. The goal of the instructor's comments, if one of engendering good behavior, is not met. In fact, just the opposite is accomplished. You have a student whose self-concept has been lowered, and who is now either bound and determined to disrupt or bound and determined to not participate at all. It's **human nature**. On the other hand, when treated with dignity, respect, and given the benefit of the doubt, **students respond in like kind**, and you will have seized the opportunity to *model* the kindness, graciousness, and respect you wish *them* to use.

What about those students who come unprepared to class expecting you to take care of them? How are they supposed to learn to be responsible? I'll deal with the notion of student responsibility a little later. Right now, however, here's a powerful tool for you to utilize. Once you've given the student an opportunity to join the class in a positive fashion, the instructional portion of the lesson is concluded, and the other students are working independently or getting ready to move to another class, ask the student if you may speak with him *"for just one minute."* These words are nonthreatening, and will allow the student to maintain a positive, open attitude. You may even wish to add that he's not in trouble. (a common question many students ask when requested to be spoken with) Some, believing themselves to be in hot water, come spoiling for a fight, which is certainly not your objective. Rather, it is a time when, in a respectful, calm tone, you ask the student why he/she was *sans* textbook, **accept** the answer without judgment, sarcasm, or any other negative reaction, reset the guideline of students bringing the book to class every day, and offer a brief suggestion as to how the student can accomplish this. Initiate this mini conversation by genuinely telling the student who he is. " *I can see that you are a good student, and I'm glad you're in my class.*" Then, proceed to the resetting phase of the chat. *"From now on I'd like for you to..."* Here, be very specific. Phrases such as "be prepared," "be respectful of others," are vague and incomprehensible in regard to how *you* interpret these qualities. Tell the student *exactly* what you'd like him/ her to do, in behavioral terms. *"I'd like for you to have your textbook, notebook, and pencil in class every day whether you think they'll be used or not. That way you'll always be prepared for whatever I ask you to do. Would it help if you were allowed to drop off your book first thing in the morning and store it on the back table?"* Remain brief, kind, nonjudgmental, and nonpunitive, and be sure to write a pass, if one is required. Then, stand back and reap the benefits of your students knowing that you **honestly believe** that they are the best, and that you'll always treat them with the respect they deserve and are expected to bestow upon others.

A final thought: There's nothing wrong with having an appropriate consequence for repeat offenders of minor rules. Be sure that it is **fair**, the student is **forewarned**, it is age/grade **appropriate,** and administered **without malice**. In other words, it would be okay to dock a middle or high school student 10 points on the assignment, to borrow a textbook, but it is not prudent to give the same consequence to an elementary school student who has to depend on a parent or guardian to prepare and send materials.

Once telling students who they are in the positive becomes second nature, instead of what society seemingly promotes via sitcoms and other types of programming, (e.g. name-calling, labeling, use of insults, criticizing and judging to procure good behavior), you'll notice your students blossoming right before your eyes, parroting benevolence, consideration, and forbearance, even accepting consequences with quietude. At this point, you'll realize that the first and most essential step toward prevention is firmly in place. **Tell Them Who They Are.**

When you raise self-concept, you raise behavior.
When you lower self-concept, you lower behavior.

Maturity, Self-Discipline, Responsibility

Whenever speaking to a group of teachers, regardless of level, type of school or district, or any other variable, I hear exclamations that surely students should exhibit some preconceived degree of maturity, self-discipline, and responsibility. This view I believe to be one of the foremost misconceptions plaguing teachers today, causing them *not* to put into place essential routines and procedures which will prevent misbehavior. Let me explain.

Maturity

First, let's look at maturity. Maturity is defined as having reached full and natural development, either mental or physical; worked out fully by the mind.[1] Not only shouldn't this be expected, but also the anticipation of such is in direct conflict with child and adolescent/teen developmental studies. I'll be the first to say that I'm no expert on the development of the brain. However, an abundance of information written by those who are anchored in this area of expertise is available for us all to read. Brain research informs us that decision-making is centered in the frontal lobe, which is not fully developed until late in the teen years. Other important research reveals that this developmental process may even continue into the early 20s, which could explain the many faulty decisions made by scores of college students. The problem is not that students have *no* maturity, but that teachers tend to expect *adult* maturity and its naturally accompanying level of behavior and thinking.

When we understand that students do not possess this depth, nor should it be an expectation, we do things differently. For example, many teachers allow students to choose their own seats or coop group members, touting the maturity expectation. Then, when students do what students will do—talk and play instead of keeping their noses to the grindstone, the inclination is to tell them who they are in the negative. *"I thought that you were capable of choosing your group members and staying on task, but since you've shown that you CAN'T..." This* is a set-up for failure. The reverse of this is to assign seats or coop group members with learning criteria, assignment objectives, and child or teen behavioral psychology in mind. This can be done with an authoritative, but fun spirit, allowing students to function as learners without forcing them to make difficult decisions they are unqualified to make. Setting them up for success in this

[1] The American Heritage Dictionary, Second College Edition © 1985

manner exposes them to organizational thinking, furthering their growth toward ultimate maturity.

Having a **procedure for everything** is key, whether teaching kindergarten or twelfth grade AP biology. Notice that I did not say having a *rule for* everything is key. Students require kind, professional guidance **throughout the day.** This is how they learn to *ascertain* what is the mature thing to do, and how to formulate good decisions. They gravitate toward significant growth by having responsible adults provide the structure that ushers them in the right direction, respectfully compelling them to work within a framework producing desirable results for them and their teachers. Each progresses at his own pace. There *is* no set degree of maturity that can be expected of all students at a particular grade. Refuse to be tempted to entertain contemptuous thoughts when students falter from lack of maturity. The indulgence can only result in the lowering of students' self-esteem, as they receive the inevitable negative messages even if your thoughts are left unspoken. Rather, develop age and grade-appropriate routines and procedures that will make it unnecessary for them to read your mind, trying to figure out what *your* particular parameters are. (See appendix)

Self-Discipline

Countless teachers have vowed to never take their students on another field trip, to another auditorium program, have another guest speaker, and so on, because of the stress generated from student misbehavior during these activities. The lion's share of student misconduct during these often unstructured times, is the inescapable result of the instructor's erroneous expectation that students automatically exhibit self-discipline. No explicit guidance is given, leaving students on their own to manage the excitement and sense of freedom associated with the events. Further complicating the matter of determining what teachers can reasonably anticipate from students in this arena, is the apparent confusion over whether one is observing self-discipline in a student who demonstrates a quiet, attentive demeanor on a daily basis, or merely personality. Many teachers point to a particular student who just *never* seems to act inappropriately, indicating that person as an example of a student who possesses a great deal of self-control. However, there are personality types, whether in a four-year-old or a teen of seventeen, who are just naturally low-key and reserved. It *does not* mean that those students are endowed with an unnatural abundance of composure, or that their counterparts are missing their apportionment of the same. Neither should educators place seemingly self-restrained students at a disadvantage by failing to employ the proper structure and procedures that will permit them to flourish.

Possessing self- discipline implies that one is an *effective* manager of self, controlling moods, impulses, and feelings, subordinating them to the situation at hand. To be perfectly honest, I know few adults who have mastered this attribute. This kind of restraint is certainly not to be relied upon from our students. They don't possess it on the scale that teachers seem to presume**, nor should they.**

Students are in the *developmental stages* of the attainment of self-discipline, and while obviously there are those who are ahead of others, none are endowed with the whole nine, namely that which can be expected from full-fledged adults. Our job, again, is to put into place the procedures and routines which spur them to behave in a self-disciplined manner. Thus, we are *teaching* them what self-control looks like without expecting yelling, punishing, complaining, and negative labeling to do the teaching for us. Then, we can tell them who they are in the positive. *"You guys are such hard workers! Thank you. I like the way you worked on your project cooperatively, and followed all of the directions."*

Let's return, for a moment, to my assertion that the field trip is one of the most stressful experiences for many teachers. To establish and ensure good behavior on a field trip, rather than relying on student self-discipline to automatically click in, several steps need to be taken by the instructor, regardless of school or level.

- **Give the purpose of the field trip. K–12**

(Students view a field trip as a day out of school to play or fraternize with classmates.) E.g. Teacher: *"We are going to the zoo to continue our study of the classification of animals."* (middle or high school)

"We are going to the zoo to see how animals are cared for and how they behave in their natural habitats." "It's going to be a fun day of learning!" (elementary)

- **Assign bus seats or have students choose seats or walking mates several days before the excursion.**

  Record the choices made so that students can't attempt to argue that another person was chosen. Unless you know that two students just cannot behave if seated together, this is a time to permit them to be with a friend. Just like us, they want to be able to chat while traveling to the destination.

- **Give POSITIVE guidelines for the trip.**
  e.g. Teacher: "*You'll chat with your seatmate or those in the seats immediately in front or behind you. Your voice should only be loud enough to be heard by the person to whom you are speaking. Backpacks and lunches are to be labeled with your full name, and placed on the floor or your lap.*"

- **Prepare a curriculum-based assignment which will last the ENTIRE time.**
  Make it substantive, interesting, and creative. It will be collected, graded, and counted toward their overall grade. This applies to K–12, and will let students know that the field trip is an extension of their classroom experience. It is the element which will keep them focused on the purpose and well-behaved throughout. If you are having them work in pairs, *you have* pre-selected the pairs, and they have been told with whom they will be working, a day or two in advance. Otherwise, this is where the fooling around and not following directions can and will occur. It's difficult for students or us, for that matter, to concentrate on working when with a best buddy or, worse, girl or boyfriend. Lunchtime offers them the opportunity for this kind of *supervised* fraternization and socializing. Let them know that they will be receiving a little longer lunch period so that they can have time to play and chat. **Warning:** Don't think that you are being "mean" by assigning activity partners. You're setting them up for defeat if you don't.

- **Go over the assignment a day in advance**, so that students understand the directions and how they are expected to find answers. Let them know that you will be there to help.

Though this procedure requires forethought and prior planning, if structured properly it is worth its weight in gold when it comes to organizing a field trip that will turn out well, both academically and in the behavior department. It also teaches students what appropriate field trip behavior looks like, without preaching to them about the dos, don'ts, and consequences to befall them should they step out of line—which they are bound to do without these preventions.

This organizational strategy, replete with specific procedures *taught* to students the first time each is to be used, should be employed for all classroom movement, and activities which take students to alternative locations on or off the school site. Here's a list of common activities requiring clear, precise guidelines for students, if student development of self-discipline is the goal.

1. library book check-out or research work
2. guest speakers: Have students prepare questions for the speaker a day ahead. Require note-taking or another appropriate activity *during the* speaker's presentation.
3. movement into reading or coop groups
4. movement to music, p.e., art, etc.
5. passing out and handling manipulatives
6. lab lessons
7. class games and social events

It's all about prevention and order, to be accomplished with consideration for the dignity and level of your students. When structure is handled in this manner, you'll notice students responding with discipline, learning when and where it is appropriate to play or chat, and when it's not. Moreover, you'll find that your students are behaving calmly and more cooperatively because they know their parameters, and are experiencing academic and behavioral success because of them. Consequences necessary to be meted out to one or two aberrant souls, will be easier to enforce because of the group's overall perception of the fairness of the classroom system. I caution you, however, to be sure that what you're requiring is within the realm of "good sense" for your age group or human beings, period. I must give the example of the primary teacher who forced her little ones to sit quietly, perfectly still with hands folded on their tables when they finished an assignment. To peer in upon that class was to evoke tears from anyone who believes that the drill sergeant method of behavior management is one which belittles students, wrenching the fun from attending school.

The alternative to prevention through the use of procedures, is what I term the **assume and criticize** method, illustrated by any instructor who assumes that because of the age or grade of his students, they will automatically know what is expected. When they fail to live up to the covert behavioral standards, berating, punishment, or negative labeling ensues. Students, subsequently, retaliate with actions intended to punish the teacher, and the whole misbehavior tangle is evidenced yet again. Remember that students are human beings who, like you and me, wish to be treated well and clearly informed of significant guidelines. The "I won't learn from you" syndrome can easily get afoot, becoming entrenched in *any* classroom where students view success as dependent upon something of which they are unaware, or something unattainable.

Finally, let's realize who our clients are—simply children. This, by definition alone, says to us that they are in the developmental stages of every single category of life. Unrealistic behavioral expectations can only lead to frustration and anger for all concerned. Our students are counting on us and other responsible adults in their lives to *guide* them through these years of extreme development. This is accomplished with the structure we institute, modeling of appropriate attitudes and actions, and the building of their self-concepts in a manner that allows them to feel *proud* of themselves as they learn from mistakes and adjust to higher levels of self-management. It takes *time*. It takes *years*. No one teaching any level from Kindergarten to twelfth grade has students that have arrived. It's the nature of the beast.

Responsibility

I believe the notion of what is and what is not appropriate to anticipate regarding student responsibility, to be one of the most egregious causes of failed relationships between instructors and students. The term, responsibility, seems to be grossly misinterpreted as it pertains to the young, with this misinterpretation leading to damaging student/teacher conflicts. Exactly what is it that instructors are looking for in their pupils? Never have I witnessed educators become more angry or animated than when expounding on the lack of responsibility assumed by their students or today's students, in general. Teachers working with third graders expect them to "take responsibility for their own learning and behavior." Many middle school teachers become livid or disgusted when a student arrives in class without a pencil. High school instructors label it irresponsible when students fail to turn in homework or projects, forget to bring the textbook to class, or fall short of studying for tests. And these are but a few of the complaints teachers stream steadily into the consciences of their students, as an indication of students not accepting responsibility. The contempt communicated is palpable and destructive.

How did this happen? For sure, these are all situations that any of us, as teachers, wish didn't exist. But they *do*—over, and over, and over again in countless schools in our land and, I would surmise, in every corner of the world where students are found. Is it really that sooo many students are *choosing* to behave irresponsibly, or are we expecting an adult level of responsibility from those who *just aren't there yet*, and *shouldn't be*? Instructors assert that kids *ought* to be held accountable for their actions. I agree, to an extent.

Responsibility – based upon or characterized by good judgment or sound thinking; capable of making moral or rational decisions on one's own, and therefore answerable for one's own behavior[2]

Brain research informs us that the frontal lobe controls planning, self-control, sorting, anticipating, and judgment. However, teen brains, let alone those of elementary pupils, are not fully mature until the very end of teen years, and perhaps even the early twenties. Now, supposing that this research is correct, what does this indicate about our assertion and cries for students to embrace and display this level of adult responsibility? Could it be that what we truly desire is for our students to follow directions, obey rules and guidelines, accept reasonable and fair consequences with a measure of civility and calmness, bring a good attitude to the table, and put forth academic effort? All of this is realistic and doable, but the question is how can it be accomplished in a more informed manner than what is being witnessed in the damaging, student-bashing jargon all too common in our schools. As a man thinketh, so is he. Thus, critical and judgmental internal dialogue raging in the minds of instructors, can permeate actions, communicating negative impressions to their students, tearing down the very favorable behavioral climate they're aiming to construct.

Responsibility is present in our students and each of us in different measures. The key is for teachers to constantly realize that it, too, is developmental, and that a student of any age can *appear* to be lagging behind, when in actuality that person is right on target for his uniqueness. It is certainly a character trait most desirable and essential to attain, and teachers can contribute to student *growth* in this area. In so doing, teachers must aid students without using negative language, condemning their parents, being sarcastic or judgmental, meting out unfair punishments, or employing undignified guidelines such as requiring the removal of a shoe in order to borrow a necessary material. In short, how can we encourage the attainment of responsibility while elevating self-esteem? The trick is to help each student experience advancement at his own pace. This is impossible if one is utilizing techniques which *create* disciplinary

[2] The American Heritage Dictionary, 2nd College Edition © 1985

hassles and broad relationship chasms between students and instructor. Recognizing that human beings *do not* perform well when feeling badly about themselves, an educator must devise a plan that steers clear of placing blame and provoking feelings of shame and guilt, but focuses, rather, on supporting individual growth by strengthening habits which lead to academic and personal success.

First, most student behaviors are indeed *not* products of a lack of responsibility. They are merely signs of children and teens being children and teens—behavior befitting their stages of maturation. It's when we *label* these behaviors as symbols of irresponsibility, calling them on it in ways which make them feel inferior, that attitudes turn sour and poor conduct erupts. Educators need to be smarter, more understanding, more gracious than this. If you give a two year old a toy with which to play, and he destroys it by banging it against the wall, would you refuse to ever give him another because it was his responsibility to take care of that one? Of course not. Well, the same is true of unrealistic expectations of our students, whatever the grade. It is *our responsibility*, as professionals, to put the procedures and routines in place which provide guidance for students to learn **age-appropriate** lessons of accepting responsibility. For example, if you *know* that students at certain levels tend to forget pencils, rather than leaving it up to them to decide how to be sure to have a pencil on a daily basis, punishing or criticizing those who forget, provoking bad attitudes and disruptive behavior, devise a procedure, suitable for the grade level, that makes sure each student will have a pencil to use in class. Set that plan in motion from day one.

The language employed when explaining any routine or procedure is ever so important. You want to communicate, regardless of the initial state of student study habits, that you believe in them as competent human beings, genuinely consider them scholars who wish to learn, and expect all students to be prepared. (This message is often omitted in schools of poverty or high minority populations, leading students to believe that the instructor harbors racial prejudice.) You are aware that there needs to be a back-up plan for student preparedness, so that everyone will be successful and comfortable in class. Further, they need to know that you realize that attending class without a pencil doesn't indicate that a student doesn't care to learn or participate. It does, however, suggest that a person who *consistently* arrives unprepared may need *ideas* regarding methods of becoming organized for school, and that this is an area in which *you are happy to provide assistance.*

A back-up plan, demonstrative of respect for your students as students, realizing that there may be those whose parents or guardians are not overseeing their organizational skills on a daily basis, is required. It could be one of requesting that each student bring two extra pencils to school at the outset of the semester, which is usually when students have an abundance of school supplies. Each pencil will be labeled with the student's name, and placed in a container to be kept in the classroom for when a pencil is forgotten. If the pencil is used, it never goes home, but is returned to the container. This will take care of the kid who needs to have a pencil awaiting him in class because something seems to always go awry. You are now teaching students that it's human to forget, but responsible to devise a plan or allow someone to help in devising a plan for that eventuality. In short, you are *modeling* for students *how* to demonstrate responsibility. This is what works—suggestions and practice in an atmosphere of patient instruction.

Having a guideline for middle and high school students to bring their textbook on a daily basis in spite of what is being done in class, helps them to develop the habit of getting the book from locker to classroom. When teachers permit students to defer bringing the textbook to class until an announcement is made prior to the day it will be needed, it is more likely that someone will slip up. Additionally, the awareness that "stuff" happens even when one does wish to learn and be cooperative, a smart teacher will **just say "no"** to discipline problems and sour attitudes *created* because a student is unprepared with the proper materials. Simply have extras on hand. This, in itself, teaches students to have extras, and allows each student to progress, mentally, at his/her own rate without the fear of being humiliated or bashed in front of classmates or in private. Instituting a fair consequence for older students who are chronic "forgetters" is okay as long as the consequence is forewarned of and suitable, not accompanied by lambasting language or negative overload for the student, and does not exclude the student from taking part in the lesson. Most parents of elementary school students are buying supplies, packing backpacks, and in every way taking charge of getting what the student needs from point A to point B. Those kids who *appear* to have this sense of responsibility are receiving this necessary aid. Those who are struggling, even with parental attention, or who have parents/guardians who are unable, for whatever reasons, to see to the school needs of their child, will need your benevolent assistance.

Making sure that students *see* themselves as capable and okay, *no matter what*, goes a long way in having each grow at his/her own pace, learning the individualized lessons necessary to move to a new level of accepting responsibility. Condemning and judging simply does not serve to change student behavior for the better. It merely causes a student to either accept the negative label and continue hopelessly sinking, using the same undesirable and ineffective habits, or generates anger manifesting itself in disruptive, defiant words and actions. Either way, both student and instructor are unsuccessful, and the beat goes on.

Therefore, whether it's getting your students to put forth academic effort, turn in homework, or pay attention in class, *you* are captain of the ship. They do not come in packaging stamped, "responsibility included." Your job is to lead them down the right path without them ever knowing that that is what they are learning. Designing incentive charts, holding daily ten minute study sessions that show students how to incrementally study for tests, requiring notebooks to be organized into sections, having time lines and checklists, establishing sound, effective routines, etc. will teach students to be responsible in ways relevant for them. These are the strategies that will go a long way toward ensuring that your students will *choose* to be responsible and to behave well in your classroom because of the fun, positive environment of success **you** have constructed on their behalf.

When we raise self-concept, we raise behavior.
When we lower self- concept, we lower behavior.

The Nature of the Beast

When considering how to design a classroom to become a kind, gentle sanctuary in which to teach and learn, an initial requirement for any educator is to be familiar with the dominant characteristics of those who will inhabit the space as learners. Paramount to the attainment of this knowledge are the teacher education classes dealing with child, adolescent and teen psychology, and the reading that teachers have done and will do on their own. Without this awareness of what can typically be expected from our "beasts," how can we plan valuable learning experiences or encourage them to bring forth their best behavior? It is imperative for teachers to not only become knowledgeable about the academics which will be presented, but, conjointly, about the habits and tendencies of those in whom they would instill these skills and concepts. Make no mistake about it, no learning will transpire if classroom management is faulty or nonexistent. With this in mind, let's take a look at what can be anticipated from students, so that instructors will be able to prevent behaviors impeding instruction and hindering students from achieving, thriving, and putting their best foot forward.

Having more than 30 years of personal experience working with students of all levels, observing them at their leisure and in other instructors' classes, there are certain things that I know for sure. These characteristics and dynamics of behavior have no stereotypical boundaries, but traverse economic, racial, religious, and all other lines, and are merely peculiar and specific, in a general sense, to children and teens, our precious students.

To work effectively with students in Anywhere, USA and at any time, educators MUST **see behavior as separate from the student**. This is so crucial that I can't emphasize it enough. So many problems are exacerbated and even initiated by teachers who label the student with the actual behavior being displayed. In other words, a student who is caught cheating isn't necessarily a dishonest person, a child who is doing karate chops in the classroom instead of taking his seat isn't a student who is defiant of the rules and just plain disinterested in learning. A child who mouths off using a four-letter word needn't be tagged rude and foul-mouthed. Behavior is just that, behavior. The behavior, itself, can be labeled, but it is imperative that the student's dignity and positive view of himself be preserved if that child is to thrive in your classroom, and for there to be any chance that the infraction will not recur in the future. Indeed, poor conduct needs to be addressed and eradicated, but, most importantly, it needs to be **prevented**.

Let me begin with an example. A mom, whom I'll call Jean, picked up her two-year old from daycare, after work. Needing to stop by the grocery store for a few items, and neither desiring to leave him at the daycare facility longer than necessary nor wanting to come back out later, she decided to take him along. Aware that he enjoyed sitting in the shopping cart as she shopped, Jean reasoned that this would add to the quality time they would spend together that evening. Upon picking him up, she asked if he'd like to go to the grocery store with mommy, and, of course, he squealed with joy! However, no sooner than he was seated in the cart and the rounding up of the groceries was underway, he began reaching for everything in sight, whining ever more loudly each time she said "no," noting that they'd be home soon. To make a long story short, his whining turned into crying and eventually into a screaming temper tantrum. This beleaguered mom had disregarded the nature of her beast—the toddler. She knew that when toddlers are tired and have been away from home for an extended period of time, the last thing that can be tolerated is another stop requiring more structure and confinement. He was simply acting out the script of a typical two-year-old. The problem lay with the mom for not realizing that what seemed so simple and reasonable to her, actually *precipitated* the undesirable behavior with which she was confronted.

Educators must be just as intuitive about their students. At each grade or level there can be preventions put into place which will thwart behaviors that are nature of the beast but disruptive in the classroom setting. Consider the following.

1. Expect students to try to take advantage of situations.

That's what they do. That's who they are. It's typical for students to grab every minute possible to chat, play, tease—whatever. As a matter of fact, that's oftentimes who we are, as well. What does this mean in application? When you must step outside of the classroom or speak with a parent, administrator, or support person at the back of the room, be sure to take a moment to provide your students with a meaningful academic task with which to occupy their time. This is called prevention. When ready to return your attention to the class, you can either continue with that task as a class, or have them set it aside for finishing and handing in at a later point in the lesson. Additionally, this is prime time for seizing the opportunity to tell them that you noticed and appreciated that they were on task, studious, and polite. Acknowledging their good conduct will help to ensure that they will demonstrate similar behavior next time you are detained and have to give them an assignment with which to be engaged. Their self-concepts as students, will have been *elevated*, promoting **good behavior** as opposed to the repercussions accompanying off-task conduct which would surely lower self-esteem.

Generalize this scenario to any other which may allow your students to drift into unseemly behavior when your attention needs to be elsewhere.

2. Expect students to want to "play" rather than to read or do class work.

All age groups have their toys, whether miniature action figures or cell phones. These items, quite naturally, occupy much of their focus time. Nevertheless, preoccupation with these objects doesn't necessarily indicate that students aren't also enjoying academic learning. It's normal behavior, to be expected. It's essential, however, that instructors set fair guidelines which prevent the use of these distractions during class. An adverse effect is brought about when students are labeled as apathetic or not desirous of learning because their attention is on electronic gizmos and playthings. This kind of thinking, alone, is divisive and can be detected by students, engendering a less than desirable relationship between them and their teachers.

Chat with other educators to see what has worked well for them in handling these common situations. Whatever you do, overreacting or confiscating and threatening to hold the toy or electronic device until a parent comes to retrieve it, is a set-up for more, even unrelated discipline problems. The best answer is to inform students in a nonjudgmental fashion on the first day of school or class, that no phones, toys, or whatever are to be brought to class. Explain that toys steer attention away from the lesson, detracting from everyone's success.

Inform them if there will be opportunities when personal objects are acceptable. (e.g. phone usage at lunchtime, toys on show and tell days) Then, forewarn of and post consequences for bringing them to class. (e.g. holding the item until the end of the day) You're not angry, just determined to preserve class time for the curriculum.

If the items are necessities, but still not appropriate to have "out" in the classroom, stress that they be kept in the locker, backpack, or can be placed for safe keeping on the teacher's desk. Your desk, then, must actually *be* a safe place for their personal belongings. Otherwise, you will be the beneficiary of tons of complaints and refusals to leave their precious objects in your care.

Upon noticing that a child has violated the rule, simply give **information and choice**. The choices are YOURS. E.g. " *Tonya, CD players aren't allowed in class. You can either put it on my desk until the end of the day or in your backpack.* " This is said with calmness and respect. There's no need to "stare her down" until she complies, and a "thank you" can be given to show that you appreciate the cooperation. This action sends the message to both the perpetrator and other class members that you meant what you said about these distractions, and that the rule will be enforced. Yet, the problem has been eliminated in a courteous manner instead of assuming that one can only obtain compliance through the use of loud, harsh language. (which, by the way, always backfires in some way) After class or once the others are settled, take a moment to have a brief, private chat with Tonya to reset your guideline. This, too, is done with preservation of the student's dignity in mind and without "working her over" with verbiage such as, *"Did you forget the rule? If you bring your CD player to class again you WILL NOT get it back. Do I make myself clear?"*

Words such as these only serve to anger or insult students AND their classmates, provoking retaliatory back talk and a resolve to test you again.

I was asked to work with a teacher whose second grade students were described by her as being completely out of control. As the children were lining up for recess one day, a little boy exclaimed, "Sean has Pokemon cards!" The teacher was ready to make a beeline for Sean's "face," when I asked if she'd allow me to handle the situation. The children were standing in stark silence, holding their collective breath, waiting to see what terrible punishment was in store for their friend. While it was clear that they had become accustomed to yelling and threats, it was also clear that neither had proven successful in obtaining good behavior. Actually, they were more defiant and contentious than ever because misbehavior is the only *weapon* children possess when confronted with someone they perceive as an unfair, unkind authority figure.

Upon reaching Sean I said, "Sean, I have an envelope for your cards. I'll write your name on the outside and put it on the desk. After school you can have them back." He stared at me with stunned, appreciative eyes, and handed me the cards with an expression which said, "I'm sorry." I gave him a reassuring smile and turned toward the desk. Barely had I taken a step when another second-grader piped up with, "Miss Dempsey, I have cards, too." I thanked him for his honesty, and handled his in the same manner. They all scampered happily off to recess. I can't tell you how many impromptu hugs I received that day, or how the students were always prone to listen up if I needed to assist the instructor in getting their attention.

This isn't an anecdote about my "greatness," and both boys were "treated" to a private chat to reiterate the school's guideline. The point here is that kids will be kids, teens will be teens. We needn't apply the lash, but do need to grab *every* opportunity to demonstrate the mature, respectful way of handling conflict. One is not striving for student approval, but seeking to not just eradicate the problem, but the behavior. To accomplish this, children must believe, on a conscious and unconscious level, your system to be a better way to "live" in a school environment, trusting that they will not be stung by negative judgments, extreme actions and language, and unfair punishments. It's out of loyalty to you, once they believe all of the above, that they honestly begin to police themselves. The good news is that when instructors set guidelines, enforcing them with authority overlaid with charity and respect, their students respond in like kind, and the instructional program is allowed to move forward.

3. **Expect a lack of maturity and self-discipline**
   This point has already been discussed, and bears keeping in mind so that your procedures and routines are in place, ready to go on the first day of school.

4. **Expect students to want to watch fights or other kinds of disturbances.**
   Were I speaking to a group of educators and a fight or argument erupted in the room, I seriously doubt that one iota of attention would remain on what I was saying, nor would I have that expectation. It is entirely human to respond to violence or disruptions of order with attention to the disruption. Your students are no different. They're everyday people who have been conditioned by society to amplify and even take pleasure in viewing certain acts of violence. We need to diminish its appeal by both refusing to inflate such incidents out of proportion, and refusing to brow beat students who seem to revel in the experience of witnessing someone else's victimization. It's important to remain cognizant of the fact that fights can and do happen everywhere. We need to be specific about the actions we want students *not* to engage in should such a conflict arise. Next, **set up and manage the classroom so that it is highly unlikely that a fight will have the opportunity to occur.**

   Allow me to give an accounting of a situation witnessed, which if permitted, could and would happen in any classroom. The instructor organized her middle school students in coop groups to work on an in-class assignment. At the conclusion of the group assignment, one participant from each group was to make a presentation to the whole class. Initially, when the names of two students were called as being group members, both the young lady and young man stated, intelligently, that they did not work well together. The teacher insisted that they give it a try, thinking that the experience would help each prepare for real-world situations. (admittedly, a difficult determination to make) After a couple of unsuccessful attempts to convince the teacher otherwise, the students kept their distance and attempted to comply. Here's the rub. When it came time for them to present, no one from that group volunteered to be spokesperson. (a problem which lay with the teacher, since no guidelines had been given as to how this was to be handled, and no "rehearsal" time had been set aside for the speaker to achieve a level of comfort) At this time, the boy snagged the opportunity to shout a negative quip about the young lady. She, in turn, having to save face, did him one better, and immediately they each proceeded to get more vociferous as classmates began to laugh and the one-up-man-ship heated up. Ultimately, the two had to be separated and sent to the office, as it was quite obvious to all that they were on the verge of a physical fight.

What was the instructor doing throughout this encounter? Well, after the first quip, she was looking at them both, smiling as though she was enjoying the exchange, waiting for them to curtail their own undignified behavior. However, once it was apparent that the situation was escalating out of control, steamrolling toward a physical altercation, she endeavored to calm the duo by saying, *"Okay, that's enough." " Stop, now."*

I contend that it was enough when the first derogatory remark was spoken. That was the time to jump in, protecting the young lady from being verbally attacked, and calmly, but clearly enforcing the guideline that no name-calling, teasing, or otherwise hurtful dialogue ever be permitted in that classroom.

(Avoid using the word, "tolerated", which can be very inflammatory). Standing by, idly watching as a student is taunted is *never* amusing or acceptable.

I imagine that there are those among us who enjoy teasing, considering it harmless. That aside, running a classroom is a horse of a different color. An educator can't know what any child's complete background or temperament is like. We don't know what is hurtful or not, where insecurities lie, or how much a person can endure before breaking. Many children and teens smile, pretending to not feel violated when being picked on by a classmate. Our job is to make sure that there is no chance, on our watch, for any student to suffer from offensive verbiage. Inaction on the part of the teacher can indicate collusion, awaken the beast within those who relish seeing others in pain, and send the message that it's okay to hurt someone's feelings as long *as you don't go too far*. Students begin to understand that they have to fend for themselves in a classroom run in this manner, rendering the environment an unsafe, unpleasant place to be. Talk about a setup for more misbehavior in the form of physical and verbal disruptions!

Significant in the above scenario, was that a "memo" was inadvertently delivered to all of her students that day. It was not one which would prevent other mishaps, but likely encourage them because it spoke of the teacher's willingness to observe a student' s discomfort without venturing to intervene.

We know that students are bundles of emotions and insecurities, so there was no surprise that the two young people went at each other in that manner. That type of exchange happens all of the time in homes, between siblings. Thus, it is up to the adults in their lives, teachers included, to show them a different way of interacting when resolving conflict.

What, then, should we say to our students about this issue of watching fights? There are **two very important concepts** for teachers to ponder and use in their efforts to dissuade kids from moving in the direction of misbehavior.

The first is to **DECRIMINALIZE.** Students are not criminals when they behave inappropriately, become involved in physical altercations, are tardy to class, or forget to bring required materials. Therefore, avoid behaving in an extreme manner in response to these common occurrences, refraining from even thinking thoughts which vilify students. When this kind of thinking is present, it manifests itself in the instructor's behavior, causing students to react negatively to being viewed in this manner, resulting in *more* disruptive behavior. Undesirable student conduct should be handled with consistent enforcement of guidelines and the use of fair consequences, while acknowledging that students are in the primary learning stages of their lives, which, in itself, means that missteps will be evident. This resolve to run a fair, tight ship will net enduring results, influencing students to

change their own behavior. It *will* happen, bit by bit, as they accept you as a trusted leader. And, yes, there will be backstrokes. It's to be expected.

In the case of thwarting the practice of kids watching fights with the intent of further energizing the participants, merely tell them what is okay and what is not **before a fight happens.**

> *e.g.* Teacher: *"Guys, if there should ever be a fight in our room or in the hall, here's what I'd like you to do.* **Decriminalize:** *I realize that it's only human to want to see what's happening when there's a ruckus going on.*
>
> **Replacement Behavior:** *However, I want you to remain seated or stand back, not taunt, tease or in any way egg on the fighters. Instead, allow an adult to get the fight stopped, and if asked, help in that effort."*

Giving these directions demonstrates that you comprehend the nature of your beasts; that what commonly happens is that a fight is made worse by the onlookers who, as in the Roman Coliseum centuries ago, egg on the fighters until "blood runs freely." Telling them what to do rather than what not to do is what I call giving your students the **REPLACEMENT BEHAVIOR**, the second important concept. Students are programmed, so to speak, with certain options with which to avail themselves, depending upon age and experience. We, too, have behavioral options from which to choose when faced with any situation. Students must be *taught* new ways of managing conflict in their lives. Otherwise, just as any of us, they continue drawing from the available choices to which they've been exposed. Their growth and competency in this area depends on how well we handle this part of their education. We'll speak more about giving specific replacement behavior in subsequent chapters. It's a vital part of establishing classrooms as havens of good behavior.

5. Expect running, jumping, horseplay, grooming

Again, this is who they are and what they do. These behaviors in and of themselves are not so egregious, but when unfurled in the classroom, can be quite disruptive and have the tendency to "spread," making it essential for teachers to forestall the occurrence of this misconduct *before* it becomes embedded in the culture of the classroom.

Running Start

Prevention is quite simple when teachers provide and maintain structure, not behaving as though students should just "know better." Taking the moral high ground, as so many instructors seem wont to do, does naught else but allow problematic behavior to get a foothold in their classrooms, and children's attitudes to turn sour as they intuitively realize that their teacher has prejudged them as chronic miscreants, and is holding a negative opinion of them, in general.

One of the most effective routines to institute, whether teaching kindergarten or high school courses, is that of commencing with a focus assignment or activity. Begin the day, afternoon, a session following a school-wide program, or each class period in middle and high school, in this manner. As soon as the bell rings to signal the beginning of class, there is a mini assignment awaiting students. This simple strategy serves to teach students to enter and settle quickly by helping them transition from the nonstructural passing period or recess interlude to the attentiveness required for the pursuit of academics. There are several components involved in this purposeful activity which are imperative if it is to become a successful part of your academic and management programs. A <u>Focus Assignment</u> must be:

1. **<u>Completely Independent For Students</u>**
   (meaning that it is either review or an easily-grasped precursor to the day's lesson)
   NOTE: This is not the time for paired or group tasks, or skills with which students are experiencing difficulty.

2. **<u>Curriculum–Based, Significant, and Substantial</u>**
   (Be creative and diverse with these mini assignments. It gets mighty "old" when tasks become repetitive and stale, promoting defiance and refusal to work.)

3. ***<u>Immediately</u>* <u>Discussed, Collected, Graded, and Counted Toward Students' Overall Grades</u>**
   (In other words, it's important.)

4. **<u>Timed</u>**
   (forces students to commence right away, offering students an added reason to be on time for class) **Tip:** Use a timer so that you won't inadvertently lose track of time, allowing too long a period, promoting the exact socializing that was being prevented.

5. Silent

The teacher **is not** speaking with or constantly interrupting students. The atmosphere is tranquil, allowing students to build academic stamina and to settle into a calm readiness for learning. (This is a great opportunity for quietly taking attendance, or collecting homework which each student has placed on the corner of his or her desk.)

Though this strategy is extremely effective, there are common mistakes which when committed by teachers render it wholly or partially ineffective.

1. **Making The Activity Too Easy, Irrelevant or Unimportant**
   (e.g. giving just *one* vocabulary term to define, allowing students to finish lickety split and commence socializing)

2. **Allocating A Meager Number Of Points To The Task,**
   resulting in students feeling that it's just not worth doing (I suggest basing each assignment on 100%.)

3. **Failing To Discuss or Grade** — having students place their papers *somewhere* to be collected on a weekly basis. Delayed gratification either doesn't or marginally works with K-12 students. Again, an adult maturity level which permits them to connect the dots, patiently awaiting feedback, should not be expected. It's a setup for failure because sooner or later, not being directly impacted by the task leads students to assume its insignificance in their lives.

Any of these missteps will negate your purpose and derail the strategy, offering your students plenty of time to waste and disrupt, and you, the annoying exercise of settling them before beginning every class.

A final word: Suppose that *during* the focus assignment you glance up and notice that a student is doing something other than what you've requested. Perhaps a young lady is unobtrusively applying makeup, or someone is reading a novel or newspaper. Should you just let it go because, after all, the room *is* silent and most of the students engaged? NO. Quietly step over to the offending party with a post-it note message. Place it on the person's desk and return to your seat where you can observe the student for compliance. What should the note say?

First-Time Make-up Offender

Jean to restroom (hurry!)
Sept. 23, 2005, 9:00 A.M.
Mr. Thomas

This method of extending "light" or graciousness in the face of poor behavior, sends the message to Jean that make-up is to be applied in *el baño* or somewhere other than the classroom, allows her to save face, which is so essential for middle and high school kids, and informs other young ladies that make-up application won't be a part of this classroom's activities. You've done it all without focusing class attention on the misbehavior or inciting a snippy attitude from Jean, as would be aroused through instructor overreaction. She, however, will not receive extra time to complete the assignment.

Repeat Offender

Remember the strategy of **Information and Choice**?
Post –it message:

"You may not apply make-up in the classroom.
Please either put it in your purse or on
my desk, and begin your focus assignment."

The same strategy would apply for a student reading a book or demonstrating any other behavior that is not what you've requested. If the student is a younger child who cannot read, or a character whose behavior is so aberrant that he or she would turn the note into a public announcement, whisper the same message either at his seat, your desk (IF it's in the back of the room), or right outside of the classroom door.

Immediately after class or when students are engaged in seatwork, ask the student who chose to "do his own thing" during focus, to speak with you for just **one minute**. Using the phrase, "one minute," as stated previously, is extremely significant because of its nonthreatening nature. At this time, restate your rule in a calm, authoritative manner, give the **replacement behavior** in very specific terms, and forewarn of a consequence should the behavior be repeated. This is imperative for even first time offenses. The idea is to **prevent** a repeat occurrence. The student is not in trouble, but being given information to help her avoid an unpleasant consequence.

Decriminalize:
"I understand that applying your make-up is important to you, but you'll need to get it done before coming to class."

Replacement Behavior:
"*From now on please keep make-up in your purse or backpack, have the materials for class on your desk, and work on the focus assignment for the full 10 minutes. Otherwise, I'll have to ask you to store it in my desk drawer until after class. That's all I needed to say! Thank you for chatting with me***."**

There's no need to say how disappointed you are, tease, become sarcastic, or make any other judgment that lowers self-esteem. The point you're basically reiterating is that when you make a request, you expect it to be followed. Be sure to tell the student who she is in the positive, and send her off to class or back to her seat with a "can do" smile. **TIP:** If the student is now likely to be late for the next class, write a pass. Otherwise, all of your work is for naught, as the student becomes angry that your "talk" resulted in her getting into trouble with the next teacher. Festering anger can actually make a student determined to disrupt your classroom at the very next opportunity.

Teachers are always modeling the behavior desired of students. Thus, when a student brings darkness, the instructor brings light – *every single time.* This concept of teaching by example is so powerful because it allows students to learn their lessons in a more humane fashion, and to recognize that their teachers actually practice what they preach. Taking a student's misbehavior personally or holding a grudge is completely over-the-top and self-destructive, for any instructor. It's not personal. Students are not out to get us unless we give them a very good reason to be, or in some manner communicate the impression that we think they are.

Consider misbehavior as "teachable moments." Handle these moments swiftly and as humanely as possible. Bear in mind that if a child is shouting—**darkness**; you will bring a quiet tone and understanding to the table—**light**. If one is using foul language—**darkness**; you will offer a different word choice rather than berating—**light**. When faced with disinterested attitudes—**darkness**; you will maintain enthusiasm and stick with a well-planned lesson—**light**.

Just speaking the words, "**I understand,**" can calm a student who is complaining about whatever, perhaps hoping to distract, disrupt, or pull you off topic, or one who truly is having a bad day. This doesn't mean that you agree, but merely understand his point of view— which, hopefully, you do. Then, continue with the lesson and address the student's concern before the day or class is over.

Comprehending the nature of our beasts and using this knowledge to better design procedures, routines, and lessons, will go a long way toward developing the kind of relationship with students that encourages them to come to class every day with the *intent* to cooperate and just plain have fun learning. It makes the job a lot easier when teachers realize that students are learning and growing in all facets of their lives, and that what occurs in classrooms is a part of that growth process. Further, it lightens the instructor's load when age and grade-appropriate procedures and **routines** basically do the work of managing students.

Mistakes To Avoid

Sometimes things can get a little tricky, and techniques or actions that an instructor honestly believes will bring about harmony and order, actually become the perpetrators of chaos and divisiveness within the classroom. With a little forethought, however, I believe that any well-meaning, determined instructor can avoid common mistakes made continually by teachers whose classrooms are fraught with misbehavior. Let's explore just what they are and how each can be prevented. However, it will be up to you to recognize if one is present in your classroom, to be willing to call a spade a spade, and to immediately take steps to eradicate it from *your* behavior. Rationalizing and blaming students for all of the ills in a dysfunctional classroom is a surefire way to continue suffering the consequences of that dysfunction. You must be willing to take a hard look at yourself to see if you are playing a significant role in the promotion of student misbehavior.

Mistake 1: Alienating or Provoking Kids Through Overreaction or Embellishment

Once upon a time, there was a teacher who considered himself to be the perfect educator. He arrived early each morning, had everything organized to the last detail, his lessons were prepared to his satisfaction, his attire and classroom décor were always in tiptop shape, and he appeared to genuinely like kids. Though all of these qualities are fine and essential, this particular person, because of his extreme attention to detail and belief that he was "all that," developed the habit of expecting the same "perfection" from his students, letting them know when they failed to measure up. How did they fail to measure up? As secondary students will on occasion, there were homework assignments left undone or not completed, materials not brought to class, the occasional tardy, a concept or skill not grasped despite the lesson being presented, and so on. When students displayed these behaviors, he immediately pounced with what he considered uplifting, motivational lectures and pronouncements of what was necessary for student achievement. As you might expect, these frequent reprimands didn't go over very well with his imperfect (beasts). They, at first, were simply taken aback, chalking it up to "the way teachers are." However, after the first couple of weeks, in light of his almost daily overreactions and embellishments of typical teen behavior, students began to do little things to "get him back." There were spit wads thrown when his back was turned, tapping on desks accompanied by looks and declarations of innocence as he attempted to teach, and an ever growing disorder, as the students who were adept at showing displeasure opened their goodie bags, taking advantage of their repertoire of revenge tactics. Others merely began to get that glassy-eyed look of disinterest or fear of failure. And, yes, there were those who tried to "buck up" and learn.

What he didn't realize was that his genuine looks of disappointment, words denoting contempt, and lectures exhorting students to *care* about their own education, were backfiring, actually causing his students to feel agitated, fearful of failing this required course, and, thus, determined NOT to allow him to penetrate their minds with his marvelous chest of information and knowledge. Their self-concepts were being lowered, he had become an adversary, and the maturity to make the decision to learn for learning's sake, was just not present. Neither learning nor order was going to take place. Even students who could pull it together and measure up were not "in his corner," because they viewed peers as being mistreated. Their quiet cooperation was never enough to allow the class to run smoothly. This predicament eventually led to declarations from the instructor of teaching " those who *wanted* to be taught." Nevertheless, his plan was foiled because all students desired to be taught, leaving those who felt denigrated by his comment to register their displeasure in the only way they knew how, through noncompliant behavior.

Instructors must be cognizant of two things. First, that there is, what I term, a society of kids. Age makes no difference. If students perceive that a classmate or classmates are being mistreated, they all seem to bleed for or identify with that person, knowing that it could happen to any one of them at any moment. When this occurs, a comradeship, of sorts, develops and they all stick together—against the teacher. Second, permitting oneself to become disappointed or disgusted because of student frailties is misguided and ineffective. It serves <u>no purpose in the quest for ways to elevate student behavior.</u>

When a student displays poor conduct, one is better served by employing the techniques that have already been put forth in this chapter, calmly dealing with the misbehavior or infraction with regard for the humanity and dignity of the student. Once done, proceed with the lesson of the day *as quickly as possible*, encouraging ALL students, even those who didn't bring materials or finish homework, to join in, feeling worthy of being taught and valued as students. Figure out ways to include even the most unprepared or disinterested individual. This is what promotes and encourages good behavior, ultimately bringing about change in undesirable student habits. Overreaction or embellishment is never beneficial to students *or* the instructor.

When you raise self- concept, you raise behavior.
When you lower self- concept, you lower behavior.

Mistake 2: Starting to Discipline Too Late

On the very first day of school or class, students are checking you out to see if you mean what you say and say what you mean. Once they determine that you do, most will settle into the system provided, and you will only have to prove your resolve to be the leader to a few obdurate souls. Often administrators or others will advise new teachers to not worry about teaching, to just "get to know students" for the first week or so. Armed with this ill-advice, unsuspecting instructors set in motion age and grade appropriate rules, but then make the mistake of allotting students "time to get used to" their new teacher and classroom standards. The intention is to begin enforcing the guidelines, *in earnest*, once they've all settled in and gotten acquainted. What's wrong with this? Students of all ages and backgrounds are astute enough to realize that there are instructors who are confident and up to the task of managing a classroom, and that there are those who are hesitant and even timid about doing so. This *perception* of timidity signals that, with little effort, students can institute and abide by their own rules, and forthwith, the testing of limits begins.

Running Start

Management begins the very first day of class, even with a guideline as simple as "raise your hand and be recognized before speaking." If a student can get away with even the simplest of infractions, the implication is that the teacher is not fully in charge, and that with more pushing of the limits students can have their way, playing and socializing while receiving unearned grades and credits. Unfortunately, many students have experienced success with instructors who, in the past, have thrown up their hands in defeat, struck bargains, and given passing grades to students who were continually disruptive and unproductive. Thus, they have reason to believe that it could happen again.

Fortunately, this behavior is easily forestalled. When a student or students disregard or disobey even the simplest of requests or guidelines, nothing more is needed than to *immediately* pause, calmly restate the guideline, and allow the student another opportunity to comply. For example, let's say that you chose the standard stated above, that of raising one's hand before speaking. You then ask a question and a student blurts out the correct answer, but without raising her hand and waiting to be called upon. Should you just chalk it up to the first day of school, respond to the student and move on? **Absolutely Not.** Neither should you overreact or make a big deal of it. Merely say, *"That was a good answer, Denise. Now, I'm going to ask the question again and I'd like for you to raise your hand. When I call on you, give me that same great answer."*

You have done two very important things. You've preserved the dignity of the student, and you have sent a message, not only to Denise, but to the entire class, that you intend for your rules to be followed. Be assured that they **will not** miss the message or fail to get your point. You have not screamed, put down, or belittled anyone. Yet, you have let them know that you are the *only one* who is in charge. Anytime during the first day or weeks that an infraction occurs, follow the same procedure, and do so with authority, mingled with kindness. Your class will soon be following your lead and the testing will become minimal. If a student chooses to test your guidelines more than once during the first day or week, be sure to set aside time for a *brief, private* chat, so that you can inform him, *personally,* that you are glad that he is in your class, but that you have noticed that a guideline or rule is not being followed. Give him explicit **replacement behavior** and explain the consequences that will follow if the misbehavior is repeated. Again, there is no need to overreact or to become judgmental or critical. However, this early chat is extremely important in establishing yourself as the person who will call the shots, albeit with fairness and humanity, but call the shots you will. End with a smile, handshake, or whatever is suitable, so that the student knows that you did not take his misbehavior personally, and **will not hold a grudge**. The next time you see this student in class, be sure to "catch him" following the rules, and give him a thumbs up or some other *inconspicuous* compliment to let him know that you have *noticed* and appreciate his cooperation. Students so desperately need our *appreciation* when they are team players, just as it is beneficial for them to be guided and placed on the right track when they're not.

Mistake 3: Peer With Students: I'm "Mean" If I Impose Structure

May I be blunt? Students are never your peers, no matter your age. I recently witnessed a young teacher of twenty-two relating to a group of high school students. As students entered, he greeted them, which was excellent. But comments made and conversations in which he became engaged, were totally as if he were one of them. It was clear that he was reliving his teenage years and identifying with them as a peer. His subsequent lesson, which began interestingly enough with a teaser, soon became bogged down with anecdotes from the students and references to television shows that had little to do with the topic. The whole lesson lapsed into such a watered down state, mired in laughter and off topic conversation, that the objective was lost and the outcome of the lesson and quality of the students' work unworthy of their academic and intelligence levels. The students liked him, but didn't respect him as their instructor. It was a class in which they could be completely at their leisure, do little or nothing, socialize, and still get by. Though, not witnessed, I am sure that it was just a matter of time before he realized that his students were not taking the class seriously, and that very little of the curriculum was being covered. This is quite common when mistake three is committed. Some teachers feel that if they roughhouse, get involved in their students' personal lives at the peer level, use certain slang terms, and, in general, behave like a student, all will go well. I have yet to see it turn out that way.

I believe that instructors are to be **friendly professionals**. Students do not need adult peers. They are looking for someone who can lead wisely, teaching them in a manner which engenders admiration and trust. Teachers need to be role models in every regard. Relate to students we must, but becoming a peer with our language, attire, or conversation does a disservice to ourselves, the profession, and our students, causing them to lose out on the very commodity we are there to provide—a solid education. Furthermore, students don't know what to do with a teacher who acts like one of them. The tendency is to jump in and try to rule the roost, to take over from the presiding hen—you. After all, someone has to be the true master. If not you, then your students. The natural order of things, i.e. structure in all forms essential to the school setting, is vital to the creation and maintenance of an invigorating teaching/learning environment. Students find it comforting, not mean, when it is done well. It simply allows everyone to relax in the knowledge that an atmosphere of balance and efficiency is solidified and continuous.

All one has to remember as an instructor is that **students will like and respect you when you set fair limits, are consistent, humane, respectful, and competent in both your management and instruction**. They beam with pride when graced with a teacher who is knowledgeable about her grade or subject, and who cares enough to make sure that students remain on track, progressing and learning. Be aware that students *of all levels and backgrounds* desire to learn, to be able to brag about and be proud of the hard work they are capable of doing. It's all part of the school experience we each cherish, and about which we love to reminisce. Don't deprive your students of the opportunity of getting to know you as a responsible adult there to help them successfully navigate their way through their academic and social lessons.

Mistake 4: Being Timid or Cajoling

A while ago, a well-known university's teacher education graduate program undertook a study of area teachers and their style of behavior management, as it impacted the effectiveness of each teacher's classroom discipline. What they discovered was that a timid or cajoling teacher had to make a request of students 8-10 times before compliance was evident. Simply put, **begging and pleading with students is an ineffective technique to employ when endeavoring to get them to follow rules and guidelines**.

I imagine that many of you may be partial to cajoling because in your home you were begged and your feet tickled until you collapsed into a fit of giggles, submitting to whatever you'd been asked to do. Nevertheless, the classroom is not the place for this strategy of moving a person toward complicity. What inevitably sets in is disrespect and, oftentimes, a belief on the part of your students, that you are afraid of them or even their parents! This all adds up to an out-of-control class and a frustrated, unhappy teacher. **Confidence is the answer**. Set up your structure, KNOW what you wish students to do, and simply ask them to do it without harboring any feelings of guilt. If a student does not comply, remember our technique of information **and choice**. Be *prepared* with fair, humane consequences, and **remain consistent**.

Note, too, that giving second chances to students only encourages them to commit the infraction one more time. Once you have given **information and choice**, sometimes there is no need for a consequence because the child just conforms to the request. However, if one is needed and you have promised a specific repercussion, be sure to deliver if the student repeats the offense. Otherwise, you can become known as a teacher who *threatens* but fails to follow through. This reputation will surely cause students to constantly test the waters of your management guidelines to see which teacher showed up that day: the one who warns, but caves in, or the one who says something and sticks with it. You'll soon get worn out with the testing, and tons of instructional and learning time will be wasted. **Threats should not be in any part of your management plan**. Calmly say what you mean and mean what you say. Keep it simple and enforceable.

Mistakes 5 and 6: Not Knowing Child/Adolescent Psychology and Not Preventing Poor Behavior

I'm going to combine these two common mistakes because they've been previously discussed. A quick word to the wise is all that's needed. There are instructors who either skimmed over the psychological studies presented in education classes, or actually never exposed themselves to the tremendous amount of important, phenomenal research done in this area. If you're thinking that you needn't bother, think again. There definitely is something to age tendencies as they pertain to the predominant mode of thinking and prevailing ways of behavior, information that can make all the difference in your knowledge and, thus, in your actions and planning. Prevention IS the key, and when that key is overlooked or omitted, the obvious result is a class of students, off the beam because they have been left on their own to discover the way to appropriate behavior. This doesn't pertain to a particular group of students or school district, but to children, in general. Treat yourself to this store of knowledge.

Mistake 7: Not Running An "Academically Tight" Ship

Students are quite the marvel. They complain about "doing work" but that is exactly what makes them feel good about themselves, leading them to fall in love with their teacher! **Know this**. Besides, this is an educator's primary duty—to impart meaningful information, facilitate skill and concept acquisition, and to, hopefully, instill a hunger and thirst for learning which grows into a lifelong love of the same. Yet, there are those among us who, for whatever reasons, deprive students of precisely these prizes. Meager assignments are given, time is spent calling roll while students sit idly chatting or playing, off topic conversation is initiated and carried on by the instructor in lieu of presenting well-designed instructional lessons. In short, more time is spent with students *not* actively engaged in learning than is spent in meaningful scholastic experiences. **This is a recipe for behavior problems.**

The moment your students' feet cross the threshold of your classroom, learning should begin. Permit no spaces without structure to invade your domain, because it's in the spaces that behavior problems hatch and thrive. While students are gathering materials from bookshelves or storage closets, sharpening pencils, handing in homework assignments, etc., *without set procedures* or reasonable guidelines and vigilance, teasing, touching, horseplay, and grooming are all allowed to get underway. The academic atmosphere, if there was one, has now been eroded. Remember the nature of your beasts? They'd rather play than to read or do class work. Not because they are inner city youth or any other stereotype, but because they are kids or teens, **period**.

You must capture and hold their attention from the first moment. It's a part of the fun of being at school. *Really!* Do so with an opening class procedure that allows them to procure materials within the boundaries of politeness and humanity for their fellow man, the focus assignment that has already been explained, and **lots of active participation throughout the instructional lesson**. There should never be a time when students are sitting idly, just listening to you. *If you're writing, they're writing. If you're talking, they're involved, actively.* All of the paperwork tasks, such as collecting or handing back assignments should be done while students are *engaged in a meaningful task.* If you're going to discuss their papers, and I hope you are, then there should be a quick, easy dissemination process for them to receive them immediately before the discussion begins. Otherwise, the chaotic movement that usually ensues as students mill about laughing and talking with friends, sometimes even victimizing those who are timid and weak, can unravel an environment that was solid and conducive to learning just a moment ago.

Students thrive on learning. Yes, they do! It's up to you, however, to make it **sound important and fun, keep it tight**, and to plan your instructional activities so that they are hands-on, substantive, and objective-oriented.

Mistake 8: Having Low Academic and Behavioral Expectations

There are educators who prejudge and negatively stereotype students before ever laying eyes on them. These stereotypes can be based upon economic level, neighborhood, school, school district, race, religion, gender, or something else, causing the instructor to establish or settle for low academic and behavioral expectations. This is a major mistake. A colleague related a story that was sad, but oh so familiar. It was an accounting of a group of teachers teaching at a city school whose reputation was poor because of many student behavior problems and low test scores. First, lessons were watered down because of the genuine belief that *these* students couldn't hack it in the real world of secondary academics. Textbooks were not permitted to be taken home, homework assignments were minimal and accompanied with well-meaning, but belittling exhortations, lesson plans were staid and stale because, after all, "the students weren't interested anyway," and so on. I submit to you, that therein lay the problem. The attitudes and actions of the instructors were so negative and demeaning that the students didn't have a fighting chance of achieving or deciding to behave correctly, though some did in spite of the reputation. However, I know what you must be thinking and saying. But, I implore you to remember the well-known axiom, "As a man thinketh, so is he." If instructors *believe* that their students are disinterested and prone to misbehavior, that is the very face and vibe that will spring forth, and their instructional planning and relationships with students will become negatively impacted by those beliefs. It can't be helped. We are who we are and what we think. Our true feelings and convictions can't be hidden, not by the patronization of students or by instructor behavior which has the *appearance* of virtue. The students will **know**, and **they will ACT out beliefs about them**. Again, it's the natural state of being ages 6, 13, or 18, and all those in between. Many a parent would also be well advised to understand this phenomenon of the human mind.

What to do? Realize that all students are capable and worthy. That ALL students, regardless of poverty, race, gender, neighborhood, or whatever variable, are just like you and me. The circumstances of individual lives may be different, but what makes us all tick is quite similar. Your students *crave* learning and success *despite what they may be showing you.* But when faced with a teacher who doesn't believe in them, they bring forth the worst—revenge behavior. This is their weapon, their only recourse in a world in which they have little power. It's that immaturity spoken about previously. Have you ever heard students say, "I'm not doing *her* work!" meaning that they will not perform for a particular teacher? This is not a statement of defiance, but one of self-preservation. They are feeling put down and "criminalized," and this is their way of expressing the hurt and anger that accompanies those feelings. It may not make sense to you, but it makes perfect sense to them. The association between the lessons you present and the relationship you develop with your students is real, and it bears keeping in mind when you expect students to perform in spite of the kind of alliance you have forged. If the bond is weak or phony, there will be very little learning taking place, if any, and behavior problems will continue and even proliferate as students attempt to maintain some semblance of self-esteem no matter how misguided and unsuccessful the course they've chosen.

A seasoned educator recently remarked with wonder at the success, recounted in a publication, of a young teacher who took a group of high school students accustomed to failing, whose academic and behavioral reputations were the lowest of lows, to extraordinary heights. In them she provoked such zeal and zest for learning that their academic and behavioral output became the highest of highs, so much so that their entire community was astonished and impressed. What did this novice instructor know? There's no mystery. It's simple. People are people, and people respond to high expectations, skills, and support. They respond to those who *genuinely* believe that they are the best, who appreciate them regardless of who they are and, as a result, set high standards which illustrate respect and elevate self-esteem. In the face of this kind of positive acknowledgment, students will give their best **every time**. It's out of loyalty to you, their teacher, that they become "all that." **Students will live up or down to your expectations of them.**

Mistake 9: Being Unaware or "Closed" to the Traditions and Core Beliefs of Your Students' Community or Culture

Our great country is comprised of varying groups of people, all with their own significant beliefs and traditions. This is a beautiful thing. When an instructor is working with students from a different culture than her own, it is imperative to ferret out just what is important, traditional, and elevating in that context. Students are watching us to see if we are going to value their traditions and beliefs, or just expect them to fall into place with whatever *we* happen to believe, perhaps ignoring vital upbringing. Just as we are filled with pride about who we are and those from whence we came, so are our students. However, they can be made to feel self-conscious about or ashamed of certain traditions or tenets if we don't acknowledge the significance of them, celebrating differences in real and positive ways.

Without a doubt, we are all more alike than different. Nonetheless, we need to learn such things as the signs of respect in another culture, how religious beliefs are carried over into everyday life, how children are taught to address adults and to behave in adult company, and which *core* beliefs, in effect, govern the behavior of a particular group of people. Then, we must show respect for these principles and customs. I did not say that we must *agree* with others' beliefs, just as they are not required to agree with ours, but it is my opinion that show respect, we must, if we are to convey to our students that they are good, great and worthy, no matter their ancestry or cultural background.

This is not hard to do. Most likely we have all been exposed to some aspects of the major cultures to which most of our students belong. Each instructor needs to take it a step further, to make himself more aware. This can, of course, be done by reading, visiting museums, attending cultural festivals, and in ways that I'm sure you've already employed. It's fun! We're educators, and knowledge and acceptance is part and parcel of who we are. Notice that I did not proclaim that "tolerance" is part and parcel of who we are. Somehow, when we just *tolerate* others' beliefs and traditions, it can still smack of criticism and judgment. We are perceived as being on our " high horse," just going along for the ride because it's the courteous thing to do. This won't work. Our students need to know that we truthfully value who they are and their conventions. Get in there and build lessons around prominent people and observances from their culture, while staying within the boundaries and objectives of your curriculum.

e.g. Science teachers who are designing lessons around human cells can surely include scientists from all cultures who promulgated theories or, in some other manner, impacted the world's information regarding cells. It can be done. Think of ways to celebrate your students every chance you get. **The payoff will be higher student self-confidence, which will translate directly into enhanced learning and exemplary behavior.**

Mistake 10: Using Faulty Instructional Techniques

One thing is for sure, the amount and depth of student learning is directly related and proportionate to the quality and appropriateness of the instructional techniques employed. Many are the students who languish year after year in classrooms in which instructors continually present curriculum material in mundane, ineffective ways, expecting students of all ages to just pay attention and do the work regardless of the proficiency with which it is presented. **This is a mistake which is all too often overlooked when student misbehavior is cited**.

Using creative, potent teaching techniques on a daily basis results in producing students who are on task and engaged in the learning process. Classroom disruptions are greatly diminished and even eliminated when the instructor employs strategies which present lessons **in an organized, cohesive, stress-reducing** fashion. Hands-on activities ensure that students are occupied with interesting learning materials, being held accountable through *continuous participation*. Couple that with a harmonious blend of curriculum skills, and you have a winning combination. They're filled with natural curiosity, willingness to explore, and the use of sound instructional techniques makes that exploration nonintimidating. Students of all ages and backgrounds *absolutely do* relish learning. That's who kids are. To reject this most basic of understandings or to take their desire to learn for granted, thinking that *anything* an instructor does or throws together is sufficient, is to simply **ask** for behavioral disruptions, as students express their disapproval or anxiety.

There are missteps leading to poor student conduct, committed by teachers who are unaware that such errors in judgment are being made. We can't know everything, but the more deeply we study our "customers," the better we can discern what makes them tick. They *want* to be figured out, because they wish to be happy and content during the school day. Teachers are beloved and cherished by their students. It's not too much to ask for each of us to open our eyes, observe, and revere them enough to learn the very techniques which will not only enhance their learning experiences, but promote the kind of good behavior that will bring tranquility to the lives of teachers and students alike.

CHAPTER ONE
Summary Points

1. Tell students who they are, genuinely and in the positive.
2. Behavior is raised or lowered with self-esteem.
3. Read the research regarding child and teen maturity, self-discipline, and responsibility.
4. Maintain high, but realistic expectations for your age group and academic level.
5. Understand the nature of your beasts. Institute appropriate routines and procedures, from day one.
6. Decriminalize and give specific replacement behavior.
7. Teach and model all expected behaviors.
8. Avoid taking student misbehavior personally or holding grudges against students.
9. Prevention is key.
10. Become familiar with mistakes that provoke student misbehavior

Chapter Two

THE DISCIPLINED CLASSROOM

There are a few keys to achieving sound, effective discipline, which are surprisingly rudimentary, and realistically work to block pesky behavior problems. **ORGANIZATION, RESPECT, FAIRNESS, LESS IS MORE, and EFFECTIVE INSTRUCTION are** major signposts leading the way to this most desirable of end results. I believe the attainment of an ultimate level of classroom management to be, not so much attributable to the rules and consequences set in place, though they *are* extremely crucial to the smooth running of any environment devised to foster learning, but to the employment of superior instructional and structural techniques. As a matter of fact, it just may be a 90/10 proposition, with the dominant factor being the usage of those master tools. With this principal assertion in mind, let's take a look at the above features accredited with being components of a masterfully-run classroom, and the impact of each on overall behavior management.

Organization and Discipline

Nothing heralds the success of an opening academic year, week, or day, like confidence emanating from an educator, thoroughly organized and raring to commence. The presence of such preparedness proclaims the fact that all is under control, signifying that the dimensions of the academic and management programs have been given sufficient forethought and are, indeed, in competent hands. This level and depth of organizational structure requires that one decide before students arrive, what the look and feel of their learning environment will be. If you're thinking, "Let them choose"— mistake *numero uno*. You're the professional, you choose. There are countless instructors who believe that kids wish to make all of these choices. They don't, and everyone involved needlessly suffers when they are thrust into roles legitimately intended for adults. However, students of all ages *do* want the professional making the decisions to know a little something about human nature, child or adolescent psychology, solvent methods of evoking learning, and yes, **organization**. (All of which we as teachers have studied—right?) You may want to take a peek at your child psychology book for a little review if you haven't read it in a while. That info will stand you in good stead.

Begin your organizational system by arranging student seating so that each student's attention is focused on you —not on their friends and neighbors. Be on guard against those who would pooh pooh placing students in rows of individual desks or tables. Once you have them eating out of your hands, you can do circles, small groupings, or whatever turns you on and works best for the lesson being presented. The optimal point to be driven home to students, is that once they enter the classroom their undivided attention is to be aimed toward participating in and comprehending the instructional lesson and its subsequent learning activities. What better way to send that message than to seat them in a manner which steers them in that direction. It sets in motion the dynamics of creating disciplined students who recognize that this set-up is designed to aid them in resisting the natural temptations of socializing. It's in their best interest. It's where the fun begins.

Further, if you are to be in charge from day one, *you* choose their seats. Control in this setting and, yes, even in high school, is not a dirty word. When students rule, the environment is unsafe, unpleasant, and teaching becomes a miserable proposition, if not altogether impossible.

The task of designating classroom seating can be done without mega student complaining which, when present, impels some educators to second guess themselves regarding the wisdom of seat assignments, caving in to pressure from students to sit where they please. Instructors who stand firmly, however, reap the early benefits of not having to deal with classroom disruptions resulting from social chatter between friends. To get the ball rolling on an upbeat, noncontentious note requires confidence and resolve. Recognizing that separating buddies, affording them the opportunity to begin the year concentrating on lessons rather than on each other, is not only educationally sound but advantageous to students, should give one the impetus to plunge right in. Prepare an initial seating chart by randomly choosing student names from your class list. Then, as they enter, direct each student to find the desk bearing his/her name. Incorporating curriculum topics or students' interests in this endeavor can actually add a little fun. If this method is chosen, instead of placing student names on desks, hand each a labeled card as they enter. To find their seats, they will look for the mate to the card received. The mates will have been secured to desks to prevent switching. Ideas for cards include numerals, formulas, names of authors, states, colors or anything curriculum-based and relevant. This activity allows them to get into the spirit of the process, forgetting that seats are even being assigned.

Now, let's address the teacher's desk—that almighty symbol of our profession and authority. As I recall from my days as a student, it was traditional to position the teacher's desk front and center. From there, the monarch of the classroom wielded all manner of power and influence. While less intimidating in today's society, this desk still carries with it, a mystique. In other words, to sit in the teacher's chair at the teacher's desk is a big deal, even today. More importantly, its placement has much to do with the success of your management program. With this in mind, I suggest that you find a way to position your desk *behind* your students. From there, you are able to observe them without their knowledge. This vantage point for the instructor has prevented many a prank or unkind act from occurring. Why? Because the student has no way of knowing whether or not the teacher will see the deed being committed! Thus, unwilling to risk the chance of being caught and "dealt with," he or she merely does the "right thing" which is exactly what is desired.

Conversely, if you are seated at a desk positioned in front of students, as they are engaged in an independent activity it is quite easy for a student to glance up, see that you are engrossed in whatever you're doing, and seize that opportunity to either disrupt or interfere with another student. It's *you* who can be easily watched without the individual having to suspiciously turn around in his seat time and again, checking to see if the coast is clear and, in effect, tipping his hand that something fishy is going on or about to occur. Thus, by being situated at a disadvantage, your opportunity for catching misbehavior before it gets underway is seriously limited.

Further, when an instructor desires to speak with a student without leaving the classroom, or needs to offer a confused learner individualized help while the others are occupied, the obvious place to do so is at the teacher's desk. Having the desk located in the rear of the room allows one to conduct a private chat with a student, or to offer assistance, inconspicuously, without drawing the attention of the class away from their work. This is of prime importance because if a student, whether being quietly disciplined or receiving additional help, notices that her peers are witnessing the process, she is less likely to be cooperative and more apt to get an unpleasant attitude if the conversation is disciplinary, or to feign comprehension about that which she does not comprehend, if the attention is tutorial. Neither scenario is desirable.

When speaking with a student, parent, or any visitor to the classroom, it is much less distracting for our students if the conversation is occurring, discreetly, out of the direct view of the class. Better behavior is fostered since the teacher is not pulling students' attention away from their work with movement, interaction with the visitor, shuffled papers, computer tasks, or any other diversion.

The next step in formulating a program to guide students toward the practice of their best behavior, entails the establishment of an academic classroom atmosphere. This requires one to gather display materials with which to create a rich learning environment. Just as any hostess takes pains to choose party decorations and trappings to infuse guests with the spirit of the occasion, so must teachers sculpt an environment that motivates students to study, raise questions, and show interest in the curriculum. The goal of preventing poor behavior is furthered when students are captivated by their surroundings—a classroom steeped in purposeful curriculum-based exhibits. They actually begin to *feel* like scholars.

It is essential that the design be both academic and soothing. A dull classroom encourages boredom and the creation of the students' own excitement, i.e. **discipline problems.** It can send the message that the instructor is nonchalant about the curriculum, unwilling to spend the necessary time constructing an inviting learning space for students, or harbors disregard for the scholastic capabilities and interests of the students. On the other hand, a room too busy or overly stimulating provokes excitability and psychological discomfort in some, therefore, also evoking the potential for poor student discipline. Find that happy medium.

This organizational piece pertains to middle and high school classrooms as well. It never fails to baffle me when I observe these classrooms devoid of all decorative learning materials, as though older students need no stimulation or motivation whatsoever. Equally as harmful, is the practice of decorating the classroom exclusively based on students' leisure time interests, such as posters of racing cars and sports or music stars. This, in my opinion, communicates one of two significant messages. Either the teacher holds low academic and behavioral expectations of his students, assuming them disinterested in academic pursuits, or is not privy to the research which clearly informs us that learners are capable of absorbing valuable content directly from the environment. Indeed, one's environment influences deportment. Thus, if you wish students to maintain an academic mindset, begin by surrounding them with age and grade-appropriate academic materials.

For those who are wondering about including a few icons from students' interests, of course, this can and should be done. The point being emphasized is that there should be a predominance of attractively-arranged, informational materials gracing classroom walls and bulletin boards. Instructors run the risk of lowering student self-concepts with a purely noneducational decor. As previously stated, students instinctively *know* when they are being respected as scholars and when they are not.

The addition of soft, background music, and plants also serve to induce tranquility. What soothes or calms you generally calms others. A word or two about music is warranted. I observed the actions of an educator who played classical music in his middle school art classroom each day. Because of its soothing qualities, the music alone could have proven a powerful stimulant for positive student behavior. However, his decision to continually extol the virtues and *superiority* of classical music over the students' music preferences netted the opposite effect. As you might guess, instead of prompting a love for Beethoven, as he wished, students began to display feelings of anger and insult. The atmosphere became toxic, resulting in a profusion of disciplinary issues on a regular basis. The lesson to be learned is that whereas instructors may not desire to use the students' choice of music, considering it unsuitable for fueling academic thought and language, remaining accepting of differences can go a long way in bridging the gap.

Actually, permitting loud, overly-stimulating music to be played in the classroom, or sanctioning the use of individual headsets even during independent math assignments, can cause students to stay *off* task, thrusting them into a recreational mood that diminishes learning. Moreover, once kids become accustomed to "kicking back" with their own music, the opportunity to help them grow in the area of developing total academic concentration is lost, and complaining becomes the rule when asked to turn music off for whatever reason, often with behavior deteriorating into harsh student outbursts and wicked student attitudes. Using the right music can be a good thing. Students are extremely pliable and will go with the flow and *like* it when new experiences are presented in a **kind, caring** manner.

Organizing instructional lessons into cohesive, ready to go units is pivotal in the quest for excellent student behavior. Each portion of the lesson should supply a bridge to the next skill or concept, providing enough **substance** and **activities** so as not to give students even *one second of* time to get naughty. Every lesson plan is structured to **begin from the first minute of class.** It's quite common for several students to ask, "What are we doing today?" This simple question can be the cause of much wasted time, actually *allowing* discipline problems to get underway. My suggestion is for you to find some method of informing students of what the day, period, or lesson will entail without having to actually *tell* them unless, of course, there's no viable alternative. This also delivers you from the pit of repetition, as unfocused or tardy students require the same information once it has already been given.

Using a method which compels students to be alert the moment they enter the room or change subjects, always works best. Some ideas are:

- an overhead projector message
- large felt board pictures
- a chalkboard message written in colored chalk
- typed instructions placed on each student's desk

Then, *teach* students to adhere to your system by orienting them to the proper source of information when and if they query you or others, directly. You are freed to smile and greet as they enter, while this strategy serves to get kids organized, *pronto,* with materials and minds ready for learning. Remember, ***when students have idle time, even at the beginning of a lesson, the potential for discipline problems increases exponentially.***

Examples

Ex. 1: Overhead Projector Transparency

HAPPY TUESDAY, JAN. 23, 2006

1. Social Studies Book, Notebook, Pen or Pencil—Ready
2. Colored Pencils Needed Today
3. Head a piece of paper for your focus assignment.

Ex 2: Recorded Song

Good morning to you.
Good morning to you.
Come sit by the chalkboard.
We'll start in a minute or two!
(Oh well, you get the point.)

Interruptions are quite standard fare in our profession. However, they need not be opportunities for your students to become disruptive and unfocused. Have something meaningful, planned and **ready** for students to do if they must wait for any reason, e.g. roll call, lunch count, unexpected visitor, etc. The mistake of the inexperienced teacher is assuming that students will automatically cooperate when the teacher is busy. This goes back to that child and adolescent psychology referred to earlier, the nature of the beast. It is absolutely human nature to take advantage of any situation to "have a little fun!" You needn't view this as aberrant behavior. Just guard against it by always being prepared.

Readiness can be as simple as maintaining a table with labeled baskets of supplementary and enrichment activities for each subject being taught daily or weekly. Make sure that the activities are **curriculum-based** and **relevant**. Otherwise, you're asking for anarchy. In conjunction with this, as part of the information given at the beginning of the school year, spend sufficient time talking with your students about the system you wish them to employ in this regard. Explain ***exactly*** what you desire of them should your attention be required elsewhere. Run through a practice of this procedure before a real interruption occurs, so that both you and they are aware of any kinks needing to be ironed out, and workable adjustments can be made. The plan to be followed will, quite naturally, include some type of academic task for which they have been prepared. They may balk at first, but consider this: when students whine or complain about doing "work," underneath the obligatory complaining, they're feeling *respected as* students, and the subsequent positive behavior reflects that good feeling. The other side of the coin is that when teachers try to "please" students by offering them something insignificant or too simple, somehow they intuitively recognize that they've been provided with an exercise just to keep them "busy," and goofing off often ensues. As one eighth-grader remarked to his teacher when she attempted to fill time at the end of the class, "Okay, now you're just making this up!"

Some examples of things to do are:

- Have the day's assistant pass out designated materials to be worked on in the event of an interruption in the lesson. This can be a review packet that changes each week with what is being reviewed. (e.g. critical thinking questions, problems to work, meaningful maps, graphs, puzzles, etc.)
- At the beginning of each week or month, assign study partners who will automatically study flash cards or do specific and relevant paired reading.
- Maintain boxes of manipulatives with specific instructions for *predetermined* pairs or small groups.
- Take a moment to give an assignment based on the current instructional lesson.

- If you're at a point in the lesson in which your students can *successfully* work on the concept or skill, it can be a moment well spent! e.g. Teacher: "*Read the next 2 pages silently, looking for statements about Ozzie's character, as we've been doing so far. When you find one, write the passage and character trait in your notebook.")*

Be sure that students are *actively* involved, requiring that something be *shown* to indicate that they have been working on the assigned activity. Again, be imaginative and plan activities that are **interesting**, **nondisruptive**, **self-explanatory**, and academically **nonthreatening.** ***When students are engaged in a meaningful, well-organized exercise, requiring a clear measure of accountability, teachers encounter fewer discipline problems during an unscheduled interruption.***

Make-Up Work

Another common occurrence viewed by teachers as an annoyance, at times, thus disruptive of the smooth running of the classroom, is the necessity of suspending instruction for the purpose of providing make-up work or an instructional explanation for a student who has been absent or is being dismissed early. Here, a well thought-out, **user friendly** and **independent** process comes in handy. Face it, there are going to be students leaving class or school for one reason or another, and students who were absent, requiring instruction on pertinent skills and concepts. It's all part of our day, so don't allow stress, anger, disapproval, criticism, or self-righteousness to creep into the equation. It's the nature of our job. Love it! Embrace it!

Forestall potentially intrusive incidents by putting into place a simple, *student–activated* plan for obtaining assignments or make-up work. Guide your students, step by step through the procedure during the first week of school, so that each will be aware of how to proceed and feel confident utilizing it. Then, be willing to keep everything organized, so that they won't have to wait on you to stop what you're doing in order to access materials. This kind of system furthers self-reliance, teaches kids to take charge of this portion of their educational lives, and leads to progress along the path to personal responsibility. In the lower grades such a system may entail enlisting the services of a paraprofessional, *trained by you* to do the job efficiently and with consideration for the children's needs. Many a student's disposition has transformed from pleasant and deferential to sour or irate after butting heads with an instructor who's out to "punish" the student for being absent or requesting to leave early. At times it's a subconscious reaction to conversations or debasing gossip about students to which a teacher has listened or participated in during a planning period. Though some banter with fellow educators is only natural, be cognizant of what actually permeates your thinking, subsequently creeping into your actions with students—**provoking student misbehavior.**

A final area of classroom structure necessitating the ultimate in instructor organization, is that of keeping accurate records. A disorganized teacher may appear amusing, providing fodder for innocent joking among colleagues and even for the educator himself. Nevertheless, daily searching escapades for student materials and graded or ungraded assignments, mad dashes to the copy machine as the rule vs. the exception, constant queries of students as to the location of vital instructional materials, a consistently jumbled, disorderly desk, et al, can *give the impression* of a person who is also topsy-turvy in his or her thinking, and not completely competent. These habits, associated with those generally assumed to not be proficient or "all over it" in the area of delivering excellence in instruction and leadership, present an open invitation for student misconduct, as any opportunity to gain the advantage is seized. Organization is a must and a plus in this profession. Maintaining orderliness simply makes the job easier, allowing instructors to put *their* best foot forward in the quest for the attentiveness and respect of students.

Respect and Discipline

The word, respect, is used so often by instructors that it could be viewed, by some, as a teacher's favorite term. Way back when, dinosaur years ago when I was in grade school, a teacher I'll call Mrs. Z taught me, *indirectly*, how to show veneration for my students. Her daily manner toward students demolished regard for us in every imaginable way. I learned from Mrs. Z how to incite feelings of fear, insecurity, belittlement, and discomfort in the presence of a teacher.

Thus, the groundwork for my beliefs and ultimate disciplinary success was laid. ***Do and say unto children what you would have them do and say unto you.*** Simply put, children and young adults are human beings who deserve politeness, consideration, the benefit of the doubt, kind greetings, and thoughtful comments. "May I have your attention, please," "thank you," "excuse me," "I'm sorry," "please," and the employment of a pleasant tone of voice, are a few tricks of the respect trade, which enhance the likelihood of your receiving a reciprocal use of good manners from your students. Conversely, screaming at the top of one's voice, "PEOPLE, GET IN YOUR SEATS!" is O-U-T, OUT. The display of disrespect on your part will inadvertently give students the signal to begin practicing the usage of irreverent language and/or actions toward you and their fellow classmates. Once this begins, it is difficult to quell.

We are teachers in more ways than one. Students learn to be respectful from our example. Just think about it. What kind of response would be engendered in you if someone screamed and referred to you as PEOPLE, or used something of yours without asking? Teachers *do* set the tone of respectfulness for their students and the student population, in general. Put them at ease on the very first day of school by letting them know that you will be treating them in the exact same manner in which you appreciate being treated. Be meticulous in this endeavor. Explain your behavioral expectations with simplicity and specificity, without enumerating every horrid thing a child of this age might do. This "listing" would merely serve to lower self-concepts, leading to student anger, insult, and determination to perpetrate the obnoxious behavior you're trying to prevent.

One high school teacher passed out his "dos and don'ts" list on the first day of class, in an attempt to set the tone and forestall behavior problems he believed to be common. The trouble began when students took a look at the list of *twenty* repugnant behaviors that "would not be tolerated." There among the don'ts was the act of writing on oneself, which elicited gasps from several kids. As more and more of the document was read and digested, more students began to display outrage. They just couldn't comprehend how their instructor could, without even knowing them, believe them capable of committing acts which in their minds seemed absurd. The resulting uproar, even in the face of his attempts to defend the document, turned into animosity against the instructor, commencing in that moment, then festering and erupting in both passive and aggressive misbehavior throughout the semester. Of course, the infamous list wasn't the sole catalyst for disruptive behavior in this case. The *thinking* which fueled the presumption of student misbehavior was ever present. Thus, other unintentional blunders were made, keeping students off-balance, feeling disrespected.

Telling students who they are in the positive nets immensely gratifying results. Genuinely expect them to be cooperative learners and *treat* them *as such.* Employ an authoritative, but pleasant tone. Then display your *like* and regard for them with *your* behavior, and reap the benefits. Dos are all that are needed. They can figure out the don'ts just by being aware of what is acceptable.

Here's a test for you. You're administering a dictation quiz and a student raises his hand to ask if you would pause a moment. Test 1: Would you ordinarily, (A) ignore him and keep going because he should have been keeping up anyway or (B) reply, *"Sure, I'll give you another minute."* Test 2: Two students are talking during your lesson. You (A) yell, "Stop talking, Laurel and Hardy!" or (B) stop, look at them and calmly say, *"You know, Laurel and Hardy, I like to chat too, but when I'm teaching I want you to listen and not talk. Can you guys handle that or do you need a seat change?"* **Preserving the students' dignity** as you discipline is a number one priority. Remember, a few drops of honey will get you further than a whole bottle of vinegar (my mother's version). In short, bestowing respect upon your students goes a long way in ensuring a sense of loyalty to you and, thus, good behavior.

Establishing Discipline

Students will fall into line a whole lot quicker if the instructor knows how to get the discipline train on the right track from day one. There are four steps.

Step one: Human beings yearn for and actually need to feel welcome and accepted. Just this simple dynamic of acting and speaking in ways which make your students aware that you are glad to have them in class, gets the relationship started off on the right foot. Don't just assume that they *know* that they are welcome. They don't. And many are experiencing stress about what to expect from *you*. This very "nervousness," created by the fear of the unknown, has spawned many a discipline problem on the first day of school. They're wondering if their hair style, skin color, skill level, gender, clothing preference, way of speaking, and a whole host of other idiosyncrasies will get in the way of you liking them and treating them well. Putting students at ease right off-the-bat, with a warm, kind smile of acceptance and friendly words of welcome, can deliver them from a ton of anxiety, resulting in them at least beginning the day or class period with a spirit of goodwill toward both you and the new school year. Too many educators and administrators, especially of urban students, in an effort to send the strong conveyance that they are in charge, end up instead conveying, via disparaging language, looks of disapproval, and prepared admonishments, that they are *expecting* students to misbehave and, subsequently, have erected guards against that eventuality. This often translates as dislike, fear of, meanness, and in many instances, racism in the eyes of students. There is a balance that needs to be struck between giving the impression that one is patronizing, inappropriately playful, or too "hang loose," and the once highly touted determination to not smile until Christmas. The way to send the message of being in charge has nothing to do with stern looks and standoffish attitudes. It's all about employing the golden rule, exuding confidence, and being totally organized.

Step two in this process of establishing discipline concerns the assigning of seats, which has already been discussed. Though their seats may not be carved in stone, you have sent the nonverbal message that you are the "official assigner of seats." Therefore, should the need arise, it will be easier for you to rearrange any or all students. Further, you've decreed, without a single gruff word I might add, that this is a classroom that will emphasize learning, as opposed to socializing. During this process, if you choose to indicate each student's seat by placing a name or curriculum-based card on the designated desk, be sure to secure each card so that it is not easily removed and transferred to a different location—nature of the beast. Then, compose a master seating chart, immediately. You have automatically, in most cases, separated friends who would have assuredly participated in social banter during class, and even thwarted victim-bully ties. Additionally, the angst of changing seats later, once they've become ensconced (which takes very few days), have begun troublesome chatter with friends, and are now determined to beg, complain, or pout in an effort to stay the course regardless of what you think best, has been avoided. Prevention, again, is key. The aim is to stave off the talking and playing that naturally accompanies sitting next to one's best friend. You are also endeavoring to ward off having to jump right in with admonishments and negative consequences to address students' talking and playing, which inevitably impedes the progress of establishing a good working relationship with the class as a whole.

Step three entails being prepared to initiate the exact beginning-of-class routine you intend to maintain for the remainder of the semester. In other words, just say, "no" to spending this day in frivolity, expecting your students to come in and "get down to business" the very next day, or to whip themselves into shape when you're ready to begin "for the reals."

A "getting to know you" written activity can serve as the focus assignment for that day. It should already be on their desks. Allot time for its silent completion as you move calmly among the students, collecting registration materials and quietly greeting each person individually, laying the foundation for a congenial teacher-student relationship. Set the timer, taking into consideration students' working and thinking pace, and expressing, up front, that each student is expected to complete this initial survey just as they will be expected to complete all future in-class assignments. Let them know that they will be receiving a grade of "A" or whatever is the acceptable mode of grading, for its well thought-out completion. Do be sure, however, if you decide to become acquainted with your students in this manner, that the questions are neither private nor invasive. Unfortunately, the young can be weighed down by unpleasant baggage just as adults are, encountering added stress by being asked to share personal information with teachers and classmates. This type of distress can usher in pronouncements of "I'm not answering these stupid questions!" and other common disruptions or refusals, including tears in younger students.

Once the assignment is concluded, follow with a session of sharing, which mirrors the discussion component that would naturally accompany the end of an academic focus exercise. Begin with yourself as model, teaching students how to proceed. Then, closely monitor and direct the activity so that absolutely no student will be put on the spot or purposely embarrassed. This may seem like much ado about nothing, but we must be ever perceptive of what will cause our students to shut down or turn to the dark side, as Master Yoda would forewarn.

Proceed to the next segment of your daily routine with the smoothness you will employ during ensuing class periods. You are, in effect, guiding your students through a well-organized, harmonious class period or day. The activities may be slightly different because of the necessity of getting things up and running with students in the groove, but beware of not designating the classroom as a place of academic work and learning, from the very first moment.

Step four of the blueprint for laying the groundwork of your management system during this inaugural day, is to have a guided lesson preplanned and ready to teach. Don't just pass out a review worksheet or assign pages in a book for them to read on their own. It's of primary importance that you establish yourself as a teacher who will guide them through lessons in a manner which will allow them to feel competent and to realize success. At this early stage, they desperately need to feel insulated from what they may perceive as inevitable academic failure or stress.

This premiere instructional topic is chosen from among those set aside for your subject or grade, has proven in the past to garner high student interest, and is introductory in nature, so as not to require your students to possess specific prior knowledge in order to experience success. Structure the lesson so that: (a) all pertinent information or skills are being presented by you (b) it contains interesting hands-on activities and (c) in essence, embodies a fun way of diving into a new class or grade. A mini, introductory unit can be written if you plan to extend the topic throughout the first week.

As you proceed with this instruction devised to acquaint students with initial, fundamental skills and concepts from the *new* curriculum, review subject matter can be interwoven and evaluated. It is designed to fit neatly, right into the overall lesson plan, instead of pounding students with page after page of nothing but review assignments, extinguishing natural student excitement and discouraging those who are apprehensive about their chances of succeeding. Concurrently, as a part of **each day's** continuance of this foundation-laying, you will need to incorporate an instructional recap of what was previously covered, for those who may just be entering or tend to learn at a slower pace. You're taking advantage of a continual overlapping technique to *ease* students into your academic program, without wasting valuable time in backbreaking, attention-busting review, or excessive "waiting" for all students to enroll.

Via this gentle, but powerful process, you are gradually becoming familiar with names and faces, and gathering pertinent information regarding students' abilities and cumulative skill levels while simultaneously, firmly entrenching their learning feet in the habit of expending maximum academic effort— all without them ever being aware of what is transpiring! To boot, this critical first step of getting students to voluntarily accept the navigational "bit" which will allow a competent educator to pilot them steadily along the trail of skill/concept acquisition as well as appropriate classroom conduct, is being accomplished in a fashion neither threatening nor intimidating to students. They are being primed for early success, which can **check unwieldy behavior problems** that just naturally originate when students are on edge, experiencing foreboding of impending academic difficulty.

The primary goal of detailing the process specified above is to prevail upon instructors to eschew the practice of engaging in actions or language which evoke feelings of anxiety in their students, either purposely or inadvertently, by "reminding" them of what they SHOULD already know, or by putting them on the spot with lengthy review worksheets and tests. Negative emotions, spanning a range of depths, allow fear, humiliation, and even exclusion—as more capable classmates have retained past concepts that others have not, to run rampant, prepping your classroom for **disharmony and substandard behavior**. A chasm is generated between teacher and students and even student to student, as the less capable endeavor to save face, shifting attention away from what they DON'T know or remember, by displaying disinterest, bravado and, sometimes, machismo. It's called self-preservation, and I believe that any of us would find ourselves so engaged were our self-image and emotional well-being on the line.

The solution to conducting the necessary evaluation of what students have succeeded in retaining, while allowing dignity to be preserved and stress levels to be kept to a minimum, is to just jump right in with mini review lessons *as* the first academic unit is being presented. It will be easy to discover who knows what, whether or not the whole class needs to be retaught a certain skill or concept, and so on.

During the first week of getting acquainted with students, in addition to making sure that all possible is done to discourage the psychological stress that can occur with pressure to immediately perform well academically, actually spend time TEACHING and MODELING the procedures that will keep your classroom operating smoothly, for the time being. Other procedures will be taught as needed. Expending energy assuming and criticizing is counterproductive, thrusting students into an adversarial relationship with you, and your classroom into one riddled with misbehavior, as students try to dismiss their feelings of incompetence through placing blame and acting out.

Once you've explained your rules and guidelines, waste no time holding back for whatever reason. Enforce each, calmly and consistently the moment it is violated. Also, don't be reluctant to institute modifications when you notice that something is not working. For example, one teacher decided to create a system for permitting his students access to the restroom with as little disruption as possible. His plan involved issuing 2, 2x2-inch construction paper bathroom passes weekly, to each person. A request consisted of a student raising his hand to receive permission, leaving the room with one of his pre-approved passes, and depositing the pass in a designated container, upon returning. Students who did not use their passes could turn them in at the end of the week for a few extra-credit points. What he learned, forthwith, was that since he hadn't provided guidelines for WHEN they could ask to go to the restroom, many of his middle school students decided to test the limits by requesting to leave right in the middle of an instructional lesson, important discussion, or even mid sentence. Moreover, the instructor discovered that there were one or two among them who decided to engage in a bit of trickery in the form of declaring that they'd not received their passes for the week. Because no notation had been made during distribution, though fairly certain each child had been given them, he ended up reissuing the precious tender to those students, who then had four! Quickly, he realized that it was the nature of the beast for students to exploit a system that was not well-thought out or tightly organized, and that **attention to detail** makes a world of difference between achieving a modicum of success or setting into motion a procedure that will work to promote and solidify stellar classroom behavior. He proceeded to make specific adjustments to fine-tune the system, allowing it to run smoothly, and sending the message to his students that he was on top of the situation. The nonsense ceased and his students settled into the process without trying to take further advantage.

The totality of what you say or do during this precarious time will either help or hinder the process of establishing your classroom as a place of order and learning. Your deportment needs to be one of authority, laced with benevolence, humanity, and veneration for your students. Assuring that they understand, *without a doubt*, that you are in their corner and will stop at nothing to help them succeed, will compel them to follow suit, putting forth academic effort instead of expending seemingly insurmountable energy disrupting the learning for themselves and others.

Fairness and Discipline

"Fair" is a kid's favorite word it seems. And you know, there's something to it. When students believe that you're fair or are at least *attempting* to be just, they behave more placidly and with greater generosity of spirit. Fairness begins with being consistent. Make a decision on rules, academic expectations, and general consequences for misbehavior. Always forewarn, and deal with each disciplinary situation from a spirit of equality, humanity, and a huge dose of humor, if possible and appropriate.

Even when a student has to accept unpleasant consequences, the medicine will be swallowed much better if you're not overreacting, or embellishing what occurred. Simply state what you *noticed* and give the replacement behavior expected in the future. **Replacement behavior** is vital. Oftentimes, teachers expect a student to know what she should do differently. This is a shaky notion, at best, because in the first place, the student *is* handling the situation as she deems appropriate. Even at the high school level, though a student may have a clue, you want to be sure that the person knows what *you* consider proper and what works in *your* classroom. (e.g. Teacher: "*Next time someone* takes your pencil without asking, instead of yelling and snatching it back, I'd like for you to politely ask once, and if that doesn't work, request help from me.")

Students **are not** experts in problem solving, conflict management, or communication, **nor should they be**. Our guidance and input gradually propel them in the right direction, teaching them how to handle difficult situations in positive ways. It takes time—years even, and they need our help! Their progress may be imperceptible, but advance they will if we just stay the course.

Once the **replacement behavior** has been explained, utilizing very specific, concrete terminology, and clarification has been given if requested, state kindly, but firmly what the consequence will be for noncompliance. If both the time and place are right, really give a listen to the student's explanation **(respect)**, then stick with your decision if you feel it to be fair. You'll know in your gut. However, if listening isn't possible at the moment, be sure to touch base with that student as soon as possible on a one to one basis if the infraction was significant enough to warrant such a conversation. Accomplished through this dialogue, is an opportunity for the instructor to honor the student's sense of self and justice by permitting the student to communicate his point of view in a concise, respectful manner. By so doing, though the student will not be exonerated of the offense, or any consequence altered unless new information has resulted in a different decision being proffered, the instructor is able to convey the message that the student's relationship with him has not been diminished in any manner, and the student is still viewed as possessing an intent to cooperate. It is most essential to emphasize this point because many children and teens are programmed by society to believe that once they've committed a mistake, their standing is permanently damaged, and that they are no longer trusted. For students, dealing with adults can be so formidable, and this "all or nothing" thinking, in and of itself, if left unchecked or not refuted, can cause students to assume a devil-may-care attitude, rationalizing behavior which has run amuck.

Further, this time of communication between student and teacher can help to strengthen the relationship, building trust and reiterating that even though high behavioral standards will be maintained, those standards will always be just and consistent.

Developing this kind of rapport at the outset of the school year or at any time, for that matter, can actually motivate the most aberrant of students to monitor his own behavior, reflecting loyalty to you. Not behaving in a patronizing manner is essential in all communication with kids. Though student reactions may *appear* to indicate approval in the face of patronization, they can " detect" it, actually abhor it, disrespect the perpetrator, and see it for what it is—fear of retribution in the form of vile student behavior should the instructor take a firm stand against unacceptable conduct, or lack of confidence in setting and insisting upon high expectations, on the part of the instructor. Thus, classroom behavior continues to plummet, at a time when an unsuspecting teacher believes he has found the elusive answer.

Running a fair and just classroom includes yet another immensely important dynamic—the avoidance of engaging in stereotypical thinking. Stereotypes are so insidious, especially those which are of negative orientation. They seem to creep into our minds and actions, sometimes without us even knowing it. Be on the lookout. They have been the undoing of oh so many classrooms run by both well-intentioned and not so well-intentioned teachers.

What is a stereotype and why are they so prevalent in our society? What is the harm? Why do people react so adversely when personally confronted by one or more? Let's begin with the what, though I'm certain that you're already familiar with its meaning. Stereotypes are generalizations and oversimplifications which assume that all identified to be in a particular group will behave, look, think in an unvarying manner, and be capable or incapable of the same kinds of attainments. It's completely nonsensical. Yet, there are those who persist in this type of reasoning, acting upon these beliefs right in the classroom. Labels and judgments become all-important, resulting in student self- concepts being scarred and even destroyed as many are robbed of their individuality and opportunity to show just who they are. Without belaboring the point, I must emphasize that students cannot and should not be branded and categorized, saddled with the burden of disproving negatives that they've not even displayed—not if you want them to learn and behave well. There are those who come to us in fear of just such labeling. They've been there before and are desperately hoping that this time will be different. Don't disappoint them. See each student as a unique individual. Grant the benefit of the doubt even when appearances seem to suggest otherwise, permitting students to make mistakes without adults leaping to the conclusion that wrongful behavior represents a summation of who the person truly is. In his biography, *Always Running,* Luis Rodriguez articulates it well when he relates the experience he and fellow classmates endured in his neighborhood high school. Coming from a community called The Hills, they were arbitrarily thought of as outsiders, delinquents, and hoodlums. Though they so desperately desired to do well, to be viewed as serious students, the stereotyping was so entrenched in the adults of the school that the expectation was that sooner or later these kids would cause trouble. They were gazed at with fear and scorn. He goes on to say that this abject belief by those in power, hindered him from moving forward, proving them wrong, since each time anything went awry, all eyes turned to the kids from The Hills. It was too much to overcome, thrusting them into the very negative behavior expected. Frustration with the system eventually led some to take pride in being disrupters.

We are all too well aware from recent events in society and just plain old common sense, that neither looks nor any other superficial variable provides a barometer of character. If you *genuinely* view each of your students as capable, honest, kind, and cooperative, those are the qualities you will most likely experience from them. They are relying upon you to dismiss common stereotypes as the destroyers of individualism and ravagers of self-esteem that they are, refusing to assign them to anyone. Treat your students as you would wish to be treated. It's that simple. Fight the impulse to take on teacher's pets, deemed to be students who are headed in the right direction, on the road to success. Make sure that *each* of your students feels that she or he is on the road to success in your classroom. **Those who detect even a hint of negative stereotyping in your behavior or speech will surely retaliate with distasteful behavior**. It can't be helped, because all human beings *need* to feel regarded and valued.

Within this framework, embracing all of your students as true equals in your sight exempts your classroom from the upheaval resulting from cries of favoritism and racism plaguing some teachers, causing them to grapple day in and day out with untoward behavior. Surprises are out. If you wish to institute a consequence, be sure to inform your students of what is on the horizon. In other words, it's not fair to rise from your seat, proclaim that the class or certain individuals have disobeyed your instructions for the past 30 minutes, and will now forfeit 15 minutes of their lunch hour. Who knew what you were thinking? Surely not the class or the individuals in question. Their subsequent, obnoxious behavior will indicate their surprise and feelings of anger at being slapped with a consequence about which they were not forewarned. It's akin to being abruptly stopped by a police officer for some newly installed infraction, and forced to forfeit your driver's license until you've paid the fine. Hard to imagine, I know, but all the same, it wouldn't sit well with you, and the same type of action won't sit well with your students.

What to do? When you notice that your students or a particular student is not following your behavioral expectations, step right up and say so in a calm, authoritative manner. Be brief in your explanation that you want everyone working quietly on the assignment at his or her own desk, and that anyone deviating from that behavior in the next fifteen minutes will be joining you for twenty minutes after school. That said, check for understanding by asking several students to repeat the expectation, if more than one student is involved. Otherwise, speak directly and privately to the perpetrator. Remain polite and respectful, inviting anyone needing academic assistance to raise his hand or come to you. Then, return to whatever you were doing. Now, if a student makes the *choice* to be spoken to again within that time period, he knows what to expect **and you must deliver.**

When detaining a student during lunch, after school, or any free time for students, beware of trying to "force" her to do school work. This actually opens the door for defiant behavior, creating a *new* problem. My advice is to be certain that your classroom is unoccupied and "boring," have low, calming, music playing in the background, direct the student to where you would like her to sit (her back is to you), and allow her to read, work quietly, or to do nothing. The consequence is the forfeiting of the student's free time, not being able to socialize with peers. It's quiet reflection time, **though you have not named it thus**. Therefore, unless you have stipulated from the outset that doing an assignment is part of the consequence, avoid trying to add anything at this point. It could be costly, regarding the student's perception of whether or not you are being fair, and, thus, in the relationship the two of you are forging.

Using a timer to keep track of the detention period always puts the student more at ease because she knows that you will not detain her beyond the stated duration. Further, you shield yourself from what some students consider as having the final word, asserted in an impudent tone— " The time is up. Can I go now?" However, should this final display of poor decision-making transpire anyway, remember that you are always bringing light. Merely reply, *"Yes, thank you for coming."* Your brief, private chat will need to occur the next day when the student is in a "calmer place" and can " hear" you. If you were to try to counsel at this point it would be all for naught, just as anyone endeavoring to issue guidance when you are in a state of anger would also be wasting his or her time. Let's keep in mind that our students, regardless of age, are first and foremost human beings, possessing the same emotions as we. When kids are thought of in this manner, instructors are open to displaying more graciousness—which is *not* timidity or weakness.

The student who accepts his consequence without exhibiting a raunchy disposition can be engaged in a brief, guidance chat during the last two to five minutes of the detention period. Keeping it short and to the point, first thank the student for arriving on schedule and displaying such a positive attitude. Tell him, genuinely, who he is (e.g. *"I've noticed that you always come prepared for class, and I appreciate that."),* describe the behavior which landed him in hot water, and terminate the chat by resetting your behavioral expectations via specific **replacement behavior.** Be sure to have figured out the exact modifications in the student's behavior you feel will bring about the desired outcome. Hemming and hawing or "covering the waterfront" can result in the student becoming overwhelmed and unwilling to attempt change. Simplicity is key.

Instructional Fairness

Fairness in instructional practices plays an integral part in maintaining an environment in which students are motivated to behave well. Many a foul attitude or behavioral disruption has been a direct outgrowth of the type of instructional techniques being employed. To proffer an example of how this can come about, take a look with me at a situation that took place in a real classroom.

It was requested that I observe the class of a teacher whose students exhibited no restraint in displaying daily, unruly and disrespectful behavior. They vociferously complained to the instructor about the fairness of her instructional practices, contending that her intention was to make them fail the class. Several had even taken the initiative to speak with an administrator about their concerns. Nevertheless, the instructor persistently denied that anything was awry except for students who were *choosing* to be off-kilter and noncompliant. Upon observing for only the first few moments of this high school class, many red flags were evident. The set-up was devoid of a beginning-of-class routine or procedure which would have provided guidance for student entry and informed them of the learning objectives for that class period. They where allowed to enter in a disorganized manner, haphazardly following their own guidelines for suitable conduct. An academic mindset was not promoted. Assuming an initial, opening-day spiel to be sufficient, the teacher never thought further about establishing a precise, daily procedure to steer students from the moment of entry, along a course of preparation for the day's class. They were simply to pick up their folders and perhaps a book, take their seats and wait for her to commence class. After all, according to her reasoning, this *was* high school and, as such, students should be responsible enough to enter class prepared to learn.

The focus assignment was scribbled on a crowded dry-erase board, not easily discernible from the writing from previous classes, with directions ranging from sketchy to nonexistent and pretty much confusing. The presumption made by the instructor was that, as secondary students, they would automatically walk in, adjust to whatever was being presented, in whatever format she chose to employ, and get started once the final bell sounded—all without any added direction from her. Instead, they did what students will do: they entered, glanced around to see what was up, a *few* picked up their folders, then most sat down to chat with friends and acquaintances, continuing even after the bell had rung. This, of course, necessitated the admonishing of students, (which the teacher often executed through the utilization of sarcasm considered to be humor), to get their materials and begin working on the warm-up assignment. Many had to be issued a special invitation to fall into line. Eventually there was a *semblance* of order once the myriad of "what do we do" questions were asked and answered.

On the several visitations made, I noted that the class had no real " kick off." In other words, the instructor didn't think to say something to garner their attention. *"Good afternoon, guys. Class has begun. You have 10 minutes to complete the focus."* This greeting, acknowledgement of your students' presence, is significant. It let's them know that you're glad to see them and gives the signal that class time is officially underway. With this routine, students will come to know that when certain words are spoken it's time to get down to the business of learning.

The instructional practices being utilized in that particular classroom continued on a downward slide as the class progressed. There was no closure to one assignment or task before another was being introduced. Students were seldom given up-front instructions as to what they should be doing while the teacher lectured. No objectives were communicated to guide learning. Information was presented in a classic bird-walking fashion. No one could put their finger on the overall theme or intent of the lesson. It swayed from front to back, side to side, with off-topic conversation thrown in for good measure. The students were in a definite quandary as to how to pass the class. Academic frustration was evident, with a myriad of coping mechanisms constantly in progress.

Many instructors reading this account may consider it to be an unfair indictment of the teacher involved, with no responsibility at all being placed at the feet of her students. I totally admit that a portion of the students took advantage of the situation to merely socialize, perhaps without any concern for whether or not they were obtaining the knowledge for which they came. However, though it would be gratifying to educators if our students would just take the bull by the horns and muddle their way through to success regardless of the level of teacher competence, it just ain't so. Neither is it necessarily done when adults are the learners and leadership or instruction is substandard. My overall contention is that teachers are trained to set the stage for student achievement, academically and behaviorally. We must hold ourselves accountable for using practices and techniques which illustrate competence in this field, just as it is imperative that students be held accountable when teaching methods *are* up to snuff. Insinuating that because we are adults we will always be right, just won't make it so! Each and every educator must continue to grapple with seeking strategies that will elevate expertise. Effecting achievement is not an easy task. All ducks must be in a row, and at least when one notices that something is not working to bring about the desired outcome, a willingness to look in the mirror to challenge the one who must instigate change, is required. As the saying goes, *If you keep doing what you're doing, you'll keep getting what you're getting*. If what you're getting from your students is what you desire, then continue moving forward. Otherwise, note that ***student behavior is a prime indicator of whether or not the strategies being employed are bringing about a thriving, productive learning atmosphere, or whether alterations need to be immediately imposed.*** It's not about placing blame, but finding solutions. Denying that methodology *is* "all that," or expecting students to rise up and automatically take the reigns of their own behavior merely lands one on that proverbial slippery slope—headed straight for offensive and obnoxious difficulties with student conduct.

Teaching your routines and procedures and making them standard helps students *develop* the *good habits* you're trying to promote. Complaining about what students "should" do is a waste of time and effort, tainting not only the instructor's attitude, but the dispositions of students, as well. The teacher in the above scenario wasn't this evil villain who was out to get her students. Her love of teaching and fondness for them could clearly be detected. Nonetheless, the absence of effective instructional techniques, organization, and guidance gave rise to the fear of failure in her students, many of whom honestly believed that she was purposely engineering their failure.

This example, unfortunately is not uncommon. It's more prevalent than educators care to admit. I believe that it stems from a lack of consciousness and sensitivity on the part of many instructors, that though the essential skills being taught are effortless and perfectly comprehensible for them, it is not always the case for their students—not even the youngest who are trying to recall that the letter "G" has two sounds. These skills and concepts must be articulated to students in such a manner so as to render acquisition as comfortable as possible, presenting learning as a series of pleasant experiences, encouraging positive behavior.

It all adds up to instructional UNfairness when we fail to expose our students to their lessons or take them through their paces in ways that quiet fears and foster a reasonable belief in the ability to achieve. **Students will create disruptions when desperation is present.** Rude outbursts, bullying peers who are demonstrating comprehension of what's being taught, name-calling, complaining, whining, refusing to work, labeling instruction and assignments as stupid or boring, and even declaring that they *already* know how to do the task and need no further practice, can all signal to the teacher that they are struggling and need a fresh approach. It's difficult to get past their poor behavior to recognize need, but get past it we must, if it is to be halted and prevented from recurring or becoming a permanent fixture.

Following is a list of areas which can be viewed by students as instructional unfairness, precipitating misbehavior in the classroom of an unsuspecting teacher and requiring a change in policy if they have, indeed, crept into the classroom system.

- reducing grades over petty errors
- refusing to answer *each* student's academic questions
- administering tests before students have had time to grasp and thoroughly practice a skill or concept
- assigning homework covering a skill introduced THAT day
- giving pop quizzes as punishment
- providing ambiguous directions for projects, then assigning a significant point total to an end product requiring specific components and standards
- giving unreasonable assignments or timelines
  e.g. Define these 60 new vocab words and be ready for a quiz over the definitions, tomorrow. (an actual homework assignment)
- testing over a broad area of information without providing a study guide or some other type of study tool
- presenting information in an illogical, confusing manner
- teaching too many new skills/concepts at once, moving students too quickly for real comprehension or mastery to take place
- assuming the worst (e.g. a student has cheated)

Testing and Fairness

Testing or any form of evaluation is another arena in which the potential monster of unfairness can rear its ugly head. The best advice that I can give is for instructors to be sure that students:

1. are made aware of and understand lesson objectives
2. are taught skills and concepts thoroughly
3. are given adequate time to practice and master those skills and/or concepts *before* being seriously evaluated.

There's nothing more anxiety-producing than being saturated with new learning material, given little time to practice, digest, or grasp it, then being required to pass a test over that material. It's stressful, frustrating, and unfair.

Students generally do not endure such predicaments with grace. Think about learning situations you've experienced in which the time allotted for mastery was inadequate for your needs, creating undue stress in your life. How did you feel towards that instructor? Ultimately, you, the teacher, will know when and if you've covered something *well enough* and *long enough* to evaluate your students. You can sense whether or not the length of the test-taking session is sufficient, insufficient, or overwhelming. Observe students and make necessary individual or class adjustments. Remember, if most students are failing, look in the mirror. If nothing changes, discipline problems could be on the horizon.

Just keeping the concept of fairness uppermost in your mind as you move through each day, week, semester, will undoubtedly aid you in sidestepping the pitfalls that accompany students' belief that their teacher is running an unjust classroom. It's truly not difficult when you follow your instincts to do what *you* would consider fair if the tables were turned, or if your son, daughter, sister, brother, friend were in your classroom. It all boils down again to, you guessed it—the Golden Rule.

Equality, Humanity, Humor

Equality

These three commodities are extremely important and indispensable in your discipline toolbox. They are actual guideposts as you work your way through each disciplinary situation. Let's begin with equality. Equal– Having the same privileges, status, or rights 2. Being the same for all members of a group.[2] Sadly, there are scenarios in which otherwise sagacious teachers seem to feel free to rationalize the use of *inequality*. Examples include girls over boys, honor students over struggling students, majority race over minorities, shy or quiet students over extroverts (or vice versa), and students with demanding parents over those with more nonparticipatory parents. Perhaps you've even experienced some of these inequities during your own school years, either personally or through a friend or classmate. Though it may be more difficult to mete out the same consequence to someone viewed as usually cooperative, than to one who regularly misbehaves, if all of your students are to view you as a fair, impartial disciplinarian, you simply cannot afford to change the consequence depending upon whom the perpetrator happens to be. The result will be angry, reactionary students just waiting to ambush and derail your teaching train.

Humanity

Humanity is so absolutely essential that its importance can't be overstated. There is a "softness" that accompanies disciplinary actions when you allow humanity to enter the picture. A sleeping student may

[2] The American Heritage Dictionary: Second College Edition © '85

have had an emergency at home the previous night, a "lippy" student may be experiencing fear of failure, frustration, or attempting to avoid academic embarrassment. These are not, I repeat not excuses. They are considerations to investigate via observation or a quick question *whispered* to the student. "Forgiveness" and empathy may be wise in certain cases. By empathizing and allowing a tired student to put his head down, or offering individual assistance *without sarcasm or an insulting tone* to a student who perhaps wasn't displaying perfect attention, you actually effectuate a loyalty that will cause students to want to "be good" for and to you. Just acknowledging a student's view of a situation on which the two of you disagree, lessens student hostility and anger.

The value of establishing a solid rapport with students and building community cannot be overemphasized. They are looking to you to be the architect and builder of this process. And why not? After all, we are professionals. Many teachers feel that they must share the same ethnic group as their students in order to be the *most* effective. The fact of the matter is, that though the commonality of ethnicity and culture does seem to bridge an initial gap between students and instructor, the bridge will begin to crumble if and when students discover that negative labeling or stereotyping exists, or that the instructor is not genuinely in their corner, for whatever reason. The good news is that we are all part of the *human* race and this, alone, supplies the connection if we will but allow it to happen. How is this feat to be accomplished in a society which seems to take notice of or exploit every imaginable difference, one that seeks to function by applying a covert caste system of sorts? It's not formidable when a teacher's absolute desire and intent is to elevate, versus amplifying perceived flaws, justifying belief in the wretchedness of certain groups of students. Simply show interest in your cherubs as individuals and human beings. Plan and deliver lessons illustrating that they are deemed capable students. Show and *tell* them that you like them. There's no substitute for actually *speaking* such words as, "*I'm glad you're here, today." "You're fun to teach." "I enjoy having you in class."* All students seek our unconditional acceptance and approval. In its presence, our relationship becomes impervious to cries of racism and unfairness. While in its absence they're taken aback, generally attributing this lack of affirming language to negative reasons, even if in actuality, it isn't. This can cause students to retreat in a refusal to allow us to touch them with the wand of learning. A prickly barrier has been erected, and the instructor can very likely be completely unaware of the problem. Therefore, we need to make students aware that we like and appreciate them for who they are, regardless of economics, race, religion, study habits, or any other real or perceived distinction.

The question of middle class values requires discussion, because so many teachers use the argument that when these values are seemingly "missing" in students' lives, those particular students are either more difficult to teach or impossible to teach! What are these magical ideals — really? Why are the possessors of such, assumed to be solely from middle and upper economic echelons? Can values be bound by financial gain? I assert that they are not. All too often, we allow our biases to masquerade as values. Biases can intrude upon our thinking to the extent of taking up residence or putting a tainted wash over all that we do, such that they become inhibitors to our ability to provide sincere, unbridled instructional effort on behalf of our students. When this happens, make no mistake, our students RECOGNIZE and REACT to these stereotypical slants with the only power they possess —Disruptive Behavior.

Personal beliefs and individual preferences for names, fashion, hair styles, music, leisure activities, entertainment, and so on should never be allowed to color who we need to be in the classroom. Ours is a global society where every child and family has freedom of choice. When students feel forced to sacrifice or exchange those choices for others in order to fully receive the opportunity to be educated, conflict is aroused between them and the very educational system that purports to be inclusive. Honesty, hard work, responsibility, pride, et al, are *human* values, transcending all boundaries. If we but KNOW that they *are* present and possible in our students, these attributes will become evident as students acknowledge our belief in them, show growth through instruction and example, and feel free to display their true character while traversing the paths on which we have placed their learning feet.

What About the Race Card?

Oftentimes, the complaint of racism is raised, forming a cultural chasm between an instructor and his/her students. Emotions are intensified and bedlam becomes the *plat du jour*. As disheartening as it is to paint such a picture, the reality is that many an urban classroom has been razed, both behavior-wise and academically by these assertions —real and imagined. When minority students truly believe that negative stereotyping or labeling will *not* be perpetrated against them, that respect for them as serious students *will* be bestowed, misbehavior *will not* automatically be assumed and expected, common failings of children and teens will not be misconstrued as proof positive of criminality, and that, in general, they will be treated fairly, receiving the same benefit of the doubt extended to their majority counterparts in both academics and behavior, the relief is enormous and cooperation unfurled. What a mouthful, but a necessary description of the apprehensions experienced by minority student groups. Whether educators believe these "worries" to be legitimate or not, the possibility that any or all could be at large in one's classroom, heightening the likelihood of the learning environment becoming eroded with ready-made tension, should be enough to influence each of us to take them seriously, working steadfastly to eradicate even a hint of any one of these concerns becoming standard fare in our classroom or school.

I'm aware that there may be students who will endeavor to use the race card to their advantage when angry or in a tight spot, but the accusation will not hit home with peers if there are no real grounds for support. The teacher in this instance, can calmly say in all good conscience, *"Don't even go there. You earned that grade and you're going to get it. Now, how can I help you avoid this dilemma in the future?"* When being dealt with in a fair manner, even those who would choose to "save" themselves by issuing a false complaint will usually back off when handled in this manner, especially since most coeds refuse to join forces against a teacher who is considered an ally. The teacher in such a case, should remain confident, resisting the impulse to take the accusation personally, but earnestly acknowledging the student's *situation* as valid, from the student's point of view. Thus, the student can be offered a more appropriate plan of action for the future. Displaying understanding seems to, somehow dilute contentious discourse.

To ascertain if your behavior or language with students is suspect, a quick and easy method to utilize is that of privately audio taping yourself for about a week during class. Once home, take a listen to what was said—noticing exact words, tone and any implications that could be negatively misconstrued as racist. Obviously, one wouldn't want to become over zealous in weighing every word spoken. This would be ridiculous, uncalled for and, in all probability, eventually backfire in some other way. Yet, without a doubt there is underlying meaning in *what* teachers say *and how* it is worded. Each realizes in his own heart the true meaning of words spoken. Enough said.

In a case presented to me, students were proclaiming racism on a regular basis, and insubordination was running rampant. When this occurs it's imperative that the instructor in question be willing and honest enough to evaluate himself in regard to the messages he is or *may* be sending. Self-effacement is essential for all who wish to reside in a place of continual personal growth. Hopefully, teachers are among that group. Sometimes, impressions emitted, indicating the presence of racial bias are inadvertent in nature. Therefore, it is vital for educators to remain cognizant of the very thoughts circulating in the mind, since they can reflect the essence of what a person believes. Thinking which focuses one's attention on common generalizations, leading to stigmatization and pigeonholing of students, places an instructor in the danger zone when it comes to committing racist actions or making racist remarks.

When faced with persistent accusations of bigotry, as unnerving as it must be, I believe it beneficial to nip things in the bud by stepping up to the plate, meeting the accusations head on. In a spirit of synergy, afford students an opportunity to WRITE (e.g. on an index card) what, in particular, they find to be racist about the instructor or the class. Guidelines are needed here. Depending upon the level, it may be prudent to *conduct a brief lesson* on how to formulate statements descriptive of behavior evoking feelings of belittlement. Employing real examples from their world (e.g. humiliating experiences in shopping malls, sporting events), and perhaps even brainstorming a list of "feeling" terms will render this exercise more meaningful and productive.

Once ready to proceed, students are to understand that all statements describing offensive acts or verbiage must be made without the use of attack or curse words, and an example of the teacher's specific language and/or behavior provided, if possible. Teachers need never open themselves up for certain attack or abuse by plunging headlong into an impromptu discussion or bashing session. This kind of session would only serve to further stir up raw emotions, damaging both one's image as leader and any positive connection already in place.

The goal, in addition to reestablishing a rapport between teacher and students which will allow a spirit of tranquility and cooperation to prevail, is to bring "light." Through the *act* of genuine listening and the installation of viable solutions, the instructor is able to model the handling of criticism and adversity, maturely and respectfully. This is how students learn!

Students are quite capable of demonstrating graciousness and reason. Simply making them aware that you "hear" them and intend to investigate and rid the class of whatever is presenting a problem or has become an obstacle to their learning and enjoyment of school, can begin the reformation. Then, once students have written their concerns on index cards *sans* names, if chosen, and deposited them in a collection box, set aside an appointed time for the actual discussion, perhaps the last twenty minutes of the next class. You want there to be ample time for adequate discussion, but not an abundance of time to be wasted on factious wrangling. Pre read student comments, discarding any to which the guidelines were not adhered. This, also, serves as an opportunity to compile like complaints and contemplate what your sincere response will be. Objectivity is paramount. Anger or denial will only result in prolonging and even deepening grievances.

For the session, establish a simple, *structured procedure*, such as having all students remain seated in assigned seats or in whatever seating arrangement you think best. The entire discussion can be treated as a learning task for which substantial points will be given for following guidelines and even taking pertinent notes **modeled by you.** (The notes would consist of recording each complaint and the accompanying suggested solution(s).) Keeping students actively involved *always* increases effectiveness. A dependable student will be appointed by you to pull a card from the box, read the concern, and then have you address it, *concisely.* Teacher honesty is of prime importance. If you refute a charge that everyone believes is true, you're dead in the water, and the situation has now just gotten worse. Should a student wish to add something, he must be recognized by the facilitator, keeping comments polite and within the decided-upon time limit.

Once an issue under discussion is deemed problematic, a class brainstorming exercise is conducted to decide on a solution. Do allow yourself the opportunity to mull over solutions, *in private,* before committing. Each change needs to be doable, comfortable, and concrete enough to evaluate. However, doing nothing places you back at square one, sending a message of disregard for student distress.

I maintain that an educator using this or any other fair, organized method of acknowledging student concerns, with the genuine intent of bringing about understanding, will find that students appreciate the attempt to rectify the situation and will work conjointly to make the agreed-upon solutions effectual. The atmosphere should begin losing its toxicity as a sense of community emerges. It requires grit, confidence, and the willingness to prove to students that we are all lifelong learners, ambassadors of peace bridging the gap between races and cultures.

The more often and authentically educators show and tell *all* students that they *are* worthy and valuable human beings, focus on the inner person and how best to engage each, academically, the stronger will be the bond that is established between instructor and students. The knowledge that the teacher doesn't, in any way, consider himself or others to be superior in the human being department, prudery will not be an issue, and that all are in this together, encourages students to ignore obvious differences and concentrate on learning. This building of rapport to this depth will serve to stave off many a grievous discipline problem, and actually aid teachers in smoothly and successfully handling the occasional difficulty that will arise—nuisances that crop up just because we're dealing with children.

Humor

Humor is not only vital, it's also freeing. There's no substitute for **not** taking everything, including ourselves, too seriously. Some mischievous antics are actually funny. I once had a student who was an absolute practical joker and definitely not always pleasant to have around. As I was walking around the English classroom promoting a rich discussion of a rather profound quote, I began to notice a few stifled smiles on the faces of my students even though what was being said was not particularly humorous. Unbeknownst to me, before class R. had placed plastic vomit in a conspicuous place on the floor, and everyone was just waiting for me to notice it. When I finally did, I couldn't help but break into laughter, which in turn gave all of the students permission to enjoy the joke and the moment. After our interlude, we continued with the lesson, and I could actually "feel" the kids on my side because they knew that I was human and didn't take either the subject matter or myself so seriously that I couldn't enjoy an innocent prank. Your good judgment will guide you in these matters.

Treat yourself and students to laughter that is not in the realm of teasing or making fun of others' deficiencies or mistakes. Show appreciation for those who are quick-witted, without permitting them to take over the class or squander precious academic time. Merely acknowledging a student's great sense of humor can lighten the mood, spurring everyone to buckle down to the task at hand with more enjoyment.

Having been asked to administer a standardized test to a group of high school students, most of whom were definitely opposed to taking the test, I knew that I had my work cut out for me. Moreover, I wasn't even familiar with these kids. I entered the classroom early, placed name tags on desks, enabling me to at least know who was who, and further organized myself so as to be free to greet students as they entered. Many hadn't remembered that a test was being given and were, therefore, quite surprised. I smiled and told them that I completely understood, which I did. After introducing myself, I proceeded to pass out necessary materials, initiating a chatting session about topics of interest to them, such as the upcoming school play and our city's football team. We had been instructed to wait for an intercom announcement before beginning, to give stragglers time to get to their classes. In a matter of minutes we were laughing and conversing, and they felt comfortable enough to inquire as to why they had to take this test, *anyway*. I honored their questions with as valid answers as possible—avoiding the standard reply that it was required of every student in the state, like it or not if their intention was to graduate, and that *they'd* better take it seriously. Remarks such as these would have been inflammatory, but are, unfortunately, answers often supplied to students who are assertive enough to question the establishment.

Once the okay to commence testing was granted, I discovered that I had a real comedian in my midst. As I read words from the manual, *"Fold your answer booklet so that you are looking at only one page,"* or *"You may use only the number 2 pencil that has been provided,"* he would do the exact opposite. Then, he would glance at me with a sly smile. I couldn't help but appreciate his humor, even though the setting was one of seriousness. I moved calmly to his desk and whispered, *" I love your sense of humor! Now get to work, please."* He smiled, knowing that his gift of humor was viewed as an asset of which to be proud, and settled down to earnestly follow the testing guidelines. I'm quite sure that had I lambasted him for "making light of such an important testing situation," his behavior would have escalated and would not have been the least bit funny. Instead, the students and I enjoyed a very quiet exam atmosphere, and I gained a new ally. Whenever I saw him around the building thereafter, we shared a friendly smile and hello.

Humor is undoubtedly more easily displayed for some than others. Many instructors, just as persons from all walks of life, are already endowed with a healthy dose of it, while others struggle to eke out even a tiny bit of laughter for themselves or those around them. Nonetheless, I believe that all of us are capable of recognizing, enjoying, and even interjecting fun into our lessons. It prevents or relieves stress and, what's more, can truly **promote positive student behavior.**

CHAPTER TWO
SUMMARY POINTS

1. Organize all aspects of your classroom **before** students enter.
2. Arrange classroom furniture so that student attention is on the instructor vs. their peers.
3. From day one, follow the steps for establishing a disciplined environment.
4. Understand that being fair is all-important to students and paramount to the goal of maintaining effective classroom management.
5. Demonstrate through your behavior, attitude, and instructional practices, that you value all students regardless of economic level, race, religion, gender, or any other distinction.
6. Make equality, humanity and respect a part of your overall strategy for dealing with students on a daily basis.
7. Allow non-destructive humor to become a part of your classroom environment.

Chapter Three

EFFECTIVE TEACHING TECHNIQUES AND DISCIPLINE

Less is More

The concept of less is more is quite simple. It has been used by many successful businesses through the years. Just consider for a moment how McDonald's and KFC restaurants initially became successful. They were structured around serving a few foods and doing them well. Likewise, as you're planning units for the year, make your objective one of simplicity. Creating an efficient teaching syllabus that encompasses the components of your curriculum goes a long way in clarifying what is to be taught and learned, and in ensuring comfort and confidence both for you as leader and students as learners.

What does this streamlining have to do with discipline? Well, when young or older students sense composure, a plan, a well-oiled system, if you will, it actually soothes, settles and, in effect, creates an atmosphere conducive to them understanding and valuing academic and social expectations. They fall into the "groove" of **good behavior** in which you have maneuvered them.

Your confidence in specifying behavioral expectations, and structuring the curriculum into prioritized instructional units will prompt students to concentrate on learning both their academic and social lessons within a well thought-out system. You will be providing **routine** and **consistency** while discouraging the confusion and poor behavior so often accompanying instructional bird walking. This mirrors the philosophy declaring that a baby's temperament reflects that of its caretaker. We need to be steadfast and self-assured about where we're taking our students. They *will* follow.

There is fabulous news regarding the positive impact of a rich learning environment and solid methodology, on the behavior of students. We know from experience, that students who achieve academic success seem to have fewer behavioral challenges in the classroom than those who struggle with learning each day. This, of course, makes perfect sense when we comprehend the powerful influence that self-concept holds over the conduct of anyone — young, old, or in-between. Self-esteem issues seem to dominate thinking to the extent of affecting what a student *believes* herself capable of accomplishing. Therefore, it behooves educators to be cognizant of specific strategies proven to be extremely sound and effective by the countless teachers who have used them.

Efficacious instruction begins with the creation of an classroom environment filled with the accoutrements of learning: appropriate literary selections, informative curriculum–based displays, word walls, exhibited student projects, and uplifting can-do language from the instructor. The *teaching* of specific vocabulary that allows them to comprehend and converse intelligently about the subject or topic further breeds interest, leading to good behavior. Vocabulary instruction is extremely crucial. Students who cannot comprehend what is being taught or read because of the terminology used, find it very easy to give up and act out. It matters not that instruction *was* given if your students failed to grasp the new terms in a meaningful way, permitting them to internalize concepts and actually transfer and apply these new understandings from rote memory to life experiences. Countless teachers overlook this fact, considering that presenting an *overview* of essential terms, speaking about them *during* the instructional lesson, or *assigning* definitions to be written, to be enough to invoke the level of comprehension imperative for learning success. The repercussion can be student anxiety and stress when the terms are consistently in use by the instructor, with the expectation that everyone is absorbing what is being spoken and conveyed. The natural student reaction amidst this sea of academic agony is one of self-preservation i.e. disorderly behavior to mask the discomfort and embarrassment of being in the dark.

I visited a classroom in which students were purported to be totally out of control. Upon first observation I noticed that "totally out of control" was an overstatement. The conduct exhibited was all within the range of nature of the beast behavior, most stemming from a lack of instructional structure which would evoke student accountability for staying on task, and centered around an inordinate amount of academic frustration being expressed in various ways. Students were chatting and socializing *as* the teacher taught, there was movement about the room without permission, many sat quietly—hoping to avoid being called upon, and others were putting forth effort without fully completing each math exercise. In short, more than half were not involved in the lesson in any way, and it was quite apparent each time the instructor queried the students, that the curriculum vocabulary being used was incomprehensible to them. Silence reigned supreme when a question was asked, except, of course, for those who were engaged in their own side conversations. Others who chose to give it a try were basically in left field, with a couple responding correctly.

The beleaguered instructor chose to teach to those few, I'm sure out of her own need for sanity and affirmation, ignoring the fact that the majority of her students were not on board. I happened to be sitting near two young ladies who obviously desired to be involved since they were engaged in writing down the examples and trying to figure them out as a team. However, it was painfully clear to me that they had no knowledge of the steps necessary for arriving at the correct answer. When the teacher left the class on their own with three minutes to come up with the appropriate response, I whispered a question in an effort to get them on the right track. They eagerly averted their thinking and energy in the direction to which I had steered, so relieved to be receiving individual assistance and the acknowledgement that the expectation that they obtain the right answer was basically unrealistic. As I navigated them step by step through the process of reaching the proper answer, eyes lit up, smiles erupted, and for the first time during that class period, when the teacher asked for a volunteer to come up and work one of the examples, the shyest of the girls excitedly waved her hand, jauntily walked up to the board and proudly wrote her answer. At the conclusion of the class, I was handed a folded piece of paper by one of the young ladies to whom I had given help. It was a beautiful scene drawn for me with her name on it to show appreciation for my assistance.

What does this indicate? It suggests that, oftentimes, teachers fail to read signals being transmitted by their pupils. They actually believe that *certain* students don't care or wish to learn. Therefore, when misbehavior in its most common forms is encountered, its causes are usually misdiagnosed as a problem within the students as opposed to the ineffectiveness of the instructional and management strategies being employed. It would be quite odd for a group of regular, everyday students *anywhere* to, as a whole, decide that they didn't wish to learn. In fairness to the instructor of that classroom, she was a hardworking first year teacher who was still learning the ropes, expecting students of that age to basically discipline themselves and, therefore, was befuddled by their constant off-task behavior. She even informed me that the vocabulary and skills being "reviewed" for a test had indeed been taught. There's no doubt that instruction was presented. The problem lay with the instructional techniques used during that particular lesson and all of the curriculum presentations which had been put forth up to that point. The strategies had proven to be totally inadequate. Almost all of her students had failed the first comprehensive test and were doomed to fail the next. They were giving up, and their behavior was a reflection of that decision.

Teachers must be aware of the art of *timing* direct instruction when seeking to garner maximum focus from students. Limiting instructional lessons requiring high levels of student attentiveness and concentration to between 8 and 20 minutes, serves to motivate learners to maintain the degree of intensity necessary to sustain focus throughout. This does not preclude one from presenting a lesson that is 30 to 90 minutes in length. However, what it does connote is that when lessons are broken up into segments of teach/recovery, teach/recovery, students pay closer attention, remain more engaged, and **discipline problems become a non issue.** Each active exercise allows them to reenergize and refresh in readiness for the next round of heavy concentration. For example, if your lesson is one encompassing 30- 45 minutes or more, you might open with what I call "priming the pump." This indicates that you have designed a brief exercise in which all students must be *actively* involved, one that will get them excited and invigorated about the upcoming lesson. Once your students have participated in this purposefully-planned exercise which could consist of brainstorming, a scavenger hunt, working with a partner on a preliminary word search or critical thinking questions, a teaser selection, etc., their brains have been primed for the lesson and they are now ready for segment two. This might be the time in which you will *teach* the vocabulary needed for this lesson or unit, requiring the utmost in student attention and accountability. Upon conclusion, do not immediately proceed to the next portion of the overall lesson. It's all about pacing. A recovery period is needed in which students will now do some kind of organized activity to cement and internalize the vocabulary to which they have just been exposed. You might choose to give them ten minutes to make vocabulary flash cards and to partner up to study the new definitions. Whatever is decided should offer a specified amount of time to practice the info just presented, and afford the opportunity to lighten up their focus a tad, while still being *fully* engaged in the lesson. The aim is to prevent students from becoming worn out from the intensity of learning new material, ultimately turning to misbehavior for relief. It also serves to guide students toward assimilating the new concepts into their store of acquired knowledge, making them more capable of continuing the lesson with an attitude of reception.

Segment three would encompass the main instructional presentation involving skills and/or concepts. Once completed, another recovery segment is provided, explained, and timed. These recovery sessions are hands-on academic activities that direct students to **use** or **apply** information just received. They may be inclusive of practice exercises, organized student discussion groups who will record and present findings or conclusions, simple projects, graphing, charting, worksheet exercises, additional reading, etc. The point is that when students are given instruction in palatable doses, provided with time to practice and digest each in its turn, and offered opportunities during the lesson for what I term *legal* movement and *legal* chatting (that which is directly related to the academic lesson), they are less prone to break away from instruction to alleviate their own feelings of being inundated, nonstop, with knowledge to be absorbed, resorting to some form of undesirable behavior.

Daily Instructional Strategies & Discipline

Let's now glance at how the actual teaching of a lesson can be presented in such a manner that offensive student behavior becomes either markedly minimized or deleted altogether. Yes, this CAN and IS being accomplished by informed teachers in every teaching situation and economic area.

Just what does effective teaching have to do with establishing and maintaining impressive discipline? Consider this. Have you ever attended a lecture, class, seminar, or sermon, and found it to be disorganized, uninspiring, over your head, intimidating, or negative in some other way? How did it make you feel? How did it make you behave? Did you fidget, get out a piece of gum or candy, survey the room, begin whispering with a friend, pass a note, doodle, or maybe search for something interesting to read? Our students are reflections of ourselves. They embody similar emotions, habits, and tendencies toward specific behaviors. Our teaching techniques must bear this in mind.

First of all, the beginning of the school year is the time to ***immediately*** involve **students** so that they commence with focus, comfort, confidence, accountability, and eagerness to participate in their own learning. How does one achieve this mighty feat? We must begin by respecting students' abilities and desire to learn, recognizing that each individual brings his/her own array of retained skills to the learning table. Placing students at their ease is the best antidote for those bad attitudes that can crop up, seemingly out of the blue on the very first day of class. Get to work on building and advancing skills, versus criticizing and lamenting over what was not retained or acquired. Many teachers lose their students from day one, and actually incite poor behavior by constantly bombarding them with what amounts to verbal and emotional putdowns centered around what the students didn't learn in the previous grade or class. Rather, to reiterate a prior point, the emphasis needs to be on building and reviewing *at the same time*, so that students are neither insulted nor intimidated. Again, instructors who are ever aware of eliminating elements that create discord in the student-teacher relationship are the ones who will be ahead of the game in averting a profusion of repugnant behaviors, producing a classroom environment with relatively few conflicts.

Effective teaching denies students both the opportunity and the desire to disrupt. Total organization is the first step, and is key. There is no substitute for sound, thorough lesson planning. Too many teachers wish to squeak by without taking this step, or by glossing over this responsibility, writing *partial* plans which turn out to be nothing more than sketchily written scraps of information about what will be *assigned* to students. All too often, no thought has been given to how students will actively participate *during instruction* to increase the likelihood of them grasping the skills and concepts being presented, literally promoting positive reactions. Further, many lessons are planned without genuine forethought as to which instructional strategies will provide the best chance of explaining curriculum basics in the most effective, engaging manner. Creativity has not been infused into the presentation. This is a recipe for student disruptions.

So often, a classroom riddled with poor behavior is simply the result of weak lesson planning which permits students to sit back while the teacher does all of the talking and practicing, do little or nothing, and still receive passing grades. Troublesome and nuisance conduct originates, festers, and thrives in this kind of learning environment. They somehow *know* when we are flying by the seat of our pants. They *know* when worksheets have been hastily thrown together with disjointed, meaningless exercises, textbook chapters haven't been read by the instructor, videos and audio tapes are neither previewed nor adapted to what is being taught, handouts haven't been proofread and are fraught with errors, assignments are doled out in a haphazard fashion. They KNOW.

Taking time to arrange the components of each instructional lesson into a standard lesson plan format with all bases covered, will get your class off to a positive start. Being certain that all learning materials are on hand in the quantities necessary, *relevant* video or audio tapes are cued and ready to play, handouts are stapled and ready to disseminate, textbook sections are pre read to ensure proper guidance, critical thinking questions are pre chosen to bring about desired objectives, and so forth, are all indicators of well- prepared instructors. These are the teachers who avoid contending with nasty student disruptions brought on by last-minute flitting around to gather materials, fix mistakes, or regroup when something doesn't quite come together.

Instructional Objectives

Secondly, students who are made privy to academic objectives for the lesson being taught, are much more apt to follow its progression, gaining knowledge and engaging in on-task pursuits as opposed to participating in wanton behavior that is on point one minute and off the next. Upon entering a classroom of high school juniors taking a required course, I whispered to a student seated nearby, "*What are you guys doing?*" She said, " I don't know." (which I admit is sometimes par for the course) Even though textbooks were open and students were jotting down a few notes as the instructor lectured, they exhibited actions which indicated that they were clueless as to what it was they were to accomplish or learn. The longer I sat, the more *I* was unclear about just what the academic goal could be. A student would read a column, then another would read, until a certain number of textbook pages—not in progressive order, had been covered, all without any mention of the purpose for the reading. The instructor, then, without making sure that what had been read was comprehended, commenced writing notes on an overhead transparency. These notes were to be copied by students, never mind that no connection between the two segments had been made. Students were to merely sit, listen, and participate when called upon. Adding further disjointedness to the lesson, was off-topic conversation initiated by the instructor! No wonder there were students with heads down and eyes closed, a couple of young ladies passing notes back and forth, and still others with that far away look in their eyes, waiting for class to end. Who knew what the plan was? The teacher was frustrated and continually called on students who weren't paying attention, to answer questions. When the correct reply couldn't be submitted, she admonished the person for being inattentive, made a request of another student to sit up or get out, and so went the class until time expired. What wasn't realized was that she had set herself up for failure by using faulty teaching methods. Though, in her mind, there was a goal, the students were not made aware of it and soon lost interest in "going along for the ride."

Many educators have come to the erroneous conclusion that students neither care nor need to know about academic objectives. Whether one believes it or not, communicating lesson objectives *is* one of the tools of the effective disciplinarian. It sets the tone for an atmosphere of achievement, placing students on notice that something important and exciting is happening in this space, taking precedence over all other activity. There's no time for nonsense. The fun is in the learning.

Therefore, objectives for each and every lesson need to be written in the same place every day, so that students, regardless of age and grade, can clearly notice and read them, becoming accustomed to having daily learning goals brought to their attention. Furthermore, just writing the goals isn't enough. Direct a student to orally read the objective(s) for the lesson, inform students in specific terms, what will be seen, heard, obtained from them as indicators of the objectives having been met. One young teacher required his students to have a weekly objectives page in their notebooks. Each day, upon completing the focus activity, they were to record the objective for the day's upcoming lesson. Afterward, that objective was briefly discussed so that he knew his students were aware of *what* they were to learn and *why* they would be asked to do specific work. Needless to say, his students were primed and ready to start once he began instruction.

Informing students of their learning goals offers them that sense of worth that accomplished students seem to own. It makes them *feel* like scholars, smart and onto something special, which can translate into appropriate, on-task behavior. This works at all levels and with students from all walks of life. It works, I believe, because feeling significant and competent is a human need.

High Expectations, Skills, And Support

The next ingredient in this plan for success with students is the establishment of lofty expectations. Too often, instructors are led to conclude that expectations should be marginal in certain communities or among certain populations of students. BIG MISTAKE. ALL students tend to respond favorably to high behavioral and academic standards. No one wants to be disparaged by having traditional guidelines lowered because they are presumed incapable of attaining the standard. Even ten-year-olds realize that something is amiss. Indeed, high expectations seem to empower kids to expand, maximizing their learning potential and allowing good behavior to blossom as a by-product. The trick, regardless of where one may be teaching, is to provide the support needed for students to meet the standards. Don't be tempted to pass the buck or use rationalizations based upon popular rhetoric. You'll be aware of what it takes to attain this goal, and the fruit of your labor will be a class resplendent with confidence, as they realize that you are determined to be an advocate for their success.

Support occurs in the following forms and through others of which you are aware.

- age/grade appropriate structure and procedures put into place in the classroom from the get-go
- teaching the curriculum such that **each** student can realize his/her full potential
- accessing support personnel and/or volunteers available to your school for student assistance
- sending can-do messages to your students through body language, choice of words, and actions
- making students accountable for every assignment, by structuring student activities to require 100% student *active, hands-on* participation
- providing the individual assistance and feedback essential for students, averting confusion, fear, and frustration that ruptures into despair and poor behavior

Teaching the skills listed in the curriculum being delivered, is a must. Yes, I know that all of our students will not be in the same place academically, and that therein lies one of the greatest challenges for a teacher. However, students can differentiate between an instructor who refuses to present certain skills because he/she doesn't consider the students competent enough to accomplish and succeed, and one who goes about teaching prerequisite skills that need to be recapped in order for students to proceed to the next level, while continually moving them forward. They know and respond with either good or poor behavior, as the knowledge may prompt. Those instructors who have become savvy in this area, will intertwine the instruction of review skills and concepts with the instruction of the new, so that students are continuing to advance. It's not easy, but it can and must be done so that student self -concepts are preserved and elevated. Positive student behavior springs forth from the realization that one is esteemed and regarded as a true learner, and from the actual pride in knowing that steady academic progress is being made. There's no substitute for students of all ages believing themselves to be scholars. It brings out their best attitudes and deportment.

Immediate Start

Begin immediately. This means that when students enter your classroom, it's ON! There is an assignment that is ready and relevant, and they have been taught to take their seats and commence once the bell has sounded. It cuts the nonsense. Stroll down the corridors of any school during the opening of class, whether it be at the beginning of the day, after a previous class, following physical education class for elementary students, or what have you. What you'll observe is the chaos that many teachers promote by providing no beginning of class, settling activity, while other instructors who have installed such a routine are cruising along in complete bliss as their students have entered, gathered materials, and are engrossed in a pertinent curriculum-based exercise. There is a stark difference in the expectations of the two. The premise is that students *need* to have a required, independent exercise to assist them in making the transition from socializing to the activation of their learning mode.

Whether settling your students in the library or returning to class after a school assembly, provide an academic activity for them to begin working on, *pronto*. They should never have to wait for you to take roll, disseminate materials, or give instructions before they become engaged. It's on their desks and has either already been explained or is self-explanatory. Again, the activity is independent, required, and timed. This will get them moving in the right direction both mentally and physically, preventing those pesky discipline problems which always seem to commandeer the class when students must be resettled.

Student Apathy

Everywhere I go there seems to be at least one teacher who inquires about student apathy and the rotten attitudes accompanying this "condition." My response to them is that we can only change or control our own apathy. Actually, it's an empowering stance, because how frustrated and inept would we feel if we considered it *our* responsibility to alter another human's emotions. The solution is teacher enthusiasm.

I recall working in a new school for about a week with no time to become acquainted with any of the other faculty (typical start-up deluge). One day an unfamiliar colleague remarked that I'd be happy to know that students were saying I was the most enthusiastic teacher they'd ever had. Frankly, I didn't realize I was displaying enthusiasm—honestly! I just knew that I felt so passionately about English literature, grammar, writing, and all things connected, and that I totally loved working with kids. That passion obviously burst forth in my teaching and dealings with the students. It was infectious. They caught it! And even when they weren't as enamored with a piece of literature or well-written sentence or phrase as I, they had to laugh or enjoy the moment because I was having such a blast. That's how you thwart apathy. You just continue being genuinely upbeat about the subject or lesson, and teach from that place, not allowing others' apathy —even that of fourteen or fifteen-year-olds, to turn your attitude sour. It works every time, because light overpowers darkness and high energy overpowers low energy.

Teach Everyone

I'll bet you're wondering where I could possibly be headed with this subtitle. It's a given that an instructor would teach everyone in his classroom—right? Wrong. You'd be surprised, or maybe you wouldn't, by how many teachers choose *not* to teach particular students based upon rationalizations considered to be valid and acceptable.

"These kids don't want to learn. I'm going to teach the students who are interested. These parents don't care about education. They're just sending their children to school because the law demands it," and so on. I contend that when an instructor contemplates the attributes of his students in these terms, even if the words are left unspoken, students will figure it out. Not only will they be aware, but feelings of insult will emerge, translating into anger and dislike, further translating into **revenge behavior**. If one honestly thinks about it, (though I admit that students can "get on your last nerve" when an inordinate amount of motivation seems to be needed in order to capture their attention), this kind of thinking is disrespectful to those students and their families. We have but to consider its application in terms of ourselves or our own offspring.

Important to remember when we become teachers, is that we will cross paths, if fortunate, with all types of people. Our challenge is to resist sitting in judgment, by possessing a determination to act impartially, focusing on instructing and influencing each student to be better academically and as a person for having come in contact with us. "*Oh, hogwash,*" you're saying. But it's not hogwash. I believe that teachers have the opportunity of inspiring more people than those in any other profession. That kid sitting in the back of the room daring you (with her negative attitude) to call on her, really wants and needs for you to do exactly that, helping her to become a conscientious student. It's unethical for educators to categorize students into two groups: those who are interested in learning and will receive instruction, and those who will be allowed to sit and vegetate in the classroom because they *appear* to be disinterested. Furthermore, acting on this belief surely backfires, as miscreants of the classroom—students who would otherwise remain everyday kids or teens, are inadvertently created due to student backlash against teachers who would view them in such a negative light. Indeed, there will be pupils who are genuinely not interested in what we are teaching. So what! Were you interested in every bloody thing you were exposed to in school? I wasn't.

The mindset to cling to is that *every* student *is* interested. Go about designing, teaching, and orchestrating each activity as though no student could *not* be captivated. This requires creativity and *perseverance.* Call on every kid, offer constructive individual feedback and patient assistance whether it *seems* to be desired or not, require participation from every student, no matter the demeanor of the person. AND, do it all with a smile, an upbeat attitude, and the confidence to not accept disrespectful behavior from a kid who is unaccustomed to being the recipient of such aid, and is leery of its sincerity. Otherwise, those very students, as one teacher said to me,

"I'll leave her alone if she leaves me alone," WON'T leave you alone. There are those who believe you to be afraid of them when they notice that their misdeeds are being ignored, or who have slumped into a pattern of debilitating thinking about their own inability to succeed in this arena we call school, have given up on trying, and assumed a gargantuan devil-may-care attitude. The insolence and bravado just increases because, actually, underneath it all they're experiencing hurt that a teacher would fear bodily harm at their hands and has prejudged them to not be serious students without even trying to "figure them out," making no effort to draw them into the fold. Educators must be bold and resolute. Remember

the lack of maturity I spoke about early on? We expect students to put two and two together, reasoning that if they were to just meet us halfway the situation would turn out better for all concerned. Nonetheless, this is not the case most of the time. The instructor is the adult and professional, with the responsibility of deciphering the avenue and approach to take in order to make each student feel valued. It's not always easy because some students are accustomed to having instructors give up on them, accepting their standoffish behavior as status quo. But fortunately, it is absolutely possible as long as student behavior is not taken personally by the teacher, and the teacher retains a positive outlook.

As educators, we cannot be aware of what is going on in the heads, homes, or lives of all of our students. We don't *know* what their life circumstances are. We don't know if someone important is critically ill, abusive, nonchalant, or just away. A stance to take is one adopted by the troops in Tennyson's Charge *of the Light Brigade*—"Ours not to reason why…" Well, ours *is not* to reason why, just teach and care. Even the most obnoxious student will come around when treated with regard. You've got to have grit! You've got to have structure. And you've got to be consistent and confident. Don't allow a sour-puss face to turn *you* off! You're on a mission to make even the most reluctant student advance from where he/she began in your class. They will thank you for it—even if only inside of their very beings. And what is your reward? You will know that you didn't allow one student to believe that you were unconcerned about his education, AND you'll be rewarded with good student behavior. The practice of neither overlooking nor accepting student nonparticipation because it's simply not good for students, will resonate with your class. When instructors display caring to this extent, make no mistake about it, the toughest students recognize it, appreciate the effort, and fall in line.

Yes, you will assuredly have to whip out that **information and choice** technique about which I have already spoken. Or, you may have to sock it to someone with an appropriate consequence. Don't be reluctant to go there. Employ the strategy I call **respectful assertiveness**—applying pressure to follow your guidelines in a respectful manner, not letting them worm out from under the rules, while adding the ingredient of positive affirmation so that they realize that you see them as wonderful human beings. The key is to not let the "I'm not going to participate" *intention* fester and grow into this monster! From the first day require involvement from each one of your students, and they will get the point that there's no free lunch in Mrs. Calabash's classroom. This requirement ultimately promotes cooperative behavior and the knowledge that you care enough to not let them self-destruct.

Ex. Information & Choice with Assertive Respectfulness

"Ken, please follow along with the outlining that I'm modeling. You can do it now with the class and receive full points, or come in after school and do it for partial credit. You can do this!" (Be sure that the partial credit is a fair # of points.)

Should Ken make the wrong choice—not doing the outlining, but is *not* normally with you at the end of the day, be sure to, literally, go and get him, or have his last hour teacher send him to you three minutes prior to the end of the final period, if you can't get away. If your school utilizes paraprofessionals or security guards to escort students to their various destinations during regular school hours, use this method. Whatever is decided, you *must* follow through if you wish to eradicate this behavior. Expecting a student to just show up may or may not be reasonable, depending upon the kid. The trick is to not give him the option of being "unsuccessful."

When he arrives, you're not angry and there's no lecture needed. Pleasantly hand him the transparencies that were to be copied in class, and when he's gotten all of the information copied exactly as it is (Do NOT accept shoddy work, which is an extension of the same poor attitude), check it over and dismiss him with a smile and *"Thank you for coming."* The next time you see Ken in class tell him what a fine job he did on the assignment. Stay after it, providing real assistance whenever needed, and experience a blossoming right before your eyes.

Over Plan

This is a fairly simple, straightforward concept. Whatever the length of your teaching day or period, your plans for each part of it need to be more extensive than the actual time permits. By so doing, you avoid the pitfall to which many teachers seem to succumb time and again. "I didn't think that they (the students) would finish the activity so quickly."

When students complete an assignment inside of the allotted interval and have been given no further instructions, the first idea that pops into their heads is free time! It's sheer folly for teachers to believe that students will just automatically pick up a book to read or decide on some other academic endeavor, while waiting patiently for others to finish or for the teacher to provide a supplemental task. Also, if you think about it, it's really a waste of academic time for them to just busy themselves with whatever.

The obvious answer to preventing the distracting commotion that accompanies too much student down time, is to plan the lesson so tightly and thoroughly that students have no opportunity to disrupt. Put a little extra forethought into attaching interesting, up-front extensions onto assignments, or employ some other proven technique about which you are familiar, to accommodate those who are fast, but accurate workers. My suggestion is to write actual estimates of time next to each segment of your lesson plan as you are designing it. Underestimate so that you err on the side of having too much lined up rather than too little. Additionally, be certain that activities planned for your students coincide with the learning objectives, and are diverse in nature so that students don't become bogged down with doing the same thing in the same way every day. When asked why he wasn't working, one consistently disruptive student replied to me *" We always do the same thing every day. I'm tired of it."* This statement is not always true, but in this particular instance I knew it to be so.

Sample Timed Lesson Plan

Objective:
The Learner Will Be Able To (TLWBAT) list the parts of the digestive system and explain the function of each.

Review Warm-up:
Label & Explain Function of Each Part of Circulatory System
10 min.

Discussion of Warm-up
10 min.

Vocabulary Instruction & Discussion
20 min.

Vocabulary Student Practice
10 min.

You get the point.

Instruction

Many instructors fail to consider the effects of the teaching techniques being utilized, on the behavior of their students. The preponderance of discipline challenges observed in classroom after classroom are a direct result of teachers not knowing how to present lessons in a way that not only affords students the greatest opportunity for mastery learning and comfort, but also forestalls the myriad of disruptive behaviors perpetrated *during* daily instruction. We seem to just expect students to follow along enthusiastically whether the techniques being used are sound, so-so, or just plain faulty. Surely it would be "splendiferous" if learning took place regardless of methodology, but, alas, it doesn't work that way. Just as parents have to find reliable and proven strategies for presenting life lessons that must be taught to their offspring, teachers, too, must be astute in choosing strategies *that work*. It's not difficult. There are ever so many books written for educators, offering a variety of teaching techniques from which to choose, not to mention the inexhaustible source of information that is at our fingertips—the internet.

Nevertheless, regardless of the techniques you choose, there are basic components that are tried, true, and continually successful in promoting good behavior and the learning that is dependent upon it, for students of all ages and backgrounds. These, I'm going to describe to you in this section. Before getting started, however, I exhort you to include the following fundamental elements *as* you teach, since they can make all the difference in the behavior you'll receive from your students during any class session.

1. Recognition of Genuine Student Effort (Benefit of the Doubt)
2. Avoid Causing Humiliation or Embarrassment of Your Students, and DISALLOW It From Their Peers
3. Kindness, Consideration, and Sensitivity During Instruction

A male high school student, following the instruction of his female teacher to draw symbols of their inner selves, to not be afraid of getting in touch with the feminine side, drew as one of his symbols, a flower. Upon noticing it, one of the young ladies in the class began to ridicule him for having drawn something as prissy as a flower. Instead of "leaping " to his aid, stating that flowers are a daily expression of gratitude, love, and appreciation for parents, friends, etc. the teacher joined in the laughter. The young man's overwhelming humiliation and embarrassment led him to not only address the young lady as a "B," but also the teacher. Unable to calm him, the teacher promptly and unceremoniously sent him out with a discipline referral. I'm sure that we can all imagine what his attitude toward participation became for the remainder of the semester in that class and, perhaps, even in others.

Step By Step Instruction

Once the skill or concept which will comprise the core of your instructional lesson has been chosen from the overall curriculum syllabus, the next job is to decide how to dissect it into a step by step instructional progression leading to the attainment of the ultimate learning objective. Whether students are advanced placement biology students or first graders learning how to tell time, this method is totally essential. Presenting the whole picture in one fell swoop, as though learners have the benefit of the instructor's years of study and knowledge attainment, is a surefire way to precipitate confusion and anxiety, leading to a myriad of annoying student behaviors. Also, laboring under the erroneous notion that only slow learners or remedial and low functioning students need this approach, has landed countless instructors in hot water on the behavior front. Simply everyone can benefit from this presentation method, whether learning to dribble a basketball, play piano, or conjugate verbs. *You* know the steps. The trick is to not assume that they can be melded altogether, skipping or glossing over what seems easy to you. It's *all* easy for the teacher, one who's studied the topic or been doing the skill for a million years! This truth is so *difficult* for some instructors to realize, accept, and consistently buy into, to the extent that every new lesson is taught in this manner.

A young protégé was teaching a high level art lesson, under my tutelage. The lesson plan was well laid out and very specifically oriented in a step by step scheme. She introduced the lesson, proceeded in the agreed-upon manner, and students were following her lead in the most marvelous fashion. In short, she had them eating out of her hands. Then, suddenly the ball was dropped. A point had been reached in the lesson where the next step was progressive and equally as difficult as the preceding ones, but because the students were responding so admirably, actually producing superior results, she reasoned that they no longer needed the step by step instructional method. Instead, the decision was made to perform a quick demo and place them on their own to proceed. The lesson took a downward turn from there, with students constantly requesting assistance, becoming impatient with waiting for that assistance, tuning out instructor comments and admonishments to refocus, chatting among themselves, moving around the classroom, and working on other projects. Though no real harm was done in that instance, the end of the class was difficult to navigate, and the teacher learned a valuable lesson regarding maintaining the use of effective instructional techniques ***throughout*** a lesson.

So, let's practice. Say that you're teaching students to divide mixed fractions. What would be the very first step to teach or review? Of course, converting the mixed number into an improper fraction, providing that you've already taught the terms, mixed number and improper fraction, would come first. As sure as your name is what it is, if you just haul off and plow through the entire process, no matter how slowly you feel that you're proceeding, how well you consider yourself to be explaining the process as you demonstrate, or how much pressure you presume to be placed on your shoulders to cover the curriculum in a particular amount of time, you are going to create frustration, fear, and anxiety in SOMEBODY. That somebody or those "somebodies" will be the students who will resort to their own devices to remedy the discomfort. Usually the devices employed are off-topic chatting, distracting others, out of seat, refusal to work, nonchalance, rushing through regardless of mistakes, or some other aberrant behavior. It's self-preservation and it's human nature.

To continue, AS you are illustrating each step, students need to be writing right along with you. They are working, *neatly,* on scratch paper, mini dry erase boards, in their notebooks, or wherever, and you are giving them the opportunity to **verbalize** the whats and whys so that you can tell if comprehension is dawning. It's essential that **"*If you're writing, they're writing.*"** There's no free lunch. Students learn by doing, not by watching. Talk through each step or thinking process as you instruct, so that students hear the words that they should be hearing in their own heads. Then, require each of them to do the same with a partner. **Just *asking* students if they have questions doesn't cut it.** Oftentimes, they don't know enough, yet, to even ask a question. They need to practice, practice, practice *with you* one step at a time until they feel that they are ready to try it on their own. Now hear this, teachers of the gifted and talented. These advanced students also need this step by step instruction. They weren't born with knowledge, just the ability to learn quickly and to retain more easily. Those of you out there thinking that gifted and talented kids experience no academic stress, and won't misbehave for the same reasons as their peers, think again.

During a demonstration lesson being presented for a teacher whose students were rarely attending or working as she taught, she marveled at the specific instructional steps I employed, and how each of her previously inattentive, nonparticipatory students was compelled to become active during the process. It's ultimately up to you, the instructor, to notice when too large a chunk of new information has been presented to students, rendering it all so complex that none of it can be fully grasped. Be observant, and once aware of confusion, simply back up and dissect each part, without adopting a negative attitude or making learners feel like THEY are not easy to teach or as smart as they should be. You will see the cooperation and *bona fide* LOVE for you blossom right before your eyes. It's no mystery. All of us desire to feel at ease and *adequate* when we're learning. The person who provides that comfort merits and receives our undying appreciation.

I know of what I speak, because nothing makes me feel more like bursting into tears than the frustration I experience when learning computer skills from an instructor who assumes that I understand the jargon without it being taught, and further assumes that each new task can be done with the lightening speed and accuracy with which he performs it! I straight up want to MISBEHAVE!!!

Model, Model, Model

Teaching is not just verbalizing and assigning. As a matter-of-fact, it's *not* verbalizing and assigning. It embodies multiple demonstrations as you explain each segment, and the setting aside of time for them to practice with you, under your tutelage, before striking out on their own. Many are the teachers who skip this step or provide ONE example *sans* instruction, taking for granted that their students have it. Then, of course, these teachers become disappointed and even irritated when students fail to perform the task correctly, refuse to become engaged at all, begin socializing with classmates, or declare that they'll just do the work at home, (intending to get help from parents, or to not do it at all).

While visiting a classroom to assist a teacher in tweaking his management and instructional strategies, I noticed that he asked very poignant questions of his students to guide their analytical and critical thinking, but never modeled the writing of their conclusions, or how one would bring closure to the litany of ideas that were bandied about. Being rather pleased with the various comments that had been pieced together, he presumed the students to be ready to move forward. Thus, he assigned the next three questions for which they were to *write* proper responses. Immediately, he was quite taken aback by their hesitancy to begin, the resistance to putting pen to paper, and how they rushed through the exercise and began talking and visiting at one another's desks—without his permission.

What was the problem? The modeling step had been omitted, and even though he had received one or two exemplary student answers during the discussion phase, the majority of the class hadn't a clue. Nor had any of them a clue as to how to convert their thoughts into well-written sentences that would do justice to the questions. The teacher, however, read their lack of motivation to tackle the assignment as an indication of their disinterest in doing anything that wasn't handed to them on a platter. He was clearly disgusted and disillusioned. Nevertheless, this wasn't the case. His students *desired* to do a good job, but had no idea of how to go about it. They chose, instead, **to avoid stress by avoiding the task**.

The responsibility was his to **teach and model**, not to assign and assume. Once he went back, had students get out paper and pencil, following as the writing of thoughtful answers was modeled, they had a clearer understanding of what they were being asked to accomplish, and were better able to attempt the task at hand. Needless, to say, when students are fully prepared to take on their assignments, *everyone* is calmer and happier.

Keep in mind that students learn by **doing**, not by merely listening and watching. Whether the lesson covers rope-climbing or dissecting a frog, there will be auditory, visual, and kinesthetic learners, and you want to reach all of them all of the time. Lofty goal, I KNOW! BUT you can do it! It increases learning and **DECREASES BEHAVIOR PROBLEMS.**

Once instructional modeling with simultaneous student practice has occurred, the lesson is still not complete. Academic frustration, one of the major causes of student misbehavior, can be further forestalled by plugging in additional hands-on practice via working in small groups on their new skills, as they reteach to one another what you have taught them. This helps to cement the process, concept, or skill in their minds, and increases their comfort level with the new material. Moreover, it allows them to sort out and assimilate what has been taught, and to share in a learning experience with their peers. You will, of course, facilitate this activity, providing individual instruction and feedback, as needed. Using this method of teaching forces students to become involved in their own learning, heightens interest, and **minimizes discipline problems**. Again, try to resist the temptation or impulse to rush through instruction for the sake of covering the curriculum. It simply doesn't work, and, more often than not, results in shallow learning for students and a rise in classroom disruptions due to confusion and fear of failure.

Coop Groups & Discipline

Providing cooperative learning activities became much more popular as a teaching/learning technique among educators in the latter part of the 20th century. What is not apparent, however, when visiting many classrooms, is the extreme significance that needs to be affixed to the teacher's know-how regarding the *structuring* of coop groups in a manner which sets students up for behavioral and learning success. Ideally, student groups should be chosen by the instructor if one wishes students to get the optimum benefit from the experience. However, all too often, teachers are heard to exclaim, " Get a group together and find a place to sit." Hearing these words immediately sends chills throughout my being, because I'm aware of what will most likely be the result—chaos, ostracizing, socializing, confusion, and at best, an unnecessary waste of precious educational time. What usually accompanies the students' attempts to follow the aforementioned directive, is a barrage of admonishments from a frustrated teacher who thought the students were "mature" enough to handle making the choice, and to do so quickly and quietly.

This is not to say that at no time may students be allowed to choose. What *is* needed, however, is forethought as to whether student or teacher choice will bring about the most advantageous learning and behavioral outcomes for any given project, AND some type of instruction detailing a *procedure* for selecting teammates and getting settled in a quick, orderly manner. Personal space can become an issue and a gigantic bone of contention among students. Is sitting on the floor appropriate? Can perching on top of desks work? What about boy-girl shenanigans? All of these questions need to be considered, *by the instructor,* before placing students into groups. The type of problematic behavior that will be the outcome of allowing certain students to work together can be prevented if one will simply make wise decisions in this department.

In one incident, it was necessary to summon the instructor's intervention to rescue a timid young lady who was being sexually harassed by one of the young men with whom she'd been asked to work. Once the announcement that the assignment would be completed cooperatively, had been given, the decision pertaining to which students would be placed in each group, was made in a cursory manner. Immediately, a young man perched himself right on the writing surface his desk, so as to be closer to the girl with whom he had been assigned to work. It was clear that working on the assignment wasn't his priority. Soon cries of *"Stop staring at me! You're making me nervous,"* were heard from the girl. Nevertheless, the teacher appeared totally oblivious to what was transpiring. The coop group task had gotten off to a rough start because of a lack of planning and structure. Educators are **always** to be teaching and guiding, on the lookout for what will thrust their students into a receptive mood for acquiring knowledge. This is how model students become model students.

Since coop group activities generally require dissemination of materials, there needs to be a system in place which accomplishes the task efficiently. I once observed the startup of a coop group assignment which was creative, curriculum-based and quite well-planned by the instructor. However, its learning value became diminished by the process used to get students going. He began by asking students to choose their own groups, which took an inordinate amount of time as the middle-schoolers wrangled over who would or would not be in their groups. One girl was excluded altogether and advised, by the instructor, to *find* a group or just work by herself. Next, there were five separate materials each would need. These items had been placed on a long table at the front of the room. To get these materials to each group, the teacher enlisted the aid of five students of questionable behavior. I believe they were chosen to quell their disruptive tendencies and to get them "flowing" in a leadership direction. (Sometimes this can work, IF a specific procedure is given, the teacher remains vigilant, and students who perform in an exemplary fashion are also chosen.) Nevertheless, what occurred was friction and chaos as each helper called out to ask certain individuals if they needed whatever it was the assistant was passing out. Then, there was teasing and refusal to give other individuals the necessary materials. In short, much time was wasted, socializing commenced, and vital directions were lost in the confusion. Before long, the frustrated teacher felt it necessary to reprimand the class for not handling the situation appropriately, and a wonderful hands-on lesson which should have gone exactly according to plan, had gotten off to a stressful and rocky start. The academic atmosphere had been lost, and the teacher found it impossible to fully regain it during that period.

What can we learn from this? First of all, pre select student groups. Then, avoid the time-wasting procedure of having several materials passed out by student volunteers, unless they have been specifically trained or prepped to do the job with efficiency. Realize that the longer students have to wait for supplies, the more involved they become in their own distractions. Perhaps a successful procedure would have been for the groups to assemble and be seated, and for the teacher to then call one member from each group to come up and collect the required materials in one fell swoop. Whatever you decide to do, just remember that **student down time is usually the enemy of the teacher and of learning.**

Additionally, for excellent behavior and learning to take place, students need to be taught a coop group procedure that:

- provides structured, *posted* guidelines which become routine (written in positive language, **Do vs. Don't**)
- provides instruction and modeling **before** groups assemble
- gets students engaged quickly
- requires each group member to do *equal* work
- grades each individual's assignment or offering, as well as the overall group's
- gives a specific time limit for the group assignment.

The "equal work" guideline bears comment. When students are permitted to divvy up work so that one is drawing the map, another is reading and recording all of the information or main points, while yet another is doing the lettering for the poster, there's going to be some kind of behavioral disruption, if only in the forms of mild horseplay, inappropriate conversation, or out-of-seat goofing around. Each student needs to cooperate on *each* part of the assignment. There is no equality between reading and writing main ideas, and drawing a map or doing lettering, (which *is* allowed in many classrooms). This kind of "planning" just opens the proverbial can of worms—complaints and cries of unfairness. Some are bogged down with the heavy duty work, while others are experiencing a walk in the park, in more ways than one. These "walk-in-the-park" individuals become your behavior problems, not to mention that they aren't learning much of anything, either. Absolutely **everyone** should be required to read and write whatever the group has to read and write. Student accountability is essential to the promotion of productive coop groups. You may need to require that individual rough copies be turned in along with the group copy to show that a cooperative effort was mounted. Having students sit around giving responses while one person writes, is just begging for off-task behavior, e.g. noncooperation, teasing, inappropriate touching, disturbing members of other groups, etc., not to mention minimal skill/concept attainment by those very students. Even in a brief, group brainstorming session, students come away with more and are totally engaged and better behaved when each is required to *write* the solutions derived by the group. You want each student's nose to the grindstone. Then, you can walk around telling them who they are as scholars, elevating self-image, while teaching academic stamina and self-discipline.

Another strategy that works well in keeping students actively involved and behaving well during coop group assignments, is the creation of a checklist that allows the teacher to evaluate each group as they work. The following is one created for a group of teachers, but whatever is significant to you can be included. Copies of your checklist can be made and stored for easy access. For this technique to be effective, the point total must be substantial, and recorded as part of each student's overall or daily grade. Specific, concrete criteria for each category is explained to students beforehand, and points given fairly and honestly. In other words, if students can spend five minutes chatting about the school's latest football game, then plead with the teacher to receive the whole 10 points for quick on task and on-topic conversation if they cease and desist for the next 25 minutes, the clout of the checklist has been compromised and maybe even lost.

Coop Group Checklist

Task _______________ Date ___________ Total Points (60) ____
Group Members: ____

_____ quick on task (10)
_____ following project directions (10)
_____ cooperation among group members (15)
_____ on–topic conversation throughout (10)
_____ completion of task (15)

Student Participation & Discipline

High student-participatory teaching takes specific planning and organization. However, it pays off in huge dividends in student focus, skill/concept acquisition, and a **pleasant teaching and learning environment**. Plan instruction and activities with this in mind. Create lessons that require ***100%*** of your students to participate throughout the lesson. This participation requirement needs to be carried out in a nonthreatening manner, lest it provoke misbehavior born of humiliation and embarrassment. You've already provided or are furnishing vital instruction and practice during the lesson, and are **sure** that they can do what you will ask of them. The expectation is, also, that you will provide them with the *respectful* support required for them to achieve a reasonable level of success as they become involved in the lesson or activity. Get them explaining, moving, repeating after you, charting, clapping, reciting, taking notes, responding chorally, even singing, if that's what it takes. And, no fair calling on someone to answer a question or exhibit a skill, and upon learning that he/she is incapable of doing so, declaring, *" This is not rocket science,"* as one instructor was accustomed to responding. This kind of off-handed, seemingly innocent remark can make students reluctant to take academic risks. It can also precipitate defiance and disrespect. One astute, assertive student replied, upon receiving the rocket science quip, " Are you saying I'm not smart?" Just keep in mind that ***the more actively engaged students are, the more they will learn, and the less time they'll have for misbehaving.***

This high student-accountability type of teaching has proven, day in and day out, to be an integral part of establishing and maintaining a classroom where management challenges are not an issue. Students *crave* explicit instructions and limits. A teacher who moves around the classroom while teaching, encouraging, soliciting responses, and in general, interacting with students as the lesson unfolds and progresses, is leaps and bounds ahead in alleviating disruptive situations. ***It's difficult to misbehave when the teacher is standing beside you, moving your way, making eye contact, smiling at you, and, generally, commanding your attention and participation.***

Don't permit your teaching strategy to be foiled or yourself to become put-off by a student who simply says, "I don't know," as a way of being left alone. Perhaps the person really doesn't know, but since you're out to procure 100% participation and to improve the self-confidence of your students as learners, a fun technique can be used to allow that student to participate without debasement or shame. Simply give hints or clues to the answer, or give the answer and ask the student to repeat it. If done in a respectful, fun manner, he or she will get on board, and you can move on to the next. Further, this technique sends the nonverbal message that each student is important, considered a learner, and expected to stay engaged. As an added bonus, students who plan to hide and disrupt are thwarted in their efforts. BE CONSISTENT and PERSISTENT.

> **Teacher:** "What kind of climate is prevalent in desert regions, Chris?"
> **Chris:** "I don't know."
> **Teacher:** "Would it be arid, which means dry, or humid, which indicates lots of moisture?"
> **Chris:** "Arid"
> **Teacher:** "Good job!"

Instructional Diversity & Discipline

Diversity in teaching techniques and materials figures significantly in keeping students attentive, interested, on task, and **DISCIPLINED**. Avoid presenting lessons in the same way every day. Once you've determined what your lesson objectives will be, set about designing a variety of activities, materials, and methods of presentation to use in meeting those objectives. This will serve to keep your students fidgeting less and exhibiting more attentiveness and stamina. ***When students shut down because one activity has gone on too long or has been used too often, diversity in the form of undesirable behavior is usually the result.*** Of course, the younger the students the more activities need to change. However, older students also need variety, not so much during one lesson (except in the case of block periods), but from day to day. Pay particular attention to objectives so that instructional bird-walking doesn't occur. Each activity has a purpose within the parameters of those objectives, and you are adhering to the curriculum. For those who are unfamiliar with the term, "bird-walking," it simply means that there is no cohesiveness or logic to the presentation of the lesson. There is flitting, if you will, from one point, topic, or activity to another, without there being a common thread linking each essential piece to the one before, rendering the lesson an unorganized hodgepodge.

This diversity of teaching techniques, et al, aids in attaining one of the most important goals that we can embrace as educators. It is that of promoting and actually *teaching self*-**discipline**. This commodity is so very essential to students as they endeavor to grasp concepts and skills which, perhaps, are not particularly compelling or captivating, but essential to their growth as scholars. Self-control is vital if students are to demonstrate patience and other virtues necessary to exist graciously and successfully in a group setting. Moreover, it's exceedingly advantageous for instructors to have students display *age- appropriate* self-discipline during classroom instruction and exercises. Of course, the larger the teacher/student ratio, the more consequential this *learned* skill becomes.

The trick here is to *not* believe that this can be accomplished by screaming, exhorting, threatening, or using other incendiary or questionable techniques. It must be accomplished through the structure and procedures you provide for your students. Asking students to just "watch" a lab experiment or listen to a storyteller or speaker without accountability, is asking for discipline problems. *As* they watch or listen, *something* must be required of them. They need to take notes, fill in a story map, make entries on a chart—**something!** Otherwise, you may find yourself constantly asking them to sit up, pay attention, stop talking, and so on. Such divisive situations occur all because teachers expect students to display adult-like self–discipline, which is an unreasonable and unwise expectation. Again, try not to assume the moral high ground, which flies in the face of scholarly child/adolescent/teen research.

Further, the more interested students are in what they're learning and doing, the more likely they will demonstrate this deeper level of discipline. The more often they actually fall into this mode of behavior, the better it takes hold and becomes a natural part of who they are as learners. It takes *time* and persistence on the part of instructors. Some students will acquiesce more easily than others, but even those who must be carried kicking and screaming in that direction, will advance at their own pace as each day, each lesson is infused with effective structure and procedures. Thus, the effort to diversify your teaching strategies, to put variety into the materials and activities to which students will be exposed, will allow them to practice and hone this precious skill.

Students come to us with different levels of self-discipline as with all physiological and mental development, leading some to better adjust to mundane tasks while others tend to exhibit antsy behavior the moment a focus-intensive activity is introduced. But make no mistake about it, you **do not** have students who have *arrived.* They **all** need our empathy, consideration, and instruction in this area. This is not to say that we rake them over the coals by telling them when they're *not* displaying it, but, again, the procedures and structure that we allow to permeate the classroom environment on a daily basis, along with the diversification of our teaching techniques and lesson plans, is what will do the trick. This indispensable framework provides the guidance and, ultimately, becomes the mirror which allows them to "see" themselves as self-disciplined human beings.

A final point to make on this topic is one that exhorts teachers to *find* ways to show that you trust students to follow the rules during learning activities that encourage freedom of movement. Again, tell them who they *are* (*e.g. "You guys are excellent at picking up and returning materials without disturbing others. Thank you!*") Praise when you see any *tiny* bit of success or effort in the right direction. Admire it, encourage it, help those who are struggling, and be persistent and tenacious. You <u>will</u> be victorious!

<u>Individualized Attention/ Feedback- And Discipline</u>

Just *how* to provide individual attention in classrooms comprised of large numbers of students with diverse learning abilities, has been bandied about in many a staff workshop and faculty meeting. It's not an easy task, but, somehow, it must be done. I can only say that it is crucial in preventing academic frustration and the subsequent learning and behavioral problems that result. Even when you feel that you've presented the perfect lesson, there's likely to be one or more students who will need that personal touch because, truthfully, there is no perfect lesson that suffices for every student. However, if educators will do what has already been spoken about in the realm of instruction and student participation, the problem is greatly reduced. Nevertheless, there is still that need for the instructor to be accessible. Your fast learners or more capable students will work on their own once instruction has been concluded, while you attend to those who need just a tad extra instruction or affirmation that they're on the right track. Don't be reluctant to offer this help by declaring that you're building independent learners. One cannot be independent when he doesn't understand what he's doing, or is feeling unsure about how something is to be completed. The result is a student who becomes angry with the instructor for creating this distress. These feelings of anger can manifest themselves in undesirable behaviors such as crying, pouting, sullenness, negative outbursts, refusal to work, and so on—all of which can be *prevented* with a little TLC.

Even those students who seem to require an inordinate amount of support can be "weaned" while still being assisted. Utilize volunteers, paraprofessionals, and the school's support system, but beware of just doing nothing. One of an educator's duties is to find a way to provide *hope* for each student. We all must try to avoid complaining and sucking air about how teachers are expected to do it all. It will only bring *you* down, and increase the likelihood that your students will adopt the same negative disposition. Usually, when an instructor genuinely does what he/she can, it works!

Last, but not least, when providing this critical **attention to individuals,** notice those who are struggling, those who are abstract thinkers and advanced learners, or those who seem to be preoccupied with some outside or personal obstacle. Each requires support. Try to forestall problems that could occur from students being exceptional in any way by initiating extracurricular, academic, or counseling support for students who appear to be in need. **Appreciate them all**, and don't be afraid to let them know it. Stick to your curriculum, while supplementing for fast learners and providing remediation and individual assistance for those who are feeling overly-challenged. Keep lessons "meaty" for *all* students so that they do not become insulted by instructional activities perceived to be "beneath" them or insulting to their intelligence. **Academic rigor** is pivotal to raising self-concepts, and uplifting to students from all neighborhoods and economic levels. **All** desire to believe that what they are learning is important, a big deal. They want to be proud of what they are accomplishing. When that pride is not present, a feeling of humiliation is sometimes the replacement. This occurs especially in students who are academically challenged. Beware of treating them as though they cannot learn. Many merely need a slower teaching pace and/or different teaching methods, to achieve success. At any rate, ***behavior problems oftentimes occur when students feel belittled by being given lessons that are too easy for them***. Considering their feelings will cause them to appreciate you, and they'll show this appreciation through their **good behavior.**

Thorough Question-Answering and Discipline

Thorough question-answering and specific re-teaching goes hand-in-hand with attending to individual and whole-group needs, helping to stem the tide of confusion and frustration which precipitate poor behavior. INVITE questions. Your students need to know that you'll stop at nothing to help them grasp what you're teaching, bringing about achievement in your class. This is what transforms them into kinder, gentler, creatures.

They know that you're not out to "make them fail." Though this may seem preposterous to you, this is exactly how plenty of students feel when struggling to comprehend what you're "laying down." You must probe for questions. Circulate the room, pointedly asking *each* student about what is being covered, to demonstrate understanding in such a way that *you'll* know if they have attained the skills or concepts just presented. This can be done in a fun, nonintimidating fashion. Whether or not they ask questions is neither here nor there. Even extremely bright students will, at times, be reluctant to take a risk, for fear of sounding stupid or less smart than everyone considers them to be. Also, there are times when students *don't know* that they don't know, so they run into glitches, later, that cause academic stress, resulting in them detaching from the lesson and drifting into undesirable conduct.

Inviting questions allows students to achieve an adequate level of comfort even when they're totally confused and on the brink of giving up. This is so very important, even when you suspect that a student has not given his/her full attention during the lesson. For whatever reason a student needs clarification, it's prudent and respectful to offer it. Then, if a private chat is needed to reset the expectation of maintaining total attentiveness throughout the lesson, or to give replacement behavior, do so. Refusing to answer questions causes negative behavior to commence or escalate, can create an adversarial relationship between students and teacher, and compounds the problem by affording the student an excuse to sit and do nothing—but disrupt, of course! Moreover, reteaching will definitely be necessary many times, and must be done without criticism or judgment, either genuine or with humor. The self-esteem of students can be very fragile. If they believe you are "doing them a favor" by reteaching, they can tune you right out or take such offense that they will not allow the lesson to be successful. It's actually a human dignity issue to *not* accept help if it's viewed as a bother. Simply reteach or answer queries with graciousness, professionalism, and a *different instructional* technique, if possible.

The above instructional strategies should be employed ***before*** a *graded* assignment is given. ***Embarrassment and fear resulting from noncomprehension of what has been taught, causes many students to display defiant or disinterested conduct.*** Teachers would do well to be cognizant of how "feeling stupid" can induce students to take on macho, impudent, or nonchalant behaviors or attitudes. Most of this can be avoided by simply not assuming, but following the teaching strategies outlined in this chapter, for each new lesson and before making independent assignments. You'll know when students are feeling comfortable with a new skill or concept. There are many relevant hands-on activities available to help them reach this point, and **an active, confident student is a *disciplined student.***

I was asked to observe a class of students who were bent on mistreating their instructor. On the day that I sat in, there was an initial assignment given which students were asked to complete independently. Clearly, they were struggling from the beginning. A few hands went up to request assistance, while others in loud voices, called out the teacher's name. Her response to them was that she had taught them how to do the skill the day before and that they were to just do it. Again, the expectation was unrealistic. They gave up, some called her names, other more passive individuals just sat and occupied themselves with whatever was in their notebooks, and still others forged ahead trying to perform as best they could. It was apparent that an adversarial relationship had been spawned between the teacher and her students. Here was a conscientious instructor who pushed students to learn a skill a day and to remember each as she moved ahead with her curriculum. The curriculum, and the pressure that she perceived as being placed on her by the school district to complete it, had become more important than her students. She was totally blind to the fact that the students required much more practice and guidance on the high-level skills she was teaching, in order to grasp and retain. She was also oblivious to the reality that she was creating the very problems that were making her existence miserable. This instructor was bent on blaming students for not wanting to learn or put forth enough effort, and they were bent on lashing out at her for the stress and fear of failure they were experiencing. It was a very sad situation, one, I am sorry to say, is being repeated in other classrooms, with similar results. **Teachers must be just as willing to alter attitudes and methods as they wish their students to be.**

The art of thorough question-*asking* takes time and requires a profound commitment on the part of the instructor. One needs to be committed to making sure that every student is made privy to what is being taught. It's not too much to request that instructors solicit a response from each student, regardless of class size, on critical skills and concepts. It can make the difference between a group of students who are "all over it" when it comes to cooperating with the teacher, because Mr. X makes sure that everyone experiences success, versus one in which there is constant tension between teacher and students. How long can it take to ask each student to give an example of a variable, a verb, an hypothesis, a state, to blow or sing a certain note, to dribble a basketball, and so on. Make a game of it, have them quiz one another in an organized manner, go up and down each row soliciting responses and giving clues. You're making sure that each is counted, noticed, and valued. The result will be students who value themselves, and who fall in love with their teacher. The result will be an explosion of GOOD BEHAVIOR.

Ignoring *any* of these puzzle pieces can place your classroom at risk for discipline problems. Embracing them as a matter of course, will accomplish just the opposite. There are professional resources that you can tap into when there is a need, and just maintaining a sense of peace while integrating techniques into your regime one at a time, can open the door to a world of teaching that is as it was meant to be—a pleasure. Though this may seem like a lot to handle, once you're rolling on a daily basis it becomes a matter of routine.

These are merely fundamental components of teaching, ones to which we are all exposed during our teacher education courses. Nevertheless, many educators do not realize just how **integral they are to the achievement of excellent classroom management**. The impact is enormously positive when sound techniques are implemented effectively, but when omitted or poorly implemented, the price exacted can be one of a classroom of out-of-control students.

CHAPTER 3
SUMMARY POINTS

1. Creating and maintaining a rich academic learning environment elevates student behavior.

2. Pacing instructional lessons is key to obtaining both optimal student attentiveness and conduct.

3. Maintain total organization so that your undivided attention can be focused on students and their learning.

4. Students who, on a daily basis, are made aware of learning objectives, demonstrate more academic focus and superior behavior.

5. Set high behavioral and academic standards, providing the support needed for student attainment.

6. Prevent playful, raucous student behavior by beginning each class immediately.

7. Teach everyone.

8. Coming up short on instructional materials or pertinent student activities opens the door to misbehavior, even with 5 or 10 minutes remaining in the class or period.

9. Employing effective instructional strategies leaves no opportunity for student misconduct.

10. Paying attention to individual learning needs provides incentive for students to behave well.

Chapter Four

DON'T JUDGE THE BOOKS

Stereotyping and Discipline

As students gather on school grounds to begin the new year, or mingle with peers before each class during those first few weeks, we tend to give them an unconscious, perhaps, but nonetheless, judgmental perusal. It's oh so tempting and human to rely upon evaluative hearsay regarding past student behavior, cultural bias, or learned stereotypes to "size them up" before becoming formally acquainted.

Though quite commonplace, teachers, who will undoubtedly have such a significant impact on these young lives, must consciously ***refuse to allow themselves to form*** preconceived ***notions of who will or will not succeed***. Many are the times that those instructors who remain open-minded and *equal-minded*, are surprised by just who emerges as a consummate learner despite a negative aura and/or initial intimidating demeanor. More importantly, what we think and feel truly comes through in actions, words, and vibes sent our students' way. Many are the students who are skeptical about us! They, oftentimes, erect tough fronts or exteriors because they are wary, insecure, and self-conscious in this new and most formidable environment we call a classroom. Self-preservation is, after all, the first law of nature.

So, how is an educator to open the doors of communication and relationship such that a positive connection can be initiated with new students? The answer is to simply smile, and be firm but friendly. ***Exude confidence in yourself as an instructor, the school, your knowledge of the subject matter, and pedagogy in general.*** Too often students can't believe in us because we don't believe in ourselves, our schools, or our school districts. Your confidence or lack of confidence in the quality of the learning experiences you'll provide, will be transmitted to your students. If you're on fire, they'll be on fire. Further, rather than making positive or negative assumptions about *any* of the students, expect *each* to care about being educated, and to possess a desire to learn. Convey that message not so much in words, as in your behavior towards them. Behave as though you are teaching sons and daughters of kings and queens. Ask the same of the tough-looking person as you do of those who appear to be studious. Because of general exposure to societal prejudices, most of us have unbridled stereotypes swirling around in our minds just waiting to be unleashed on any unfamiliar person with whom we come in contact. However, maintaining honesty and awareness about the biases one possesses, renders it far more likely that reason will overpower ignorance. Additionally, when students are embraced with an attitude affirming them as willing scholars, you'll be surprised that those tough, disinterested-looking exteriors will smile *with* you, and are often undercover lovers of learning versus the ready-to-pounce offenders too many instructors surmise them to be. Nonetheless, if even a *hint* of prejudice or negative stereotyping is perceived as emanating from you, there'll be time bombs in your classroom just waiting to explode at the slightest provocation. So be sure to exorcise yourself of those demons. Then, go ahead and break the ice with fun, academic activities.

Countless teachers guiding students from cultures or backgrounds different from their own, disbelieve that they are harboring negative stereotypes. This can be twice as dangerous and lethal as fully recognizing that one has this dragon to slay. The more common generalizations are the ones about which your students are aware, and for which they are on the lookout. Many have experienced prior unpleasantries or brutal difficulties in this regard, with their families or as individuals. These disturbing experiences can place that proverbial chip on their shoulders, disallowing them the grace of giving each subsequent individual the benefit of the doubt. Following, is a listing of some of the negative stereotypes which when permitted to creep into or inhabit an educator's mind, will assuredly create havoc in the area of building positive student relationships leading to good classroom discipline.

- wannabe
- "don't care"
- gangster
- dumb jock
- spoiled
- at risk
- special education student
- inner city/ urban
- slow learner
- streetwise (in a negative sense)
- punker
- race
- ethnicity
- cultural background
- religion
- single parent home
- tough
- hyper/ ADD

These are representative of an array of vexatious labels which can move a teacher to *not* offer students a fair chance to prove who they really are. When this kind of labeling occurs, consciously or unconsciously lowering an instructor's opinion of his students, the teacher involved is headed for trouble in the areas of delivering effective instruction and promoting positive student behavior. Students will simply refuse to learn from such a person. The risk is too high. The trust too little. The pain too sharp.

I imagine that this position seems a gross overstatement or overreaction to a systematic practice so customary among schools across the nation, one which places students in categories as a matter of course. But it's not. This factor has been flagrantly underestimated in its importance and contribution to student misbehavior and low academic achievement. Students must feel at ease with their instructors in order to learn and relate in a productive fashion. As a matter of fact, don't we all have this need?

I recently assisted a teacher who, after teaching for years in a suburban area, relocated to a new city, receiving a position to teach urban students. With successful years of experience under her belt, one would have expected the transition to progress with relative smoothness. Nonetheless, it was anything but. The problem? "Culture Shock," she stated. Though possessing many tools of an accomplished teacher, her insistence upon feeling "shocked" by differences she noted between the two student groups, accompanied by an unconscious display of superiority, wreaked havoc in her classroom, eventually resulting in her demise as an effective teacher. The students were having none of it, even though they were unable to verbalize just why they disliked her.

I believe that there can be initial culture shock when one is totally unaccustomed to dwelling among or associating with those from another culture or economic group. However, students are everyday people who, like all of us, desire to feel proud of themselves and to be affirmed as "good people." This, she couldn't provide. Though her words were well-chosen, her tone subdued, they just didn't have the ring of truth. Thus, students, *seemingly* without provocation, behaved badly on a daily basis. There were daily refusals to sit in assigned seats, brazen walking around the classroom, blatant inattentiveness during instruction, loud outbursts, throwing of items when her back was turned. Need I say more?

The disrupters had simply fulfilled her unspoken expectation of them as students who didn't behave, kids who possessed no interest in bettering themselves through education. Yet, most endured the discord, quietly waiting for her to obtain full control and teach the class. Ordinary "testing of the waters" behavior from the more assertive souls grew routine, and the classroom atmosphere became toxic and extremely sad for both students and teacher. I truly believe that in her heart of hearts she desired to succeed with her new students, but the inability to just say no to negative stereotyping, blaming the kids for the contentious conditions being experienced by all, led her to eventually call it quits.

Make no mistake about it, the teacher *is* the person who determines whether the classroom will or will not be a place of order, an environment conducive to learning and positive energy. Necessary strategies can be learned if one is willing to relate on a human to human basis, regardless of who sits in the student desks. A brief article discussing student behavior as it pertains to the amount of genuine deference afforded them, noted that though students may not know how to *define* dignity, they certainly know when theirs has been violated or trampled upon. Something to ponder.

As previously mentioned, to be effective with students in this all-important quest to procure cooperative behavior, they must feel at ease in your presence. My advice is to **relax and relate**! These two rs seem to soften the most awkward, emotionally- charged situations. Take time to study the age group you're teaching. What are the movies, music, toys, or issues of importance to them? Once discovered, don't just fake interest, actually look into your life to find areas of common ground. Talk to them in a natural, friendly manner. They will reciprocate! Surely, we as sojourners of the same time in space have mutual experiences, regardless of individual differences. Certain things in life are unifying: feeling ill, tired, or excited, news happenings, sporting events, sense of family. Complimenting students or making affirming comments when the sentiment is genuine, lets them know that you embrace your oneness with them. Whether the student is 6 or 16, a nice hair day, cute outfit, intelligent answer, great effort, leadership moment can be noticed and remarked about, as long as it's done in a manner which neither is nor can be misconstrued as improper. The list is endless when one is determined to accentuate the positive, elevating self-image and bringing out the best in students.

Relating also means displaying empathy. If a student is coughing, ask if a drink of water or a peppermint would be helpful. A continually yawning student seems to perk right up just because a teacher acknowledges that he or she seems tired that day. Conversely, when teachers choose to attack those displaying less than perfect attentiveness, using criticism or sarcasm to make a point, students fight back—with defiant behavior. The student-teacher relationship takes a step backward and an opportunity to model graciousness has been lost. Students learn from and advance to new heights of desirable conduct as a result of consistent, exemplary role modeling from instructors.

The lasting effects of the two rs are priceless in the establishment and maintenance of good classroom discipline. When you display your human side, students tend to bond with you, "choosing" to discipline themselves. They are relating to you relating to them. There is elation that they're not being unfairly judged for just being who they are. They're relieved that they have a teacher who likes and appreciates them, differences and all, and, in fact, one who enjoys and applauds the differences, while guiding them toward their best selves.

Just as loving, competent parents seek to find the right balance in forging relationships with their children, so must loving, competent teachers find that balance. Relaxing and relating doesn't mean that you are striving to be a peer with students. On the contrary, this would place all at high risk for failure. The responsibility is to communicate acceptance as you build solidarity.

Alienating or Provoking & Discipline

Believe it or not, there are times when educators literally incite the very student misbehavior they find so offensive. Though indeliberate, the outcome is the same. I suspect that sometimes adults forget that children and teens are just people—people with less life experience, but people, nonetheless. They are incensed by the same actions or words about which we become incensed, insulted, maddened, infuriated, exasperated by the same things that cause these emotions in us. What more can be said? Teachers must be mindful of this fact if they are to engender good behavior in their students of any age or description.

When contemplating writing the first edition of this book, I began to *really* pay attention to specific actions and remarks impulsively made by colleagues communicating with students considered to be misbehaving. Comments and conduct provoking student outrage. Sudden outrage surfaced in otherwise low-key, well-behaved students, as well as in those with horns peaking above strands of hair, students who just naturally responded badly to any and all perceived assaults to their dignity. What I discovered was that there are certain behaviors displayed by educators which automatically propel students to the edge, ready to defend themselves by any means available. These practices teachers would be wise to shun, if cooperative, decorous classroom, hall, lunchroom, or field trip student behavior is the ultimate goal. An important point to remember is that students are not called upon to be mindful of instructors' self-concepts, though the positive atmosphere generated from the use of good manners and human kindness by students, can hardly be minimized. Nevertheless, it is imperative that those who seek to educate, remain mindful of not trampling on the self-esteem of the very students needing to be receptive of direct guidance. The more instructors honor the responsibility of goal-oriented leadership, refusing to misuse or abuse authority by allowing anger and vengeful actions to creep into the picture when dealing with students, the better will be their days, weeks, months and years as teachers, and the more desirable the behavior garnered from students.

With this in mind, lets look at conduct to avoid if the objective is to establish the kind of relationship with students that will induce them to accept discipline with a measure of civility and compliance. They will. Students realize when they have overstepped their boundaries. They know, and expect to be called on the carpet. However, calling them on the carpet doesn't have to, and shouldn't include disrespect.

- **Invading Student Space**:
  Respecting a person's personal space is just good manners. However, some teachers feel justified in overstepping this boundary when attempting to administer disciplinary correction. When a teacher stands so close that student discomfort is experienced, he/she is alienating and provoking. This seems to be especially true with kids in middle school, and high school freshman, instigating rude reactions from students. However, all students must be regarded, out of general respect. Speaking with students from a comfortable distance discourages the crudeness that occurs when students take offense, and encourages student cooperation.

- **Finger in the Face**:
  In the "Leave it to Beaver" days, it appeared to be standard fare for an adult to wag his finger in the face of the child being admonished or disciplined. Let me just say that this doesn't work. It alienates and provokes.

- **Using Sarcasm or Cynicism**:
  Sitting in the classroom of one young teacher, I noticed that her manner of control was to become sarcastic and cynical whenever a student was

observed not following directions. As a result, even though she was quite personable otherwise, there was a constant cloud of impending disorder hovering overhead. The room was never quite peaceful or free from discord. Upon speaking to her about the practice, she appeared surprised, expressing that she considered it okay to be sarcastic. Well, it's not. It alienates and provokes.

- **Embarrassing or Humiliating**:
  Who among us would relish being reprimanded or "called out" during a faculty meeting? Would it promote good feelings or contrition? I think not. In the heat of the moment, instructors forget themselves, lambasting a student who is out of order. However, wisdom is demonstrated when perspective is maintained, noting that the goal is to change student behavior for the better. Unfortunately, some educators believe that students *deserve* to be verbally manhandled when off track behaviorally. These same instructors wrestle, daily, with grievous disciplinary struggles. If defiance, name-calling, loud outbursts, rude gestures, and other negative behavioral reactions are not the goal, then this is not the strategy to use. The one-upmanship relished by some teachers, once a student has been "put in her place," fails to net the desired result of a contrite student, eager to make amends. It merely inspires feelings of victimization, with peers identifying with the pain of their classmate, leading to more bruising classroom misbehavior. Further, an opportunity for the instructor to model a mature way of handling conflict has been squandered. Letting a student know what you desire, exhibiting confidence and calm assertiveness, is the road to take.

- **Assuming the Worst:**
  Can we talk? Nothing gets a student's dander up more than being accused of something he didn't do. I'm going to keep this simple. Unless you actually SEE or KNOW that a student is cheating or has stolen something, you can't make an accusation. Sooo many teachers make this mistake, alienating the entire classroom of students. Students should and do have rights. Nevertheless, there are instructors who believe themselves to possess special privilege of search and seizure, superceding the personal, privacy rights of students. This is a very harmful notion. Give the benefit of the doubt. Employ the golden rule. If you think that something is awry, just say so to the class or

to an individual, privately. Students are able to hear that something is missing, that you don't know who has taken it, but that you'd like for it to be returned in a specific manner. **The key is to avoid making students feel like criminals.** Preaching and berating simply doesn't work. It alienates and leads to retaliatory misbehavior.

NOTE: Keep personal belongings and valuable school materials in a secure place just as you would in any workplace. Remember that schools are public buildings.

If a person appears to be cheating, but you can't tell for sure, get rid of the problem. Using a post-it note or discreetly visiting the individual's desk to state that you'd like for her to place her notebook in her backpack until the test ends, is sufficient. You've gotten your point across if she, in fact, is cheating, but if she's not, no false accusation has been made.

The same technique works just as well when it's obvious that cheating *is* occurring. A private chat comes later—without judgmental or self-concept-lowering verbiage, stating the facts and issuing a fair consequence. Actually, all testing guidelines should be procedural, taught to your students at the time of the first test. Just be sure that rules are not insulting, such as not permitting students to wear long sleeves on the day of an exam. You *are* going to take care of any problem arising in your classroom, you just are not going to do so in an alienating or provoking manner.

- **Snatching Things**:
When a student is fiddling with something that is captivating his or his classmates' attention, or is creating a disruption of any kind with said item, use a simple rule of thumb. Permit the person to handle his own property. This just prevents the nonsense surrounding a teacher's attempt to snatch something away from a student, or the demand that it be placed in the teacher's outstretched hand.
A middle school young lady was "terrorizing" a fellow student with an ink pen. Her male teacher's request to cease and desist, fell on deaf ears. Finally, in exasperation, he approached her with the intent of grabbing the pen. At that exact moment the girl shoved the pen into the breast pocket of her blouse, forcing the teacher to remove it from there. You guessed it. She accused her instructor of touching her breast, to a chorus of oohs and guffaws from her friends. The principal had no choice

but to suspend the teacher on the spot, in the wake of an investigation. Fortunately, several of her classmates were honest and courageous enough to aid the teacher in proving his innocence.

A P.E. teacher requested that a young man turn off and put away his CD player during class. Recognizing that compliance was improbable, the teacher moved toward the student in an effort to grab it. A brief tugging struggle ensued until the student realized that the player could be damaged. He gave a final tug just as the teacher abruptly let go. The student fell backward into a locker, and later reported that the teacher had pushed him into the locker.

In each of these instances, the problem was not solved by the instructor's action, but exacerbated. Again, the educator is the mature thinker. The objective is to have the offending item placed where it can no longer create havoc or become a disruption. The method to use is **information and choice.** Two choices are issued **by the instructor,** and, ideally, though both are acceptable to the instructor, one is more desirable to the student. This allows the student to feel as though he can make a decision that works for him. (Avoid the mistake of proffering an insulting or otherwise inappropriate choice.)

e.g. "Jason, the swinging necklace is making me uncomfortable because it could hit someone. Put it around your neck or on my desk until after school."

Immediately tell him who he is, avoiding "staring him down" until it's done.

e.g. "Thanks. You can do this. Hang in there for 15 more minutes."

Move on with the lesson, but notice whether or not he complies. (Remember the nature of the beast.)

If you observe that there is no compliance, forewarn of a consequence.

"Jason, do as I asked, now, so that you won't have to turn your necklace into the office and get a call home. Keep it simple."

Again, no staring, but follow through on the consequence, promptly, if it appears that your instructions are being ignored. Not only Jason, but your entire class needs to be aware that you say what you mean and mean what you say, though it will be said in a respectful manner.

Information and choice generally works by itself when communicated with respectful assertiveness. Teachers, all too often, feel that harshness is required. It's not. Harshness alienates and provokes.

Culture and Discipline

One can hardly speak about stereotyping without spending a moment or two on culture. Many years ago, it was my pleasure and good fortune to hear a professor expound quite eloquently on culture and the need for educators to comprehend just what it *is* and what it is not. First, as we are all very well aware, our country is one composed of a multiplicity of cultures embracing both traditional and nontraditional belief systems. Many of our schools are multicultural in student population, but not so much when it comes to the cultural backgrounds of faculty and administration. This common predicament has spawned many a distasteful situation resulting in widespread student misbehavior. **When students perceive that preconceived notions are held by their teacher or teachers, notions which are negative toward their cultural background, the natural responses are ones of anger, revenge conduct, and refusals to demonstrate academic progress under those instructors**. Critical judgments based on broad generalizations, ignoring the uniqueness of each individual, limiting rights of expression, and assuming superiority of a particular way of life, are tremendously hurtful to students. Even when left unspoken, such views somehow come to light, creating a climate promoting and fostering student misbehavior, behavior born of a passionate need to claim one's worth to society by retaliating against negative stereotyping.

Educators need to be careful. Careful to honor and respect students' cultures, even when radically different from their own. Tolerance is not enough. Acceptance is more potent and inspirational. When endeavoring to teach, all obstacles that could potentially bar us from penetrating the minds of our charges with the knowledge and information we've pledged to impart, are to be circumvented. If we wish them to attend with cooperative, open spirits, then we must embrace *all* of who they are with the same deference we wish to receive for all of who we are. Verbal comments escaping from our lips, facial expressions and other gestures labeling their lifestyle as somehow substandard when compared to the one we practice or endorse, not only ravages the relationship being cultivated between instructor and students, but, indeed, ravages the self-images of students. They are confounded over what to do with this stern rejection of the very fabric from which they are cut! The solution, in their young minds, one easily accessible and at their disposal, is to show their displeasure with the affront, and pride in who they are by rebelling against the rules and guidelines of the assumed perpetrator— a.k.a. their classroom teacher.

Culture is not solely embodied in the songs we sing, the dances performed, or the foods eaten. These are just the outward trappings of a particular way of life. Culture denotes the core beliefs, habits, customs, and ideologies that are learned and shared among a group of people. These very beliefs shape values, behavior, and attitudes. When I was growing up, it was a definite sign of respect to address any and all adults by their surnames only. To do otherwise was a brazen show of disrespect. This, along with other customs and beliefs were drummed into my very being, so much so that even today they are part and parcel of who I am.

"Okay, you say. What has all of this to do with establishing and sustaining that all-essential daily classroom discipline?" Everything. Along with knowledge of curriculum and pedagogy, instructors also need to know something about their students' cultural beliefs. What makes them tick? What makes them proud? What matters? This needn't require a long drawn-out process of study, or necessitate visitations to students' places of worship, cultural events, or ancestral sites, though these experiences would, of course, expand one's information and appreciation, offering valuable insight. Some kind of ***positive-content*** reading, visiting, or viewing, leading to gaining an understanding of the *core* beliefs of the culture, is warranted. Just *listening to those from the culture* can be extremely instructive. This would aid in preventing educators from making unintentional mistakes which backfire, spurring student misbehavior as they view teachers as not being interested in or accepting of the very essence of their upbringing. As my mom was wont to say when, in her presence, someone else's way of doing something was criticized, "There's more than one way to skin a cat!" In other words, I'm okay, you're okay.

Being educated is purported to infuse one with *more* open-mindedness and acceptance of others' views, simply as a result of becoming broadened by exposure to tons of knowledge and information substantiating the expertise and achievements of all peoples and cultures. It is so imperative that we convey, naturally and as a matter of fact, this message of affirmation to our students who are of a different culture than ourselves. No, they don't automatically know that we honor and respect their roots. They are waiting to see how their culture is regarded, by observing our attitudes and words about their customs, our actions in response to specific cultural patterns, and through the inclusion or exclusion of their significant historical and celebratory events in instructional plans. A bone of contention can be raised between teacher and students when it is perceived that the teacher views students' core beliefs and values as inferior to her own. Misbehavior will surely arise, creating an adversarial relationship which, generally, leads to a proliferation of *mean-spirited* student disruptions. They are feeling angry and insulted, and they're letting you know in the only manner at their disposal — putrid, noncompliant behavior.

One very well-liked teacher, not realizing how important the traditional teachings of the Catholic church were to her students, decided to show, in a history of the bible class, a modern video version of Christ's life in which it is hinted that Christ entered into a sexual relationship with a woman. Though the entire class was appalled, several students came unglued. They couldn't believe the disrespect shown in this film. They would not be quieted or reasoned with. One of their most important beliefs and images was being trampled upon and massacred right before their very eyes. It was an affront to something held dear and sacred. The saving grace was the love they already felt for their teacher. Knowing that she wouldn't purposely disregard their convictions allowed them to listen to her sincere apology, and the teacher to terminate the film and move on with the class. All could have been avoided had this teacher known a little something about her students' core beliefs and values.

Another incident related by a teacher-ed student, involved high school teachers supervising students in attendance at an all-school commemoration of Dr. Martin Luther King, Jr. The instructors' misinterpretation of clapping and singing along with the gospel choir, as being actions of disrespect and rudeness, created such ill feelings among students as teachers rushed in to demand that they sit quietly during the performance. At first, there was shock at being quieted and reprimanded. Then, many became up in arms, ready to take the matter to the administration. The incredulous students felt that they had been unfairly targeted and accused. They were merely doing what had been taught, expected, and praised all of their lives — to not be spectators, but participants in praising the Lord — to not be ashamed of doing so no matter where they were. The teachers, on the other hand, unaware of their students' traditional customs, believing nonparticipation to be the proper response for all, unintentionally transformed an affirming program from an uplifting moment into an occasion requiring disciplinary admonishments and actions. The fact that the teachers were uninformed became the issue and the problem.

These kinds of sticky situations are being played out in more classrooms than you might imagine. The splendid news is that they are preventable. Treating others as we wish to be treated is a maxim we've all heard, perhaps *ad nauseam* to some. It's, nonetheless, valid, and if tucked away deep inside of your very being, so that it is the automatic response to your students in *every situation*, life in the classroom will become that place of comfort and good will that is essential for reaching *all* students, cultivating good behavior.

Common Reasons for Misbehavior

When working with groups of teachers regarding methods of achieving effective classroom management, it seems extremely beneficial to those instructors if clues as to **why students misbehave**, are provided. Once revealed, you'll have no trouble recognizing tell-tale signs of them at work in your own students, others in your building, or perhaps even in your own home. This list was derived by being observant of student actions—cause & effect, and recalling circumstances of student misconduct in various situations and classrooms during my years in the profession. Surprisingly, at first, I realized that the same factors leading to student blow-ups were present time and time again in classes in which poor student behavior was the norm or even occasional. I began to know what was going to happen before it actually happened when witnessing students in their relationships with teachers. Because much of student behavior is quite predictable, possessing this knowledge helps teachers guard against perpetrating negative circumstances in their classrooms.

Reason 1: Retaliation for Perceived Unfairness or Mistreatment

As stated in a previous chapter, a kid's favorite retort is " That's not fair!" Thus, when there is the *perception* of unfairness regarding rules, grading, consequences, equality of treatment among students, or what have you, there's going to be trouble, right there in River City. This needs to remain uppermost in the mind of any adult working with students so that all matters pertaining to them will be handled in a justifiable, humane manner. I am aware that many teachers are fond of saying that being fair doesn't always mean being equal. Whereas this may very well be true, the fact remains that maximum attention to overall fairness when dealing with your students will net better classroom behavior. It will help rid your domain of the toxicity accompanying negative feelings engendered toward a teacher who appears to treat some students more favorably than others, or who generates a stressful learning environment by failing to *graciousl*y prepare students to achieve academic success.

This last statement deserves a closer look, as this reason for misbehavior is sorely overlooked in countless classrooms. When instructors neglect to invest the amount of instructional time and energy essential to ensuring student learning, leaving students to feel inadequate in their abilities to acquire pertinent knowledge, questioning their worth as students, those instructors are setting up conditions ripe for delinquency, as students endeavor to avert attention away from what they "can't" do, to activities which provide comfort.

Reason 2: Academic Frustration

Thumbing through a national education publication a number of years ago, I came across an article stating the foremost reason for new teachers exiting the field of elementary and secondary education as that of experiencing classroom management difficulties. I believe this to be true even today, and contend that **academic frustration** is a covert contributor to many of the student behavior issues driving educators away, declaring that kids today are rude, crude, and unattractive. I've simply witnessed **academic frustration** and it's profound behavioral effects time and again, involving an entire classroom or on an individual student basis. Further, the corresponding behavior accompanying this form of student distress seems to be constantly misinterpreted by the adults concerned, as conduct *purposely* defiant or disinterested. The fact is that many educators are unaware of its existence, extreme significance on the education front, and the signs for which to be on the lookout. Apparently, this source of distress among students is not one about which teachers are usually forewarned. Additionally, many who *are* aware, remain staunch in their insistence that their students just *try* to complete schoolwork about which they are confused, reasoning that the skill or concept has already been taught or discussed. However, it makes perfect sense that when a child encounters fear of failure, illuminating his inability to comprehend or perform according to a teacher's expectation, creating a "diversion" becomes a viable solution. Rather than sitting, enduring the frustration and discomfort of being required to do something a student considers himself unable to do, other options are chosen. Entering into social conversation, artwork, writing notes to friends, or merely declaring the assignment "stupid" and refusing to do it, are some of the more common student choices. Again, it's human nature and self-preservation.

What can be done? First and foremost, teach *all* lessons utilizing effective instructional techniques and adequate practice sessions, omitting instructor assumptions regarding ease of skill or concept attainment. Then, teachers will do well to remain attuned to signs of incomprehension and anxiety. When students are asked to perform a task independently, but instead are requesting help from classmates, many hands are raised to procure assistance from the instructor, some are quietly choosing to engage in off-task artwork, idle sitting is observed, and the more assertive are refusing to even begin, you are witnessing manifestations that something is amiss! Avoid negating these obvious tip-offs, attributing conduct to student laziness, disinterest, not desiring to think for themselves, or to students who are accustomed to being spoon fed. Know that you are beholding students who are experiencing **academic frustration.**

I consider it safe to say that most human beings are eager to demonstrate expertise, and will do so for acknowledgement, praise, or self-gratification. Our students are no different. Yes, there are those who would rather not work on their own, and will do anything to get out of doing so, but they're not in the majority, and they're not the ones about whom I'm speaking.

When, as a group, your students are purposely off task or are requesting help with an assignment, STOP, just on general principle. Take the time to regroup and to lead a *guided* lesson, using the assigned material. Merely acknowledging that you, the teacher, may not have quite explained everything sufficiently or provided enough practice, informing them that you desire to make sure that everyone is on track, helps them relax, and stops the nonsense. Never mind that *some* student *may* be getting a free ride. We MUST hold our students in high esteem. Giving them the benefit of the doubt will encourage better behavior many more times than not, not to mention the advantage gained by extending good will. It just naturally makes them *want* to behave well.

When pausing to reteach the lesson, include these strategies to ensure success with this exercise.

- <u>Step by step instruction</u> with **active** student involvement provides an opportunity for comprehension holes to be plugged.
- <u>Give an "A" grade</u> or full points to all who are participating and will, thus, turn in an A paper! This gets you their undivided attention, provides an incentive to participate, and increases the likelihood of enhanced comprehension.
- <u>Provide additional practice</u> under your tutelage and/or in small coop groups.
- <u>Communicate no criticism</u> via sarcasm or cynical remarks regarding students not listening during the real" lesson. Not even in jest!

  Seemingly innocent comments can incite anger and resentment over being considered incapable of learning it the first time, lowering self-esteem and provoking " I don't need your help" attitudes which can result in revenge behavior. After entertaining questions, feel free to give them a similar independent assignment covering the exact same skill or concept with **no additions** or tricks.

The same process can be employed with individuals or small groups of students experiencing academic frustration. The difference is that the instructor would invite them, inconspicuously, to join her at an instructional site, preferably out of the direct focus of their classmates. Then proceed with the reteaching and practice sessions. Sometimes, very little clarification is necessary to get them smoothly and happily on their way. Nevertheless, giving them the impression that you're in a hurry, spurs them to quickly feign comprehension, leaving the problem unresolved, and the undesired behavior to resume.

<u>Feelings of Powerlessness</u>

Let's face it, if you're alive you long to feel a sense of power over some portion of your day or life. When constructing guidelines and rules, it's imperative that educators keep this in mind, giving the utmost attention to formulating guidelines which honor the dignity of students. Whereas I don't ascribe to the contention that students be allowed to make significant decisions, those better left to the professionals in charge, I do understand their need to feel that they have choice and control over some areas of their day. The one that comes readily to mind is the area of bathroom privilege. Though this issue will be discussed at length in a later chapter, it's inclusion here is pertinent to speaking about the prevention of student feelings of powerlessness, and the misconduct that ensues.

When students feel that they will be denied or limited in their opportunity to take care of this biological need, fear just automatically sets in, and fear in any of its forms leads to objectionable behavior. Such behavior encompasses crying, defiant language or actions, use of foul language or lewd gestures, rude outbursts, leaving the room without permission, and so on. It's simply preventable by establishing humane guidelines and procedures which allow students to experience the comfort of knowing that they can maintain a semblance of control in this area. Educators *must* figure out ways of preventing student abuse of the privilege without inflicting the enormous amount of stress imposed upon students, feeling that they will be required to walk on hot coals before being permitted to go to the bathroom! **(Golden Rule Opportunity)**

Teachers can also wield power unjustly in the areas of grading, dispensation of points, and in the punishment of entire classrooms of students for the misbehavior of a few. The last of the aforementioned misdemeanors which unquestionably wreak havoc when it comes to creating an environment in which students *desire* to be compliant, is never fair or the right thing to do. Students exhibiting proper conduct have no control over others' indiscretions. Though punishing a whole class for the faults of a few can *appear* to work, what it eventually accomplishes is the addition of disruptive students, ones who were initially among the ranks of the cooperative. They are now determined to disrupt and *earn* their disciplinary stripes because they feel powerless to control their own fate with *good* behavior.

The trick to preventing these everyday, common, and pesky predicaments, which are of major concern to any and all students, is to give forethought to guidelines, making sure that they are equitable and in tune with students' needs and individual rights as learners and people. There's no substitute for thoughtfulness on the part of the instructor in charge. Find workable solutions or keep tweaking until every person in your class **knows** that he is esteemed and revered. Cooperative behavior, reflecting the pride that they have in themselves as important human beings, will be your reward.

It's incumbent upon teachers at each level or grade to resolve power issues of significance to students at that level. Beware of going overboard in allowing them to make decisions that no child or teen should make. This, too, will lead to student misbehavior since they are neither intellectually prepared nor mature enough to make prudent decisions in certain areas. For guidance, read the brain research and consult those who have attained a degree of mastery in this area.

One teacher, considering himself to be fair and kind, and, in all honesty, one who indeed displayed caring toward his students, nevertheless, declared that each student would be permitted only one trip to the bathroom during class time per six-week period. The moment this proclamation was issued, his middle school students became alarmed, and rightfully so! This was a teacher who had a reputation for saying what he meant and following through on what was said.

They were afraid, already, that something embarrassing was in store for them in his classroom. When their expressed concerns were disregarded, making it apparent to them that this was the system under which they would have to abide, their behavior became disruptive even though the instructor was, for the most part, benevolent. Further, this same instructor exhibited a similar problem with dispensing instruction. His methods were fast-paced and unyielding, as he smiled and told them that they could do it. The difficulty arose from his refusal to offer the practice or reteaching which would have catapulted them to the point of realizing their prowess in his subject, and his inability to realize that that was the missing piece. Needless to say, though his classes were never totally out of order, they also were never totally orderly. There were spitwads on the walls and other sneaky disruptions that wouldn't cease. He just couldn't understand it.

Dislike or Anger Aimed at the Instructor

When an adversarial relationship is somehow left to develop and flourish between students and teacher, many of the most vicious and difficult-to-quell behaviors surface and proliferate. The bulk of these problems occur when students feel that they have been unfairly or negatively labeled, an instructor's determination to be obeyed or taken seriously leads him to take too harsh a stand, or the students themselves, perceive in their instructor's demeanor or manner a dislike, arrogance, or aloofness aimed at them. It evolves into a contest, of sorts, as to who will win and survive— the teacher or the class. Basically, the students are experiencing insult and hurt over not being liked or regarded as good people or serious students, and are bereft of the conflict management and verbal communication skills with which to handle their concerns in a positive fashion. An admonishment, intended as valid counsel, such as this issued by an instructor who recommended that students read a certain book and participate in an oral activity practiced in class, *instead of spending the weekend partying, eating junk food, and putting-down those with whom they were at odds,* can inadvertently send a message that invariably lowers self-esteem, resulting in even the most sure of themselves questioning their self-worth. Though the teacher making a statement to this effect had no intention of demeaning students, the dastardly deed was, nonetheless, done.

What can occur when students view the instructor as an adversary is a daily battle between the more assertive students and the teacher, while the passively aggressive ones sit back, unwilling to soften the blows of disruptive conduct dealt by the others. Many become either innocent bystanders caught in this web of wills, or silent cheerleaders for the outspoken souls who are making the teacher pay for his transgressions against them all.

In one such classroom where an adversarial atmosphere reigned supreme, several students began the class period by entering the room with loud, boisterous noises and raucous horseplay. Storming right past the *offending* teacher, they consciously ignored any and all directions he endeavored to give. Upon being tracked down and "called on the carpet," they merely pretended that the teacher had the problem. "What did I do? You're always picking on us," were typical comments.

While observing these actions, which didn't end just because I was in the room, it was apparent that we had a mammoth job ahead of us. They were angry alright, and bound and determined to punish the teacher with their behavior. Throughout the class period students waited to "catch" any little mistake made by the instructor, and worked him over with derision and putdowns. The ringleaders complained about every assignment, remained off task no matter what, mimicked the teacher's attempts to obtain order, talked to one another across the room, and either refused to participate when called upon or usurped another student's opportunity to participate by blurting out errant responses. It was truly classic.

To stop the bleeding, I received permission from the instructor to teach a portion of the lesson. I wanted to determine if the response would be the same no matter who was leading instruction, and to demonstrate teaching techniques that would work to break the cycle of misbehavior. The students cooperated, as I figured, affirming my thinking that we were dealing with self- concepts which were lower than low, and the kid solutions which are the eventual aftermath. The self-esteem of the students had been unwittingly crushed by their teacher's ineffective disciplinary and instructional techniques and the distinct negative vibes being emitted toward the students, making it imperative that *this* teacher somehow prove to them that they were not being stigmatized and devalued. It was going to be tough sledding because now that the students' behavior was so abhorrent, the stress level of the teacher was over the top, and though he desired to turn the situation around, simply entering this classroom every day was already a challenge.

Upon returning the instruction and management of the class to their teacher, I noticed, right away, that one young lady who had been so cooperative only a moment ago, was now choosing to revert to her previous misbehavior. I knelt beside her desk and asked her to work with her teacher. "He's mean to us, and we're going to be mean to him," was her calm response to my request. Another young lady, whose extreme intelligence I had earlier observed, added, " He thinks we're stupid," as she moved without permission from her assigned seat to one near a friend with whom she began chatting. It was painfully clear that significant and swift changes were dire.

What had initially happened to bring about this dismal set of circumstances for all? The teacher, who knew very few effective teaching or management strategies, but who was attending sessions designed to bring him along at a pace conducive to achieving success, had begun this assignment, also, without knowing any of the 'truths" that are in chapter one of this book. Right away, in response to a few students' noncompliance, he became harsh and unkind. He made little or no eye contact with them, there was nary a positive remark, even when what they were doing *was,* for the moment, productive. His screaming set the tone for their screaming. His admonishments and constant criticism conveyed the message that they were B A D and difficult to teach.

Since they were receiving no affirmations to the contrary, they naturally fell into line with his low expectations. Moreover, the teaching strategies being used required little or no active student participation. They were sitting idly a large percentage of the time, or given work to do in *insignificant* bits — Self- Esteem Busters.

Let me hasten to say, that misbehavior is *not* justified because a teacher employs ineffective techniques. It's not justified, it just happens. Kids know no other way to respond to injuries to their dignity other than with their conduct. Indeed, MOST students actually *endure* these injustices and breaches in professionalism without exhibiting any outward signs other than quiet resignation. Nevertheless, their attitudes toward learning and, sometimes, society are being soured.

What we must remember as leaders of classrooms, is that we have a great deal of power over the lives in front of us. They are people who want to trust us to create a daily atmosphere which allows them to feel good about who they are and what they bring to the table of learning. The onus is on the teacher to find the midpoint between being permissive or mean. I use the term, mean, because that is how students view extremes in discipline. Discipline, as we shall discuss in a future chapter, is a total positive. But, when negative attitudes about our students, the students of a particular area or school, or about young people, in general, are allowed to infiltrate our minds, there's no other outgrowth that can materialize save contemptuous actions toward them. It's inevitable, and inevitably leads to anger from our students and the profusion of obnoxious behaviors in which they choose to persist, hoping to get their point across.

Because of their belief in fairness, younger students tend to overlook or "forgive" ineffective teaching techniques when there's a sense that the instructor *genuinely likes them and is working hard on their behalf.* Even middle and high school students who are displeased about not receiving adequate instruction, will generally try to "help" the instructor to succeed. No, the behavior will not be pristine, but it will also not be malicious and mean-spirited, making it easily revertible to exemplary behavior with the insertion of sound instructional techniques and procedures.

The lesson to be learned for instructors, is to present oneself as a confident, caring, sincere individual, who appreciates and reveres students—one who will lead the class to the height of their potential as a group and as individuals. Then, to set about doing just that on a daily basis, embodying the attitude and persona of a friendly professional.

Perceived Weakness of the Instructor

There's really very little that needs to be said on this topic. In all probability, each of us has sat in the classroom of a teacher whose very essence was one of weakness and fear. My experience as a student was with a social studies teacher whom I'll call Mr. F. His behavior was typical, and will serve to illustrate the prototype of an instructor who exudes weakness and angst. First of all, Mr. F wasn't completely lax and out of it. He knew that he was *supposed* to "control his classroom," and he set about giving the *appearance* of doing so. Therefore, each day as we filed past him to enter, he made shallow comments to individual students aimed at demonstrating that he was in charge. "Go straight to your seat. There'll be no talking in here, today," he'd proclaim. The trouble was that he was speaking to students who had no intention of misbehaving. They were the students who came in every day, sat in their seats, and waited, no, *hoped* that something valuable would be taught and learned, and that the chaos which had become run-of-the-mill would somehow *not* exist that day. Nonetheless, because Mr. F behaved nervously when "naughty" students got started, perhaps spoke to them once with great bravado, but when ignored pounced on some unsuspecting student who was really not out of order but was easy to trounce, the daily routine of disruptive behavior *by a few*, continued throughout the semester. He yelled and they yelled. He became inappropriate in his comments. They laughed. He turned his back to write on the chalkboard and a roll of toilet tissue would barely miss his head. They, the few, the proud, those who probably went on to become lawyers and politicians, had figured him out. They *knew* that, for whatever reason, he was *afraid* to adequately challenge them on their interrupting conduct. He lost their respect and, moreover, his teaching techniques were insufficient to capture their interest. What was occurring? Well, when students meet us, the teachers, for the first time, many are sizing us up to discern whether we are confident or tentative. Do we have all of our ducks in a row, are we willing and able to enforce the guidelines put forth, will we shy away from an obviously wayward student, will we come unglued or become disoriented when challenges or complaints arise?

They take notice of how we handle ourselves. The question is will students witness smooth, seamless, but kind and courteous authority, or recognize nervousness tinged with anger and fear when a student throws down the gauntlet. Does the instructor have to *prove* that she's in control by shouting or lambasting, or does she just *know* it and can, thus, "put a student in her place" without demeaning the person or becoming flustered herself. It's human nature to test the waters of power. Teachers tread the same path with their administrators, checking to see if they can arrive late for school or meetings without retribution, grade papers during faculty discussions…but, I digress.

However, when students discover that initial affronts to authority will be handled swiftly, deftly, and consistently with <u>confidence</u>, <u>competence</u>, and humanity, the nonsense stops or becomes minimal and manageable with the use of effective techniques and appropriate consequences. Respect has been won. Everyone is now aware of just who is in charge, and that those deserving to be "called out," *will be,* without regard to how rough and tough they *wish to* appear, who their parents happen to be, or any other variable.

There will always be one or two students who feel the need to "get by" without doing any school work, and will make your class the one in which they usurp control, if you ***allow*** it. That's the core, it has to be *allowed,* or it simply won't happen! They're not that powerful. YOU ARE! And they want you to be! Actually, students are generally taken aback when their teachers exhibit fear of them as though they are criminals. They view their challenges, initially, as "having fun," until it becomes apparent that the teacher is experiencing trauma, without the ability to get a grip. Then, just as sharks who smell blood in the water, go for the kill, those who are adept at resisting authority and disregarding the adults in their lives step up to take the reigns from the teacher, establishing a daily system of disruption and anarchy.

Oftentimes, these are our most proficient students, who in other classes wouldn't even consider misbehavior. Other times, they are students who have a long history of agitation, kids who subconsciously view themselves as disrupters, disinterested in learning. They go from class to class, year after year testing each instructor to see who *cares* enough to curb their destructive behavior. I believe that underneath they are wounded each time a teacher buys into their offensive persona, ignoring or doing little to correct their poor behavior, leaving them to persist in creating turbulence and proving them right yet again, that they are not "nice" people. One young lady accustomed to running roughshod over her teachers, announced to me as I was treating her with dignity, respect and *discipline*, "I'm not a nice person, Ms. Dempsey."

I realized that she was shocked, first and foremost, that I had the guts to speak to her about her actions, and, secondly, that I spoke without fear or anger. She saw a different view of herself through my eyes, one of a cooperative student who could be spoken to and expected to conform without taking issue.

When students experience a new, uplifting view of themselves in your presence, that's who they'll become, *in your presence.*

Response to A Disorganized Environment

How many times have you rushed into your classroom at the last minute, glanced at your "junk" table or into a filing cabinet, and realized that you couldn't locate, or simply didn't have the materials required to effectively carry out your lesson plan? If this has happened on one or two occasions, there's no need for concern. Stuff happens. However, when it's the norm as, trust me, it is for many educators, the groundwork for discordance is being laid. There are teachers who honestly believe that organization is just not their *forté*. Their homes are in constant disarray and they, laughingly, proclaim to be totally incapable of maintaining any sense of order at school. Students are aware of the teachers for whom this is true, and know that when they enter class they will have time to socialize and "kick back" until the teacher gets things rolling. This very kick-back time becomes the undoing of so many instructors who just can't believe that their students won't "busy" themselves productively until the necessary materials are located, a student assistant or paraprofessional scampers to the copy room to make additional copies and returns, or what have you.

Further, the very same instructors, even when considering themselves prepared, often have not procured enough markers, novels, protractors, or whichever essential learning tools are indispensable for the planned activity. Instructional materials have not been gathered beforehand, so as to be in adequate supply for each student to have his own and for the lesson to proceed smoothly. This is considered, nonchalantly, as not presenting a problem. Thus, the behavior challenges associated with students required to share or to sit idly awaiting their turn to use essential materials, come into play. Indecorous student behavior is *invited* when the television and DVD player have not been reserved, and are, thus, unavailable, resulting in cacophonous complaints from disappointed students. The field trip bus is late arriving because mandated paperwork was not filled out correctly, necessitating last minute calls by the secretary, and a hurried, rowdy entrance at the field trip destination. Not enough brochures or free materials are awaiting students, since an accurate last count of students participating wasn't submitted according to plan, or at all.

The list goes on and on, and the inevitable student disturbances occurring are the same, whether the disorganization centers around transitioning students from the reading circle back to their desks, handing out parts for play tryouts, assembling students into workable coop groups, or divvying up pizza at a classroom party—each without a plan. Coarse conduct, as kids do what kids will do when disorganization is the rule of the day, becomes the bane of the teacher's existence. Many students endeavor to take charge and fix it themselves, or opt out of the entire process by participating in their own "fun." These confident individuals are often labeled uncooperative and defiant when, in fact, their **misbehavior stems from the absence of an orderly environment.** The entire class suffers as a result of existing under a dysfunctional, haphazard system. It's all preventable when instructors insist on keeping *themselves* on track by paying attention to every detail.

Before leaving this very important topic, I must touch, again, upon discipline problems invoked as an outcome of disorganization in the realm of handling student grades, assignments, and projects. Unfortunately, there are educators who routinely lose or misplace student work, through lack of vigilance suffer projects to be damaged by others, or somehow *forget* to record hard-earned grades. These behaviors are simply unprofessional. They incite the wrath of even the most docile and committed of students, many of whom become cynical and disrespectful about their instructor's academic credentials, often rudely questioning his or her qualifications. Countless disciplinary "scenes" have been brought about during the passing back of graded papers or the handing out of periodic grade reports or report cards, as students notice that a significant grade or assignment is missing. For sure, teachers are not perfect, and are literally handling hundreds of papers. However, just as you and I wouldn't put up with or accept missing bank deposits or statements just because the bank is handling hundreds of accounts, our students shouldn't have to resign themselves to receiving inaccurate accountings of their grades and assignments. It's maddening and it provokes poor student behavior which simmers, spilling over in other areas of the day, diminishing the teacher-student relationship.

All of this can be easily prevented by creating a workable system to keep both yourself and students thoroughly organized. If you're not prone to this level of personal structure, look around and find another educator in your building who is. Then, copy their system to the last detail, if necessary. Your colleague will be flattered, your days will be less stressful, and your students will be better behaved. Win-Win!

Response to an Unpleasant Environment

The current climate of the educational environment nation-wide has much of society either determined or interested in stopping the violence in schools. Though outbreaks seem senseless and spur of the moment, I believe that most are not. Creating an atmosphere of peace begins with each and every adult in the building being vigilant and mindful of, presumably, "harmless" assaults on individual students and groups of students. The classroom is ground zero, because it is where students spend most of their time and where the foundation for peace needs to be laid, practiced, and enforced. Teachers ought never be too busy or too focused on the curriculum to notice when negative actions or words are being perpetrated right under their noses. All too often, instructors place the responsibility of safety on each student's shoulders, especially in middle and high schools. The pervasive rationale goes something like this. "*You're old enough to take care of yourselves. If someone is bothering you, just ignore them and they'll usually stop.*" Those who have ever attended school know that victimizing *doesn't* stop most of the time. Further, it's NOT the responsibility of students to fend for themselves in the classroom, *including the physical education classroom.* It happens to be one of the most important duties of the instructor or adult in charge, to make sure that each student is mentally and physically safe whenever they're in the presence of that adult. Saddling students with this responsibility all but ensures that the weak will suffer, and though the strong may survive—at what price? It also ensures that violent outbursts and actions will be the order of the day in your classroom, and that learning will become minimal.

Conflict management for any of us is tricky, but for our students who've had neither time nor training to develop skills in this area, it's extremely improbable that negative situations left *solely* in their hands will be handled satisfactorily.

Know This!

Observing the instructional lesson of a teacher, I noticed that a couple of young men were, not so quietly, verbally harassing one of the girls. The first took it upon himself to call her a prostitute. She replied, softly, with something that I couldn't hear, and tried to ignore them. Then the other, gaining confidence because of the instructor's apparent obliviousness to what was going on, laughingly proclaimed her a whore. At this, receiving still no response or aid from her teacher, noticing that peers were beginning to pay attention to the slanderous taunts, and seeing no end in sight, the young lady arose from her seat during the lesson, and fired off a loud threat to the boys. (You're probably wondering why *I* didn't immediately respond. Though ready to spring into action, my job was to observe the techniques of the instructor vs. taking charge. I was *hoping* that she would act, since it was extremely improbable that the very first comment had not been heard.) Upon witnessing the girl's outburst, the teacher, who could no longer feign ignorance of the situation, quickly brought it under control. In this particular incident the boys cooperated and the girl was low-key enough to settle down. This is not always the case, and who knows what continued during passing period or occurred the next time she came in contact with those guys. It was an unnecessary experience for this student to endure, and would not likely make her want to return to that class or willingly participate, once there.

Though the incident went no further at that time, it was troubling. The fact that the instructor, a kind person herself, permitted any manner or degree of taunting and teasing to take root in her classroom, raised the question of how many other students had been or would become innocent victims of bullying or just plain teenage meanness, on her watch.

Oftentimes, instructors who enjoy being teased or are diehard teasers themselves will not only permit, but even join in against a student, considering certain remarks to be innocuous or just good clean fun. When a student participating in oral reading or verbally answering the instructor's academic question, happens to commit an error, allowing other students to pounce with negative comments regarding the student's ability or to shout out corrections, constitutes an affront to that person's dignity. These actions, sanctioned by an instructor's silence, can instantly spawn poor conduct ranging from sullen refusal to speak and work on the part of the victim, to the initiation of physical fights. This, you may not wish to hear. Nevertheless, the teacher is at fault when disruptions occur because taunting behavior is suffered to go unchecked or is encouraged by instructor inaction or participation.

Teachers *cannot* permit personal preferences to overrule good judgment. Our charges deserve to not have to wonder or worry about whether or not the learning, athletic, lunchroom, or any school environment will be vigorously monitored, and not offered up as a breeding ground for tortuous dealings among students. Putdowns and teasing are *never* funny or okay, even when the student "appears" to be unaffected. Humiliation, in any of its many forms, damages self- esteem *and the spirit*. Its residue lingers, backfiring on an unsuspecting teacher by providing sustenance to an environment filled with antagonism and cruel one-upmanship. Putting out fires, constantly exhorting pupils to calm down and cut it out become the order of the day, further stifling learning among an already self-conscious population.

Academic Standards Too Low Or Insulting

There are educators who take it upon themselves to predetermine what their students can or cannot learn, thus, limiting the skills and concepts they will even *attempt* to teach. Usually, this occurs not because these instructors are malicious people wishing to cheat their students out of an excellent education, but often due to some type of unfavorable labeling of the students prevalent in their minds, buildings, or communities. This type of thinking is dangerous and untenable. Dangerous because it deprives students of the opportunity to pursue the same level of achievement as other students not being negatively categorized. Untenable because there is a set curriculum, developed by those whose job it is to make the decisions regarding the skills and concepts to which each and every student is to be exposed. Untenable because no one can cast his gaze upon a student or group of students, instantly ascertaining the level of accomplishment which will be realized or the amount of effort which will be exerted. Untenable because by the very act of signing a contract, I believe that *each* instructor has promised to teach to the best of his ability, whomever shows up to be taught. For sure, this may not always be easy, but teach, we must. Many an educator has been astonished by who turned out to be proficient learners and who, though seemingly "all over it" initially, required tons of assistance to achieve. We can't forecast, nor do we have the right to predict the future for any student. We are to be, *purely*, willing to teach the curriculum to the fullest extent of our abilities, and to *make necessary adjustments in instructional strategies and techniques* to meet the learning needs of our students. Learning needs may run the gamut from those of the highly gifted and talented to those of the academically challenged. When we, as educators, *refuse* to judge or to be swayed by what others say or think about our students, the sky is the limit for them and for us! **They respond positively to our belief in them as scholars, or react badly to the impression of them as incapable or unwilling to learn**.

There are several ways in which this notion of incapacity is asserted by teachers and transmitted to students. Even if, initially, students are unsuspecting, an instructor's skepticism regarding student ability eventually becomes crystal clear, and the obvious occurs—a profusion of objectionable student behaviors. Self-esteem has been negatively impacted and the result is substandard behavior. Check out the following list to be sure that you have not and will not succumb to any actions indicating disdain for your students' abilities to succeed either academically or as good citizens—actions which propel students, unconsciously, toward poor conduct.

- giving low-level assignments (beneath grade level or insultingly easy)
- purposely omitting instruction of certain curriculum-based skills and concepts, considering them to be beyond your students' grasp
- assigning minimal student work
  (e.g. Though a substantial paragraph is more appropriate, saying: "*Just write 2 sentences for me!*")
- refusing to permit student-usage of the approved textbook, with the rationalization of it being too difficult for them
- usage of daily patronizing remarks
- overuse of incentives (e.g. countless pizza parties or videos, as though they will only work if rewarded)
- wasting daily class time in off-topic conversation, inappropriate joke-telling, or peer–like banter
- assigning shallow homework, having nothing to do with the class (e.g. *Write a paragraph stating your opinion of the dance program presented last period in the auditorium.* For Math Class)

There are, surely, other actions or remarks conveying to students the conclusion that they are not expected or believed to be capable of reaching levels synonymous with their potential, or that, somehow, their potential is inherently less than others. While many instructors sending these signals are well meaning, but misguided in their thinking, there are others who are not so innocent. Whether intent is virtuous or not, the effect is the same—feelings of belittlement and injured student spirits, provoking the defense mechanism of raucous behavior.

When You Raise Self-Concept, You Raise Behavior
When You Lower Self-Concept, You Lower Behavior

Finally, there are instructors who erroneously contend that if student assignments are made easy or minimal, students will be more amenable, and behave. Often using the words, "these students," they reason that the students are not interested learners and, therefore, cannot be expected to perform as such. Special education students are especially vulnerable to this type of thinking. Many are the times in which teachers dismiss or explain away poor student behavior by merely remarking that it was a special education student who was the perpetrator of the misdeed.

Let's take a silent oath to rid ourselves of this thinking. Any student will rise or fall according to the expectations set by the instructor. They are aware of our thinking, even when not openly stated. And though they may be unable to verbalize their emotions or suspicions succinctly, displeasure at being presumed inferior is displayed via misbehavior. They rant and rave, complaining about even the most miniscule of learning tasks, chase one another around the room instead of taking their seats, and participate in a myriad of other inappropriate behaviors. They're feeling "crunchy" without being able to explain it. It's instinct. They just *know* that the potency of their intellects is being disrespected, regardless of the kind words or tones which may be emanating from their teachers.

A couple of former middle school students ran up to greet me as I stood watching a high school football game at their new school. They happened to have been special education students who had been mainstreamed into my English class the previous year. Both had been hard workers, determined achievers, and very pleasant young ladies. In the course of our conversation, I inquired about how their first year of high school was going. They became visibly infuriated when explaining what was occurring, showing me the low-level work routinely assigned them. They had literally been transported, via class work, back to elementary school, and were vehement about their displeasure. Feelings of insult and anger, in fact, were so strong that cutting class had become their way of handling the situation. Their "solution" had transformed them from eager, cooperative students into rule breakers.

Lest I give the impression that I believe all students in any grade or class group capable of achieving or succeeding at the same level or rate, let me quickly state that I'm aware that this is not the case or even realistic. However, it's also not the point. Just as every educator in your school or student in your teacher education program is endowed with his/her own unique package of capabilities, making personal achievement consistent with potential and effort, the same is true of our students, regardless of who they are. We must shun making predictions of success or nonsuccess, based upon presumptions. Instead, wise educators will see the possibilities, treating each student as capable of *potent* performance. This is simply conveyed and accomplished by giving them our best, and *holding their feet to the fire* in a caring manner, so that they are encouraged each and every moment to give their utmost. It brings out the dynamic in them. This manner of expert instruction releases the *desire* that spurs them to go the extra mile, because they see us going the extra mile with an upbeat attitude, creative instructional strategies and techniques, and high expectations, skills and support. Students see us putting forth maximum effort in our determination to aid them in accomplishing the learning and behavioral goals set before them, and guess what—these are the actions which cause them to exhibit behavior that is *boldly* cooperative and gratifying to teachers.

A newspaper article extolling the virtues of an educator who, in a single year, took previously negatively-stereotyped, underachieving high school students, to exceptional heights of performance in advanced placement classes, and further to acceptance into respected colleges, said it all. How did he do it? One of his students simply stated that it was no big deal to work for a teacher who worked so hard for them.

Though previously diminished by the contempt of society and prior instructors, these students were infused with pride about who they were as individuals, and affirmed as serious scholars by this wise teacher. There's really no mystery. **Student behavior is a direct result of what an educator does or doesn't do**—what educators cultivate.

Genuine belief in the goodness and greatness of human beings is totally awesome. It just naturally colors everything done and said to such an extent that those on the receiving end recognize their own power to slash the nonsense from their lives. Under the security of this inspirational aura, unfurled by instructor over students, students recognize and embrace the power to channel their own energies toward allowing something positive to take hold in their lives. Inspiring students to eat from your hands, to remain focused on their own academic success and the good feelings engendered and encompassed by that success, is a precious gift. Those genuinely desirous of igniting the wills of students to this depth reach this highly attainable goal through sincerity of spirit. Somehow, it just seems to happen when an instructor's good intentions are authentic, moving him toward professional skills, strategies, and attitudes commiserate with the effective guidance of students. The rewards are obvious. Students are on track, academically, self-esteem is high—rendering uncouth conduct unattractive to all, the teacher-student relationship is “all that,” and all is harmonious in the kingdom.

They Simply Ain’t Misbehavin’.

CHAPTER 4
SUMMARY POINTS

1. Students, perceiving themselves negatively stereotyped, respond with retaliatory disruptive conduct.

2. Teachers can and do provoke the very student misbehavior they find abhorrent. Note specific actions and verbiage, which when used, alienate and provoke students. Avoid them like the plague.

3. Culture is extremely important and an integral part of who each student is. Dealing effectively with students includes awareness, acceptance, and respect for their culture.

4. There are common reasons for student misbehavior. Know them. Prevent them.

Chapter 5

TAMING AND MOLDING YOUR STUDENTS

Just as Petruchio of Shakespearean fame displayed method to his madness in his determination to tame the fair Katherine, so must educators choose reliable methods for taming their shrews. As mentioned in a prior chapter, one of the first precepts teachers must fully grasp is that **sarcasm doesn't work.** Not only does it not work, but it assuredly backfires in several ways. I admit that it can feel mighty good to fire off a particularly witty bit of sarcasm when confronted with a consummate brat or, worse, an accomplished Smart Alec. Nevertheless, the result of acquiescing to a moment's weakness can be the lowering of a student's self-image and the promotion of belligerence or vulgar comebacks from the student. In addition to these negatives, the instructor's professionalism is compromised, and the positive role modeling that needs to be ever present becomes tainted, taking a nullifying, ugly turn. Students can actually begin to hold *you* in disesteem. Needless to say, none of the above furthers good classroom discipline.

At all times, teachers must endeavor to exercise governance over the classroom environment, working to prevent or diffuse destructive situations, avoiding being drawn into power struggles. The best way to accomplish these lofty feats is to create a "kinder, gentler" classroom. When a child chooses to be impolite, the instructor must respond with politeness. When a mean remark is uttered or a raunchy attitude displayed, the teacher's response is always one of tranquility, wisdom, and charity, delivered firmly, but without allowing oneself to come unglued or to follow the example of the child. Instead, <u>restate the expectation</u>, providing **information and choice**, and meting out an <u>immediate and appropriate consequence</u>, if necessary. Never should the actions of an undisciplined student be permitted to derail standards the instructor has set for the classroom. It is a daily effort born of stubborn consistency and repetition that teaches students to adhere to the higher concept of group preservation. Commit to it with confidence and conviction, knowing in your heart that to discipline is to care.

This gentle approach in no way indicates the forfeiture of power as commander in chief, or that your stature and authority will be diminished. Actually, your power, in essence, is in the restraint and benevolence exhibited in the face of an out-of-control student. Employing this course of action also does not mean that you're not strict and take charge. You are both, neither of which is undesirable nor outdated. You are simply and wisely refusing to follow suit with a naughty child or rude adolescent. Maintaining calmness should work to diffuse the emotion of the student, and prevent his or her peers from joining forces, becoming overly sympathetic, resentful of the actions you'll need to take in order to handle the situation with expertise. When peers, especially older students, *perceive* a classmate as being dealt with unjustly or as suffering humiliation, even though they realize that their classmate was in the wrong, the inclination is to support that person in spite of the fact that the misbehavior caused the problem. Therefore, proper handling of poor student conduct takes on more importance than initially meets the eye.

This "taming" teaches students that they cannot control you with emotionalism, whether it be crying or profane outbursts. It also teaches them, through modeling, to be composed and rational when things go awry. Further, it saves your energy, which would surely be wasted on retaliatory remarks and screaming, as is often observed in ineffective educators. Again, state your disciplinary expectation and consequence in a firm, but mild tone, and follow through quickly. *"Jon, there won't be talking during the lesson. You're welcome to listen quietly, or give up 15 minutes of your lunch recess. I know you can do it."* Once said, don't "wait" for the student to comply, or otherwise draw attention to the situation. Move on so that the student can quietly get on board and *save face*. Should there be no compliance, immediately apply the consequence and continue. One thing to remember is that your consequence must be substantial and unpleasant enough to deter the behavior, but also appropriate for the offense. A consequence too minimal provides no incentive for the student to conform, while one too harsh can provoke anger, dredge up the fairness issue, and actually precipitate escalation of the misbehavior. Therefore, give some thought to common problems and suitable consequences during your daily jog, or discuss with other colleagues those that have worked for them.

Accompanying this kinder, gentler style of communication, is a quality we've already discussed— humor. You'd be surprised how far possessing a sense of humor will carry you in the taming process. Many classroom occurrences really *are* funny. Don't be reluctant or too stiff to laugh. If a student does or says something that cracks up the class, something that truly *is* creative and comical, it's easier and more human to laugh with them. Admit that the person lightened things up for a moment, thank him or her (without sarcasm), compliment the wit, and say, *"Now let's get back to our lesson."* There are very few students who won't appreciate your humanity and ability to have a little fun, and return to work feeling kinder toward you for giving them permission to enjoy a joke or humorous remark.

Being a person who can laugh at oneself carries a lot of weight in the discipline game. If you've made a mistake verbally, written, or otherwise, go ahead and say, "*Oops, I goofed!"* and allow laughter or amusement to erupt. This is not to say that students should be permitted to lose all control and stretch the moment further than considered prudent. Common sense and manners are always to prevail. Therefore, stating behavioral expectations around laughter is a lesson that cannot be neglected. The fact that laughter can be an instrument of cruelty must be expressed to students should the need arise, and **absolutely forbidden** under those circumstances. There is an obligation for you, the caretaker, to keep the classroom environment safe for its inhabitants and deferential to you. The willingness to take academic risks can be seriously undermined if and when instructors do not understand this distinct responsibility, not to mention the proliferation of student self-defense behaviors which arise when they fend for themselves. ***Discipline problems are more likely to occur when students' feelings of embarrassment and humiliation are not prevented, making it necessary for them to defend themselves.***

Seeing humor in what some would view as misconduct can go a long way in your effort to maintain a humane classroom. If a student comes sliding across the threshold of your classroom door just as the bell is ringing, you have two options. One is to blast him for running, and expound on how he's still tardy because he was not in his seat when the bell rang. The other is to ask, jokingly, if he's practicing for the baseball team, and commend him on his excellent effort. If you choose the first, you risk giving the impression that you've never been tardy, being tardy is a capital offense, you'd just as soon have him *be* tardy than to put forth effort to respect your rule to arrive on time. And last, but certainly not least, you risk the likelihood that the student will now feel angry and embarrassed by the reprimand in front of his peers, and at the lack of understanding on your part that he was actually *trying* to please you, regardless of whether or not he exercised good judgment. The mood of that student will almost assuredly change from cooperative to sulky—if not worse.

By electing to use the humorous approach, you have the opportunity of receiving that student's appreciation and, most likely, loyalty from both him and his classmates. In addition, you can still **restate your expectation** of being on time, by querying him later about what occurred, offering pertinent advice, privately. Thus, you've saved both yourself and the student the stress of beginning class with a sour attitude. In other words, it's perfectly okay for teachers to lighten up and chill out. If we will but reflect on our own school days and some of the concerns and situations that impacted us in either negative or positive ways, we'll be better able to separate the vicious and repetitive misbehavior of our students from that indicative of just being kids.

Though the use of humor can be one of your most effective tools in the taming process, one must be astute enough to not allow oneself to be viewed as a buddy or pal. You are ever the teacher, the one who creates and structures a wholesome, harmonious environment. Be careful to not sanction the creation of an irreverent, wisecracking atmosphere that erodes the respect students must maintain for an instructor in order for good discipline to be sustained. Guard, also, against suffering your students to endure the discomfort of peer on peer teasing and putdowns. There's a very fine line that's important to find and not cross.

Taming Through Building Community

Building community is a relatively new term as it pertains to educational strategies effective in promoting student togetherness and team spirit. However, it's not a new concept. Many teachers of old just seemed to know that molding their charges into a working unit was essential to the propagation of a good crop of students. Further, though it wasn't labeled as such, they knew just how to go about accomplishing the creation of a learning environment which valued each individual, while honoring and maintaining that individual's worth as a part of a **cohesive group**. The "we're a team" concept is extremely powerful when teaching each kid how to see herself as a member of a learning *family* who is allowed and must, in turn, allow others to thrive and learn in an environment of patience, acceptance, and unity.

The initial step in bringing about such a climate is in the construction, by the instructor, of a pleasant, uplifting, *academic* classroom environment which lets students know *why* they are there. They are there to obtain additional knowledge and social skills which will serve to increase the likelihood of them becoming productive, positive citizens. This academic environment needs to be in place on the first day of school, and is comprised of attractive displays depicting the curriculum which will be forthcoming. There's no need to include posters or quotes that debase and assume the worst behavior or manners, in the hope that upon reading the admonitions, students will take heed and change their evil ways. These kinds of displays, though viewed as humorous and harmless by some, can have the opposite effect, that of *enticing* students to mimic misbehavior not customarily a part of who they are.

When students enter an academically inviting and intriguing classroom, the taming process commences. Those who were expecting to spend the first two weeks goofing off and "getting acquainted" on their own terms, are immediately *informed*, nonverbally, that there is a larger, loftier plan *already in place*. They notice that the room isn't stark and naked, devoid of all symbols of learning, in limbo until the semester is in full swing. They sense the determination of the instructor that no nonsense will be afoot here, and though this may come as a surprise to some instructors, they "catch" the excitement and can be kept in that place through the use of functional management and instructional strategies. Once the lessons are underway, which hopefully is on the very first day, the room will be further enhanced with samples of student work. EACH student should have some kind of academic paper or project immediately on exhibit. The idea is to install the impression of a learning family as soon as possible, and to get each individual drawn in as a member of that family. Though it's common knowledge that students will distinguish themselves academically, based on the quality of their work, this is not the time to accentuate that difference. Quality makes itself perfectly clear to all who look upon it. Thus, students will naturally recognize who among them puts forth more effort or possesses more skill. The duty of the teacher in laying the foundation for community is to set each student up for success, so that what is displayed on the bulletin board or wall is his or her very best, something about which each can be proud and complimented. This initial groundwork is crucial because students hunger to *belong* on some level. They, generally, don't wish to stick out like sore thumbs either positively or negatively, and when they do, something ugly is usually on the horizon from the individual or his peers.

The second step in fashioning a coalition of students who as individuals feel revered and literally *desirous* of maintaining the peace and comfort of the group, is in building the self-esteem of the **entire class**

as good kids and able learners. Note that the use of the term, "kids," doesn't seek to separate the ages. All ages desire to know that they are on a winning team. Therefore, the strategy is to compliment the *class*, just as often as one would compliment individuals who distinguish themselves by meeting or exceeding instructor expectations. *"You are a great class, good students, great listeners, fun to teach, hard workers,"* are all comments that, when said time and again with genuineness and *from the very beginning*, influence students to remain on the right track, seeing themselves through their teacher's eyes, as kindred learners. This acknowledgement makes them much less likely to perpetrate the cruel teasing and meanness toward one another, or the immediate onslaught of "testing" behaviors so often perpetrated in classrooms of every sort and size. The teacher's model transfers to the students. They become "in this together," all for one and one for all. Whew! It's a beautiful thing.

When one steps out of line, momentarily, the group is not behind him. He is met with *somebody's* comment informing him that no one is more important than the group, that graciousness and courtesy is the way things are handled in this space. These, in all probability, won't be the "kid" words used, but the sentiment is the same. This taming and molding is just what is required to help them make it through the tough times of feeling insecure among their peers and with their new instructors. Conversely, when an individual student deserves and receives praise, the others are more likely to not take issue or comp a competitive "who cares" attitude, because they realize that they are **all** valued and will be celebrated when the situation warrants. Just be sure that your words, as the instructor, don't pit student against student or class against class, as with one seventh grade teacher who announced to her period three class that period one turned in more homework and made better test grades. The student reaction received was not the one she expected, or for which she was prepared. Her period three students immediately took offense, assumed a defensive disposition, and let her know that they didn't care what their period one counterparts did. This threw many of them into a funk for the remainder of the class, during which they purposely became inattentive, feigned disinterest and, in general, behaved poorly. Few students, if any, are pleased or *inspired* by being compared *unfavorably* to others. It's not motivational and it's not uplifting. As a matter of fact, with students it seems to have the opposite effect.

Step three of the community-building process embodies the skill an instructor possesses in the area of making every student feel accepted and welcomed. This is a mammoth undertaking for some instructors, because from the outset many pre-select the students whom they will like and to whom they are willing to offer approval, based on looks, grades, and other superficial attributes. This is a community–buster and a deal breaker. Students somehow become aware of the covert preferences possessed by their teachers. Indeed, those who have experienced prejudice of some type, in the past, are on the lookout for any signs of the same. How can we ask and expect students to display impartiality and tolerant spirits if we don't? When bias is recognized or merely perceived in their instructor, a fractious atmosphere proliferates in which a student or group of students is pitted against another, and rancor over favoritism becomes a reason for a profusion of rebellious, disruptive behaviors.

How one communicates this entirely critical acceptance to one's students is worth contemplating and planning if it doesn't come naturally. The key ingredient is sincerity. I believe that simply smiling, greeting, and literally saying the words, *"I'm glad you're here,"* on a daily basis, covers a lot of territory in accomplishing this goal. Just as those in couple relationships thrive on hearing "I love you," on a regular basis, so is there an authentic need for your students to constantly hear that you *like* them, **despite any offense they may have committed the hour, day, or week before**. How easily we forget that assurances are the stuff of which human beings are kept feeling secure and comfortable. There's really no need for teachers to negatively dwell on uncommon hairstyles, clothing fads, body art and piercings, or what have you. The trick is to take in the outer crust of each student without allowing personal preferences to affect your opinion of them as serious, cooperative students.

I can recall a high school student entering the classroom after lunch a few minutes before the initial passing bell, stopping by my desk to show me his latest piercing. He said, "Look, Ms. Dempsey," as he poked his tongue out with pride. I smiled and inquired, *"How does if feel so far?"* He smiled right back and informed me that it was a little uncomfortable, but that he'd get used to it. I remarked that I was sure he would. Satisfied with the acceptance, he trotted happily off to his seat.

Nothing further was necessary to be said. He simply wanted to share his excitement and to be acknowledged for who he was, not being negatively judged because I didn't choose to pierce my tongue. My next step was to move on with greeting other class members as they entered, and to not take class time to draw attention to his new acquisition. This, in my opinion, would have or could have been misconstrued as patronizing and disingenuous. It certainly would have been a misuse of class time, a presumption that my students would rather spend time in discourse about a peer's personal preference than on the fun of learning the English curriculum. In other words, I would have sent the message that I didn't view them as serious students who came to learn. There is no doubt in my mind that a conversation centered around J's latest piercing could have easily begun, and the students would have joined in, eagerly relating and sharing their own personal tastes. However, by so doing, in essence I would have been disregarding them as scholars, who, yes, enjoy relating to their peers, but who are capable of conversing with just as much enthusiasm and fun on an academic level. Too much of this off-topic banter, and self-concepts are lowered. And **when you lower self-concept, you lower behavior.**

I imagine that this may strike some as an extreme position to take. Nevertheless, it is, indeed, the *seemingly* insignificant things which become the undoing of an otherwise proficient teacher, and the source of wonderment about why one teacher is more cherished and successful than another.

The building process continues as the instructor teaches community through the daily *invitation* extended to students to ask *any* question which will clarify a skill or concept, coupled with guiding them to respect the questions of others regardless of whether or not the answer is one that expresses a personal need. This aids in eliminating or lessening the fear and stress that can cause students to drift into misbehavior in an effort to alleviate academic disquietude or embarrassment. It also permits an emotionally safe learning environment to prevail and flourish merely by communicating to *all* students what accomplished students everywhere know—to ask is a sign of intelligence, not one of ignorance. Questioning is valued.

As intuitive educators are well aware, most middle and high school students are reluctant risk-takers in the realm of academic uncertainty. The practice of cruel teasing is alive and well in classrooms, corridors, and each school's nooks and crannies. Though impossible to police every area, it is up to the adults of the kingdom to refuse to become parties to, and, indeed, to prevent this sabotaging custom, if the learning environment is to be untainted and behavior problems averted. It's just as essential as establishing and maintaining a physically safe environment. Feelings of community cannot co-exist among those of fear, trepidation, and precariousness.

Humane, consistent rules and routines round out the picture. When students live in a classroom society which considers each individual to be productive and agreeable, wonders never cease. There is an intense level of relief and pride that comes just from their knowing that each is expected and *believed* to be capable of stepping up to the plate of good character and gracious living among their classmates. It brings smiles to their faces and a resolve to do better each time they err in judgment. It's a higher order of thinking and living. It's *th*e level they crave to achieve. If you believe otherwise, you're doing them and yourself a disservice.

A male middle school student who was an absolute handful for all of his teachers, and who reveled in that reputation, provided a recent opportunity for me to further affirm the above assertion. He was a fire-spitter, a bully to classmates and teachers, and a wholly miserable kid, masking anxiety surrounding personal issues by making everyone around him suffer. I knew when I took over the class during his block, that I, too, would be tested. He began by not sitting in his assigned seat, refusing to move at the request of his teacher, and hissing mean comments and threatening looks toward the teacher who had referred him for disciplinary action the previous day. He was awaiting suspension which would begin at the close of the day. What did he have to lose? He was as good as gone right then and there. I realized that and was also aware that he possessed no sense of community. However, what I know is that all human beings wish to be validated as worthwhile individuals, in spite of the behavior being flaunted.

My first obligation was to get the class underway and students actively engaged in the lesson. He noticed this accomplishment and saw his power already diminishing. I smiled in his direction, letting him know that he was in this *with* us, but also verbally informing him that he wouldn't be allowed to disrupt. He hissed, but I detected an aura of calm and a shadow of indecision emerging as to what his next tactic would be. I seized the moment to move in his direction as I taught, whispering an explanation, showing him the next step in the lesson, and praising the meager amount of work he had already begun. The crony sitting next to him, timidly "appreciating" his every action, I moved to another location so that there would be no temptation for him to further "perform" for anyone. At first there was protesting from my "spitter," but upon realizing that he could engage me in neither anger nor a power struggle, he relented. In that instant he looked at me and asked, "Why can't you be our teacher?" The question was not a criticism or indictment of his current teacher, who was quite a caring person, but a plea for help, I believe. Students are not pleased when they misbehave without provocation. They desire and need their teachers to lead them to higher ground just so they can respect themselves! Many are ignorant of how to exist within a flourishing community just as are countless adults. They are mirror images of society, at large. Nevertheless, when instructors grab the bull by the horns, not in a hit-or-miss fashion, but with an all-out plan and determination to bring this kind of dynamic environment to fruition, triumph is achieved and a lucrative atmosphere of learning and growing becomes the fruit of their labor.

Taming Through Relating to Students

When anticipating a new experience or actually embarking upon one, what do we all seem to feel? Angst, to some degree is usually the result. Our sensibilities are heightened and defenses raised. However, once a positive relationship has been established with the one in charge—the head honcho, anxiety subsides, allowing us to settle in and take full advantage of whatever is being offered. It's wisdom, *savoir-faire*.

As instructors, it's dire that we understand that our students are in the throes of this predicament—trying to remain true to themselves and peers while simultaneously desiring to feel at ease in the presence of teachers. Taking care of their academic needs is insufficient. In fact, they won't permit us to be even marginally successful in that regard if we haven't forged an authentic connection with them. It's the fabric of which human bonds are made, and it's the bread and butter of every educator's managerial strategic system. A sound, professionally friendly relationship with one's students is worth its weight in gold. Their ears are open to what you have to say. Their hearts are attuned to the lessons of life, those essential to be imparted if the lessons of the brain are to be grasped in an atmosphere of peace and solidarity.

So and so is my favorite teacher. How often have we heard or said these words? This doesn't occur by accident. Somebody knew how to relate to students in a way that showed sincere interest in them as individuals. Frankly, we do it all of the time with people who are dear to us. It's an extension of that same mindset that needn't gobble up class time, but does need to demonstrate a resolve to show one's human side during *all* encounters with students. Simply remarking about a sporting, music, or cultural event of significance to a particular or all of the students, appreciating an outfit, hobby, talent, or accomplishment, lets them know that you are down-to-earth, unpretentious. It accentuates the similarities between teacher and students, and **allows them to view the instructor as ally rather than foe.**

Believe it or not, many students do initially see their instructors as foes, and are apprehensive and intimidated by this vision. This very perception can cause short fuses to explode in the classroom, as students erect protective barriers against failure, humiliation, or any conceivable harm considered possible as an outgrowth of their instructor's conduct or verbiage. However, when a sound, trust relationship has been established, during those disconcerting moments when students are unprepared or disciplinary action is warranted, tranquility can prevail because they are certain that their fragile egos won't be bruised by abrasive words or behavior from their teacher. They're buoyed by the love and caring of which they believe themselves to be recipients. Otherwise, the very thought of absolute power at the complete disposal of another, one's instructor, is both frightening and a cause for panic. Benevolence helps to ensure them that they need not fear exploitation at the hands of the adults in charge, **they need not safeguard themselves by raising the roof**.

Additionally, it's essential for students to believe that their teachers aren't on a superiority trip. The most successful educators relay, in an effortless fashion, the fact that having knowledge to impart is not synonymous with being "better than" their students. It doesn't even cross their minds to be contemptuous or condescending, and students sense it. Poverty is not an issue, parental occupation isn't an issue, race or cultural background aren't issues, neither ability nor skill level is an issue, music preference isn't an issue. NOTHING is allowed to drive a wedge between instructor and students. It's a relationship created and nurtured by modeling respect and generosity of spirit, on a daily basis. You're *never* finished proving to them that you like and appreciate who they are. And if they sense that you dislike or hold them in disesteem, for whatever reason (it's palpable, you know), the obvious result will be misbehavior. Their feelings of inadequacy in this area can produce absolutely incendiary conduct.

Demeanor is everything. Those teachers who are nervous and edgy, furtively waiting for their students to "abuse" them in some fashion, fool no one with disingenuous smiles or patronizing remarks. We all have instincts. If one doesn't figure it out, you can bet that another student will, and he or she won't remain mum about it. Assuming a genuinely smooth, comfortable manner when in their presence aides in convincing students that you're on their side. This doesn't mean that one should be careless with valuables, tempting those prone to taking advantage of situations, to falter. That wouldn't fly in any workplace, not even a venue of worship. Too many teachers fall prey to the aforementioned missteps of viewing their students as threats, postulating judgments based upon negative societal labels, putting on the cloak of superiority, or withholding respect from students if students are considered to be less than resplendent in exhibiting esteem for the instructor. Subsequently, when surprised by the derogatory reactions of students, placing of blame and guilt ensues, further alienating their charges and destroying the delicate relationship being forged.

We all understand what it means for someone to truly take pleasure in knowing us or to delight in being in our company. Since this is exactly the way in which we wish to be regarded or to have our own children regarded by their teachers, this relationship-building process needs to take center stage in the minds and planning of educators. A relationship steeped in patience, support, and willingness to guide—*no matter what*, brings out the best in students, spurring them to cooperate without first wrestling and wrangling, and permitting instructors to retire to their homes at the end of each day feeling gratified that they have touched the lives of students in the most propitious way. It encourages each student to put his best foot forward, arriving with a mind open to the exploration of knowledge, and the readiness to make productive, purposeful changes in behavior. It allows them to rid themselves of the angst of being rejected because of some mold they do not fit.

Yes, there is that student who is difficult to love. Nonetheless, the onus is on the professional to ferret out that *little something* which permits her to see that student as capable of stepping up to the plate of good citizenship. It's there. And the more of it that the teacher provokes the child to bring forth, by giving positive strokes, establishing structured procedures and routines, providing meaningful consequences, and the use of any of the other *uplifting* techniques at one's disposal, **the more control and effort the student will allow to emerge**. They want it to happen—this feeling great about themselves as model citizens. Sometimes, it's a formidable task for those who have been mired in misbehavior for many years, to climb and claw their way out of it. They need *help*! They need *guidance*! They need understanding without patronage or acquiescence to their poor behavior.

Favorite teachers, those who receive cooperation even when students aren't in a cooperative mood, have passed the relationship test. Their students are willing to reach deep inside of themselves, going the extra mile out of loyalty to their teachers. A prime example of the potency of a well-grounded connection with students was so poignantly illustrated during a high school class that I was teaching. Upon asking a young man to change to another seat, he replied, "I don't want to, Miss Dempsey, but I'll do it because I love you." That says it all.

Attending school, learning to accommodate and please a variety of personalities, from administrators to instructors, peers to support and other building personnel, is a daunting task for anyone, much less for those who are still developing physically, mentally, and socially. No wonder they seem to be on overload and out-of-sorts, at times. Parents and educators underestimate the pressure under which kids exist day in and day out. They need to be able to count on us to know our stuff, how to help them forestall some of their challenges. The taming process is a humanitarian approach, preparing them to successfully maneuver their way through this system of educational and social streams, canals, rivers, and oceans. Being empathetic to their struggles and concerns in and out of the classroom, is a must if we are to influence them to, in turn, practice this very valuable life skill of showing empathy to others, furthering the demonstration of proper classroom behavior.

Taming isn't merely indicative of the behavioral management strategies purposefully employed to guide students toward the deportment considered most suitable for order and maximum productivity to be realized. It also encompasses the day by day construction of a framework which gently and *incrementally* nudges students toward setting reasonable and appropriate behavioral parameters for themselves. It's this nifty by–product, parameter-setting, which allows them to begin molding themselves into mature individuals capable of traversing the spectrum of academic and life lessons with some degree of finesse and comfort. This doesn't come automatically, no matter who your parents are, how much money is available to you, or any other factor. It just is *not* automatic. It is *learned.* Each year that passes allows students to grasp more of this individual power over themselves, provided that the taming instruction is consistent and humane. We are supplying them with strategies for behavioral success. The raw animal instincts which each human must eventually corral and control, are on the loose and existing unabated in our students—just because they are embroiled in the developmental phases of their lives.

By remaining observant when they are under our tutelage and in our space, we can assist them in navigating many of the rough paths and waters encountered on a daily basis. They need not have to rely on their own untamed, unsophisticated methods of grappling with difficulties and entanglements with classmates or learning material, if instructors will but intervene with some degree of wisdom and understanding upon noticing a brewing situation in which students are out of their league. It is a gross error in judgment for the educator on duty to sit back, watch, and *wait* for a child to falter before stepping in to lend a hand. Psychological studies have informed us that the more often a practice or habit is repeated, the deeper the entrenchment. This depth of comprehension on the part of educators is vital if arguments, fights, pushing, shoving, name-calling and all such "solutions" to student problems are to be averted. It's painfully obvious that conflict management intervention and instruction is essential on the spur of the moment. Spur-of-the-moment intervention is imperative for teaching them how to handle frustration precipitated by confusion surrounding the use of learning materials such as computers, textbooks, research sources, art supplies. It's needed to teach them how to curtail the stress of dealing with a difficult curriculum. And it's needed to teach them how to tackle everyday conflicts that inevitably crop up just because they're endeavoring to comfortably exist in such close proximity with countless others.

Graciously jumping in to proffer a more amiable way of managing a disagreement, keeping tempers cool *before* they erupt, and, in general, offering students viable alternatives to the negative response behavior so prevalent in what they are exposed to via television and movies, is a part of our responsibility as mentors. It tames, and molds them into people who can take a moment to step back and consider their options. First, however, they must be aware of options! They also must be allotted plenty of time—meaning days, months, years—and adequate opportunities to practice positive responses, hone their skills, and to, hopefully, alter destructive patterns, before we pounce on them with denouncements of their unwillingness to be peace brokers or agents of harmony.

When we fail to guide them through the process, *as often as it takes*, and to allow them *structured* opportunities to try out their new self-discipline skills without lambasting comments, critical judgments, or sarcastic rhetoric, hostility arises from them. They are nonplussed that *immediate success* in reversing untoward behavior is required of them by their teacher, regardless of the effort being put forth. This expectation of **instantaneous improvement** in behavioral patterns ingrained in a child's very being, results in a setback for some students and can be even more damaging, lowering self-esteem, promoting apathy, and leading to a reversion of what comes naturally —**self-destructive, but familiar behavioral solutions.** They have thrown up their hands in defeat and placed the blame squarely on the shoulders of the instructor in charge.

Taming and Power Struggles

When teachers consciously refuse to engage in power struggles with their students, they are furthering the taming process and the advent of desirable student behavior. Notice that I chose the word, conscious. It's imperative for instructors, especially those who are novices on the frontier, to make a conscious determination to have antennae raised in an all out alert to recognize when a student is on the prowl for an honest-to-goodness power contest of wills and words and the glory that accompanies victory. The most innocent-looking kid can seek to get his fifteen minutes of fame by drawing an unsuspecting teacher into a juicy, no-win game of "whatever you say, I will refute." Cut it off at the knees when you've been suckered.

Three of the most common of these struggles involve the teacher trying to *convince* a student that he or she will learn to *like* a particular area of the curriculum, become accustomed to performing some skill or concept, or attempting to justify an assignment. On one such occasion a student declared, "I will NEVER like math, and I don't see why we have to learn something that we'll never use!" Another asserted, in disgust, "This is math class, NOT English. Why do we have to write in complete sentences!" This was, of course, not a query, but a challenge to the teacher to defend his assignment requirement and to engage in a debate. Whatever the case, as soon as it rears it's ugly head, RETREAT. Respectfully and *briefly* state or restate any information or explanation that is absolutely essential. Acknowledge that you heard and understood the student's point, modify if prudent to do so, or quickly move on with *your* appropriate decision without taking personally any attempt to confront, complain, or reroute.

e.g. Teacher: *" I hear you, Elizabeth, and I understand that writing sentences in math class may seem senseless to you. But, sentences make explanations clearer, lets me know that you guys fully understand why an answer is correct, and helps everyone practice using the format required on the state test.*

Elizabeth: *"It's just stupid and makes the assignment longer."*

Teacher: *"Again, I hear you. But this is the way we're going to do it.*

I'm moving on. Hang in there."

This method of managing the situation, in effect, models for students that it is okay for persons to hold differing opinions, illustrating evaluative thinking, but that all such differences of opinion can and will be handled in a positive, nonargumentative manner. It models a civil way of dealing with conflict of opinion, which defies following the lead of those who would drive communication into a pit of disagreeable remarks and attitudes.

Further, an extremely vital message is being sent: you *are not vulnerable to contentious wrangling over professional decisions made for the good of the class, and the academic curriculum won't be ambushed and replaced as a result of students ranting and raving.* In a nutshell, it acquaints students, **via example,** with a method of expressing themselves in a courteous manner—graciously accepting decisions that they cannot alter, or reaping the benefit of putting forth an idea which changes something for the better.

Taming while Respecting Student Privacy

A final point to make in this matter of taming and molding your lovely students, is one concerning respecting student privacy. All too often, teachers assume that students have relinquished their right to regard personal information as theirs to proffer or withhold, when a request is made. What exactly do I mean by this? In an effort to get to know our students or to have them become an integral part of the group, at times their rights to privacy are inadvertently trampled upon. Circumstances, usually arising from innocence on the part of an educator are, nonetheless, capable of precipitating student blow–ups. When requested or pressured to divulge presumably harmless information, but information which is somehow a source of embarrassment to the student, otherwise represents a breach of trust to someone they love, or is just extremely personal, students can become testy. Younger students are especially vulnerable since they are less skillful at expressing their unwillingness to share. *Open discussions* of topics such as parental work schedules and occupations, roles of family members, ability to afford school supplies or field trip fees, religious beliefs, unconventional holiday traditions, or divorce and guardianship issues, can create discomfort for many students and, subsequently, **provide a reason for acting out.**

When completing a "getting to know you" activity for his new teacher, one high school student shouted, "These questions are too personal!" Of course, the teacher had no intention of committing this violation. He was merely attempting to break the ice for his students by having them share information that would allow them to get to know one another better, revealing common interests which could build congenial relationships in the classroom. However, the unexpected outcome was raucous grumbling and complaining by some, and quiet refusal to respond to the questions, by others. When it was time to share responses, the experience was tarnished by reluctance to speak on the part of those who were offended by the questions and by those who didn't wish to alienate their peers. The activity was sound, but questions needed to be formulated so as to constitute nonpersonal, teen–friendly topics, (e.g. favorite color, games, sports, foods).

In matters of ferreting out those who need financial assistance of any type, or sending students to school psychologist, counselor, or social worker appointments during the regular school day, the utmost in discretion is imperative. Many educators forget to be sensitive to student confidentiality needs. Unwittingly, students are set up for cruel teasing or, at least, uncomfortable questions and comments from peers, when instructors *publicly announce* that so and so's mom is waiting in the office to take her to a medical appointment, or state out loud to an economically deprived student, that her book will be paid for by the school. These are occurrences that make students crazy. Crazy with humiliation and fear of mean taunting from peers. Crazy with anguish, wondering when another such pronouncement or announcement will be forthcoming from their teacher, sending them into further convulsions of embarrassment.

There are students who seem to always be leaving class for this or that "special" appointment. They are, oftentimes, the ones who have to "perform" for the class, spouting some kind of inappropriate or what they consider to be humorous remark as they exit, causing further interruption to the instructional lesson, prompting rude, disruptive come-backs from fellow classmates. Many are feeling so "crunchy" as a result of the virtual emotional pain of sticking out like sore thumbs, that they believe taunting or some other obnoxious action to be the salve. Ever so many teachers fail to recognize the underlying cause of this conduct, as pain. It's generally considered as just another incident of misbehavior by Joey. And they're understandably, "sick of it!" However, we have to be more savvy than this. **There's always a reason for misbehavior**, valid or invalid, our own misbehavior or our students'. When the root problem is unearthed, a "cure" can be researched, discovered, invented, and the students involved, mercifully put back on track.

Misconduct originating from these kinds of student concerns can be halted. They can be prevented by prudent instructors who realize that standing out in *any* sort of way is the bane of existence for most students. Managing students' private matters, privately is the ticket, i.e. waiting until other class members are dismissed before speaking about an economic issue, refraining from speaking with a student regarding personal issues *even in the presence of another colleague*, offering the opportunity for students to write notes concerning personal matters, delivering messages in a *whisper* to the student whose mom is waiting to take him to an appointment or who has to go to the social worker's office, and disallowing cruel or teasing remarks to be made regarding a student's daily obligation to sit with the student advisor or visit the psychologist. Using tact, teaches tact. It's part of the taming process and is critical to the promotion and sustenance of a comfortable, congenial classroom environment.

Taming and molding is a process which infuses students with invigorating social traits, pivotal for turning an ordinary classroom of students into an extraordinary group of young people who function as a learning team. It's a priceless strategy requiring unflappable resolve on the part of the instructor, but paying huge dividends when accomplished successfully.

CHAPTER 5
SUMMARY POINTS

1. Create a kinder, gentler classroom environment by using taming and molding strategies.

2. Use appropriate humor. Refusing to take oneself too seriously, in addition to not sacrificing a humanistic relationship with your students to assume a get-tough stance, nets gracious, cooperative conduct from students.

3. Begin the school year *purposefully* building community with each of your classes. Cultivate and nurture this commodity throughout the year, for the maintenance of positive student behavior.

4. Relate to students as a friendly professional and fellow human being. A sound relationship serves to lessen student anxiety, forestalling disruptive, revenge behavior.

5. Avoid engaging in power struggles with students.

6. Respecting students' privacy promotes comfort, preventing behavior blow-ups originating from circumstances of embarrassment.

Chapter 6

WHO'S THE BOSS?

"In Yo Face"

It must be acknowledged that there are students who are so persistently negative or off track discipline-wise, that they require what I term the "in yo face" technique. These are the ones to whom you must prove, in no uncertain terms, that you're the boss. You must get up close and personal with them from the outset, not in a disrespectful, confrontational manner, for this would only serve to provide them with the necessary rationalization to continue displaying perverse behavior, and soil your reputation as a professional of respect and dignity. Nonetheless, special attentiveness is essential. As soon as you discover that the taming process and structured procedures, in concert, are failing to fully do the trick of engendering the compliant, cooperative behavior requisite for the well-being and educational success of the individual, and no positive signs are appearing— indicating that an appropriate level of self-discipline is being embraced by a student whose behavior is consistently disruptive, here's another technique to try. Be aware that the taming process does not have to be in effect for weeks or even days before you get an inkling that a particular student requires a little something extra. You can tell by behavior responses displayed on the first day, as you begin the building and molding process. Subtle actions betray the student's intent, such as insistence upon snippets of misbehavior sprinkled throughout the period or day, or resolutely engaging in minor disruptions, necessitating the teacher's continued attention to reset expectations or restate guidelines.

These are the students about whom I will speak in detail later, those who may have been ensnared in misbehavior for years, and who are really and truly unaware of how to disentangle themselves from the mindset and conduct of a chronic disrupter. Their self–concepts have been tarnished, slanted toward the notion that they are outlaws of the classroom. Some have embraced this view of themselves solely because there's no other view available to them. Until now no one has influenced them to see themselves differently—as good citizens. They are earnestly trapped. They've fallen and can't get up. This, you can recognize even if demonstrated in a passive aggressive manner. Not all behaviorally off-target students are overtly obnoxious. Some insist upon reading a book as you teach, pretending to be sooo much smarter than their classmates or even you, or far ahead of your instruction. Others listen intently for every mistake you make in order to arrogantly and saucily challenge you in the middle of each lesson. These students are displaying a dysfunction, and though they will not openly admit it, would be oh so happy if you were to just nip their naughtiness in the bud, enabling them to escape from the enslavement of their own poor conduct and allowing them to begin feeling good about who they are as citizens. Many have become imprisoned by their own poor behavior and the negative, superficially powerful reputation it has fostered.

The prime opportunity for turning even the worst of these students around is as soon as you notice they're not getting on board, before the misbehavior has a chance to escalate and rise above the dam. This is usually the first day or week. Even a week of unchecked misbehavior can transmit the wrong message to the perpetrator, creating a monster who could have been otherwise and relatively easily salvaged. Kids desperately desire to fit in, even those who have become accustomed to usurping their instructors' authority, taking charge of whole classrooms. As they witness your genuineness and respectful take-charge techniques, they may attempt to disrupt, but when thwarted, show signs of enjoying the calming opportunity to shed their prickly surfaces to become productive members of the group. You must remain strong and resolute in your methods so that the confidence exuded sends a clear message of who is and will always be in command. They are counting on you to get them off of this destructive treadmill.

There are educators who recoil from the use of the word, boss, thinking that there should be no boss in the classroom, that students should be permitted to share in the decision-making process that structures guidelines. Nevertheless, boss is not a vile four-letter word. Having one capable person responsible for creating the operational framework, whether those involved in a group endeavor are age five or fifty-five, is preferable when the overall goal is one of consistency. Where two or more are gathered to accomplish something, there *will* be a boss. If not chosen, one will *emerge.*

Recently, a young instructor took a leave of absence from his high school teaching position. His students were on track both academically and behaviorally, and from all angles the job appeared to be a piece of cake. However, unbeknownst to his successor, he *was* the boss, and his students knew and pleasantly accepted that fact. The teacher hired to finish out the year, on the other hand, quickly and confidently declared her conviction opposing disciplining high school students who were "*perfectly capable of monitoring their own behavior.*" She, further, revealed that she just didn't see herself as a disciplinarian. Unfortunately, in short order, the students instituted their own daily routine—one of socializing throughout the period, ignoring her admonishments and pleas for order, shutting down any attempts to present instruction. It was soon apparent to their new instructor, that the harmonious system in place when she took over had been badly crippled by her inaction, in a few short weeks. A couple of assertive, astute young men had managed to slip the reigns from her hands to theirs, leading the class down a path to behavioral chaos labeled: Having Fun. The students lost out on valuable instruction, and her bubble completely burst as she ran from the room in tears, proclaiming them to be incorrigible and impossible to teach. While not all similar situations turn out this badly, the fact remains that each instructor needs to be comfortable and confident in the knowledge that he or she is the indisputable leader of the classroom. Don the cape. Your students need and deserve a competent and kind commander-in-chief.

The Heart to Heart Talk

For those who would rip off your cape and place it around their own shoulders, or who fail to exhibit even the remotest of cues indicating cooperative intention, *right away*, take the time to set up a private, face to face talk that very day. The advantage is that you are not angry, frustrated, or in orbit about repeated behavioral offenses, as you assuredly will be if you wait, enduring adverse conduct for days or weeks. You are in a gracious place because you've not allowed this student to perpetrate his or her brand of nonsense to the extent that the classroom environment has become overwhelmed by its toxicity. You're doing the class, yourself, and the student an enormous favor by addressing the issue early on, nipping it in the bud, compelling the student to become "someone else" — someone positive, someone admired for her goodness rather than the pseudo admiration received as a result of her intimidation.

Coming from a calm, nonjudgmental place within yourself, make an arrangement, with a smile, to meet with the student on your planning period, a time uninterrupted by other students or faculty. This may necessitate making a request of a fellow instructor to dismiss the student 5 or 10 minutes early from class, so that you may pick her up. Once begun, try to avoid any interruptions whatsoever, and *please* don't allow your student assistant or even a paraprofessional (unless an adult witness is necessary) to be present as you speak to the student. Immediately ask *anyone* who shows up, to return at another time. You wouldn't want the student to feel embarrassed, compromising her ability to offer complete focus and collaboration. Avoid, if at all possible, requesting that the student meet with you after school or at some other time precious to the student. With such a request you're simply inviting noncooperation or a raunchy attitude. Think of your disposition when asked to stay after work for a meeting when you'd rather be working quietly in your classroom, or are looking forward to leaving for the day. Reflect on what you are trying to accomplish. You are endeavoring to establish a positive relationship with this student; one in which she can let down her guard, turn from the dark side, and fall into line with your behavioral guidelines and standards. This kind of considerate thinking is what sets apart instructors who bring out the best in their students, from others who *seem* to be doing everything right, but are continually raising the ire of the exact same students, achieving little in the realm of promoting "changed" behavior.

Should your classroom prove unsuitable for this confidential chat, or is off the beaten path, raising a question about the wisdom of meeting in such a secluded space, decide on a public area on school property—one which lends itself to privacy, but is observable by a responsible party. This can be especially important for male teachers who are speaking with upper elementary, middle, or high school female students, for obvious reasons. It's also important for young teachers of high school students. You don't want there to be an opportunity for *any* student to "get fresh" or to report that you maintained anything less than a professional demeanor.

Though there's a definite advantage to handling this alone, If you feel the need for support, enlist a colleague, administrator, or parent to sit in—not to glare, admonish, threaten, or to inflict guilt on the "chatee," but to be an observer of this early process. This is definitely something you want to handle yourself, so be sure to have your observer accept that he or she is there in that role only. The talk involves several components delivered in a no-nonsense, yet calm, respectful manner.

1. **<u>Tell Her Who She Is</u>**

   Teacher: "*First, I want to say that I appreciate the way you participate in class when called upon. You're putting forth effort, and I enjoy having you in class.*" (Say whatever is TRUE. FIND something positive without going on and on.)

2. **<u>Describe the student's misconduct</u> or infraction in terms of actual facts.**
   Teacher: " Jean, I've noticed that during the last 2 lessons you've shouted across the room to one of your friends. Do you agree that this has happened?" (A simple yes or no answer is all you want. State, politely, that her turn to explain or expound will come later.) Thank her for her honesty, if there is an honest admission. However, if there is denial, just move on, disallowing a power struggle to commence, *"Perhaps that wasn't your intention, but that's how I saw it."*

3. **<u>Decriminalize and Display Understanding</u>**
   (Understanding does not mean agreement.)
   Teacher: *"I know that it can be difficult to hold onto a comment when you want to share something with a friend right away."*

4. **<u>Explain the effect of the misbehavior</u>**, making sure that the greatest negative impact involves the student in the chat. Otherwise, you risk receiving the "I don't care about them" attitude.
   Teacher: *"However, shouting across the room interrupts the lesson. It pulls both you and other students off focus, gets you into trouble, and prevents you from being successful in this class. My goal is for you and all of the students to achieve, and I won't let anyone stop that from happening. Does this make sense*?" (Again, only a yes or no answer.) Note: Avoid belaboring the point or preaching.

5. **<u>State your behavioral expectation(s)</u>**: **Replacement Behavior**—addressing only the issue at hand, without harshness, **but with total confidence and authority.**
   Teacher: *"Starting tomorrow I want you to* (be very <u>concrete</u> and specific) have *your book opened to the correct page, have your pencil and notebook ready for note taking, follow lesson directions when given, and be absolutely quiet until it's your turn to participate. You may talk to your friends either before or after class."*

   Be sure to tailor language and number of expectations to the age of the child. You wouldn't want to give a plethora of expectations to a first or second grader. Nor do you wish to use the words "I will not tolerate," with *any* age. These words are positively inflammatory, giving rise to anger and sub par results.

6. **<u>Ask for questions or comments</u>**. Listen politely and carefully, making sure that the student understands that she must also speak respectfully and in a sedate manner. In other words, if she begins speaking with an inappropriate tone or volume, or displaying irreverent body language, calmly stop her and say "*I want to hear what you have to say, but I need for you to speak to me in the same manner in which I am speaking to you."* Then, smile and say, *"You can do it. Now what would you like for me to know?"*

   Limit comments to a reasonable length of time. However, should the student refuse to speak now that you've asked her to modify her tone, just stay pleasant and move on. DON'T CAJOLE!!! You would be transferring the power to her—which you DO NOT want to do.

7. **<u>If there is a conflict regarding the expectation</u>**, or a difference of opinion, acknowledge it. Briefly and confidently state that your way will have to prevail for the benefit of all concerned, and for the reasons you have already stated. e.g. Teacher: "*I hear you and I understand. If you need to tell Ryan something, quickly jot it down so that you won't forget. It's just too disruptive for any student to shout across the classroom. We need all of our class time.*

8. **<u>If a compromise is in order</u>** for whatever reason, clarify <u>exactly</u> what it will entail. e.g. Teacher: "*Since this is a block period, Jean, there is a 5 minute break every day. That is a time when you can sit or stand with a friend and talk quietly.*"

9. **<u>Issue a *simple* contract that has been prepared by you ahead of time</u>.** It should contain:
   - **a brief description of the infraction(s)**
   - **the expected replacement behavior—do vs. don't**
   - **firm, fair consequences** should the infraction(s) be repeated

   NOTE: Forcing a student to issue an insincere apology is tantamount to promoting lying and deceit. An apology should only be given when a student *truly* feels sorry, not because someone else *thinks* he should feel remorse. Additionally, hastily writing a contract with guidelines that are nonspecific or unclear, or with consequences either too harsh or too lenient, requiring altering later, can lead to a loss of credibility or the risk of the instructor being viewed as one who lies or goes back on her word.

The contract is quickly and pleasantly explained to the student, then signed by both the student and the instructor as a symbol of the chat and the agreement. Decide on a signal that can be used between the two of you, reminding the student of the agreement. (e.g. thumbs up)

Unless the misbehavior is of a serious nature, I personally believe that for the first infraction a student deserves the opportunity to "fix" the problem on his/her own without the intervention of a parent or guardian. It can be empowering for that student, the instructor has already given him/her precise tools for achieving success in the form of **replacement behavior**, and it's a chance to stimulate student growth while displaying confidence in the student's willingness to be cooperative. Parents and guardians also seem to appreciate not having to be burdened with every little infraction committed by their child. It's a decision to be made based upon the circumstances and the policy of the school.

- As the student enters your classroom the very next time following your talk, either use the signal to briefly **remind her of your agreement,** or **give a word or two of encouragement**.
  This should be done kindly and discreetly. The student's peers should not become involved in this process.

- **Praise successes immediately**, in an *inconspicuous manner.*
  (ex. thumbs up, a whispered compliment, or an appreciative tap on her desk as you pass by during the lesson)

Following this very significant and potent heart to heart talk, monitor the student's behavior, closely, as you move through the regular duties of your classroom. If the misbehavior is repeated, **enact the forewarned of consequences immediately** and **with composure. No Second Chances, No Additional Punitive Measures**

If this step is left undone, the student can quite naturally assume that you are a teacher who bluffs and threatens, one who can be challenged again. Rest assured that the opportunity for that student, and perhaps others who are watching, will not be relinquished.

Otherwise, follow up with "mini" talks *as needed* —to praise, encourage, reiterate, address new concerns. Don't overdo this. Use good judgment and common sense. If all is going well, leave well enough alone, while being certain to *notice* the progress by informing the student that she is succeeding in her effort and that you're appreciative of her turnaround. It's vital that little changes in behavior not be taken for granted, or an attitude quite prevalent among teachers not be assumed, that *there's no need to praise students for what they are supposed to do anyway*. Countless human beings require encouragement and approval in order to stay on the right path. It simply feels good to be affirmed. Don't underestimate this psychological tool so readily at your disposal. Finally, remaining consistent, fair, and **not singling out the student** as a consummate behavior problem, no matter what, will allow her to eventually blend in with the rest of the group, held accountable for the same standards required of her classmates.

A properly conducted heart to heart talk is indeed effective. However, there are times when a student's misbehavior is so revolting or persistent that he needs to be removed from the classroom until you have a few moments for this talk. In some instances, *mean-spirited misbehavior* is an indication that the relationship between teacher and student has somehow become damaged. Check to be sure that you are not transmitting signals of disdain or disregard, in any manner. Sometimes it helps to audio tape oneself, listening in on just how academic and procedural directions, as well as disciplinary statements are being delivered. It would genuinely surprise some educators to *hear* how they come across to students on a regular basis, unintentionally provoking fits of temper and feelings of ill will.

In any case, be sure that you are not overreacting and that the situation cannot be diffused by changing a seat or doing something else innocuous. If this is not the case and the impossibility of maintaining order with the student in the classroom is apparent, do not waste your or the other students' time by arguing, screaming, or using some other ineffective measure to achieve control. A civil admonishment in the hallway may get you through the class until there is an opportunity to conduct the real talk. At other times, it may be prudent to enlist the aid of an administrator, the referral system, or whatever process your school employs. Nonetheless, you are the one who will need to take the bull by the horns, gaining respect and moving the student toward behavior in concert with your management system. Even if an administrator becomes instrumental in meting out an appropriate consequence, you will still need to have "the talk," establishing your own authority. After all, it's *you* who are being disregarded, and *your* class that is being disrupted.

Therefore, *you* must obtain each student's compliance and respect. When entering class each day, one wishes to do so with peace of mind and a feeling of happiness to be there. This comes from knowing that you, and not the students are in *complete* control. Therefore, **taking care of problems while they are mere annoyances, not allowing them to become the norm, is the goal to be achieved through early intervention.**

Avoid Power Struggles: Yet Another Warning

In the process of establishing oneself as the indisputable boss of the classroom, teachers must be aware that students may attempt to instigate power struggles, vying for a share of the control pie. Some student efforts may be perceived as harmless or even humorous. These power-grabbing ventures are not limited to those who are known agents of disruption and difficulty. Many students come to us having experienced success in manipulating the best of parents through the initiation of such mind "contests" in the home. Quite naturally, to achieve similar results with instructors, they seek to utilize their acquired talents in the classroom. Their success can spell the undoing of an otherwise competent instructor.

Therefore, though I've mentioned power struggles previously, because being drawn into daily power struggles can precipitate such heinous disciplinary repercussions for educators, it warrants another quick look. Some attempts appear to be harmless, but in the long run the teacher's stature as the leader of the classroom becomes eroded. Accomplished "artists" begin to attack every issue or decision made by the instructor, in hopes of changing the teacher's mind. Even those instructors who claim to like being challenged by students, eventually tire of the ever-present complaints—being under siege and second guessed on a daily basis. Flare-ups occur in which teachers lose their cool, plunging headlong into ineffectual disciplinary techniques, or destructively giving up and giving in. Students are very intuitive and smart when it comes to obtaining their way. They can tell when a teacher is unsure of a decision or is determined to have students share the power.

Be very cautious. Students are not prepared to share power. Narcissism, to an extent, is yet taking precedence over altruism. Nor do they possess adequate knowledge or maturity to assume such massive responsibility. Though they may *seem* adult-like, remember that you are the "trained and mature" one. "Share-the-power" thinking can become a slippery slope for those who believe that their students should be permitted to make pertinent decisions regarding curriculum and behavioral guidelines. Favoritism rears its ugly head, in many instances, and the inexperience and ignorance of the young, though exhibiting academic adeptness, makes this a risky position to assume. In most cases, the education of the group is compromised, and those students who have been allowed to "institute their wisdom" must be put back in their places, usually kicking and screaming all the way. There is a way to listen to your students, offering them reasonable opportunities to participate in planning. Actively engaging in power struggles is not it.

Preventing Power Struggles

When Challenged:

- Stay Calm, Avoid Taking Offense
- Voice Control—No Screaming
- Listen if Possible and Appropriate—Maintain Timeliness
- Display Confidence & Understanding
- Disallow Disrespect: Restate
  e.g. Student: "*This book is stupid!*"
  Teacher: *"It may seem stupid, but it contains information that will bring you success in this class."*

- Restate Decision or Expectation Without Preaching, Judgment or Trying to Convince
  e.g. Student: " *Why do we have to study clouds? Who cares! Let's talk about something we can use!"*

  Teacher: *"Thank you for your comments. They show that you are thinking, and I appreciate that. However, this is a part of the curriculum that is essential, so let's continue."*

- Send Acceptance Messages Apropos For The Situation
  e.g. "*You'll get this." "I can see that you've tried." "I realize that you're disappointed." "I'll help."*
- State Consequence For Persisting, If Necessary
- Move On As Quickly As Possible—*Respectful Assertiveness*
- Require 100% Student Involvement and Accountability (hands-on activities)

- Avoid Holding A Grudge Against Perpetrators and Maintain Pleasantness

Tough Cookies & Discipline

At some time during the career of each teacher, he/she will cross paths with students accustomed to and accomplished at taking over a classroom. These students who have been *allowed* to rule the roost in other classes and, frequently, in the home, present a real threat to the well-being of their peers, educational goals, and the presiding instructor's ability to hold down the fort. For certain, numerous teaching careers have been abandoned due to a lack of adroitness in controlling the behavior of a few tough cookies. Some "toughies" have morphed into genuine misfits, while others are just doing what has come naturally to them for years. Indeed, most of these students began their careers as incorrigibles in kindergarten and even in preschool. They have been afforded the opportunity of running amuck and roughshod over set rules and regulations to the detriment of their own and others' educational environment and possibilities, by educators who either considered themselves incapable of meeting determined delinquents head-on, those who attempted but were unsuccessful, or by those who were not caring enough to accept a fundamental responsibility of teaching: maintaining law and order.

One *must* be savvy in *immediately breaking the cycle of misbehavior* while simultaneously preserving the self-esteem of the student, thereby building a positive adult/child relationship which leads the student to modify behavior without feeling that she is sacrificing sense of self. That sense of self most often needs to be redirected, without the student necessarily knowing what is occurring. Students laden with severe clinical issues are not the ones about whom I'm speaking. Ideally, they will receive service outside of the classroom by professionals specifically trained to handle clinical problems, with pertinent strategies being shared with their instructors. There are plenty of students who experience no underlying medical conditions, but continually display difficult to manage behavior. I daresay, however, that employing techniques which seek to *restore* self-esteem as serious students and gracious human beings, will aid most children and teens who are consistently "acting out."

Contrary to what many of you may be thinking, it doesn't require loud demands and harshness to move these individuals into a status of behavioral success "*Pre-write discipline referrals, kick them out, spare not the admonishments, snare them with clever sarcasm and constructive criticism,"* many workshop participants have expected to hear me declare. However, these are not answers. There is a delicate balance of *caring* reproof and stealthy redirection that must take place. It's not trickery, but it does require that the teacher have his/her own secure sense of self in tact, a lack of fear, and patient, persistent consistency.

There is a distinct difference between discipline and punishment. Too often, the mind of the instructor heads pell-mell towards punishment for students who are consummate disrupters, when what they truly *need* is consistent, fair discipline, coupled with a genuine understanding of the arduousness of conquering oneself. Discipline is guidance—guidance that dares to teach a person how to behave so that his actions are constructive, conducive to his own prosperity, as well as considerate of the rights of others. Punishment, on the other hand, is vengeful. It seeks to condemn and penalize someone for a perceived offense. When an instructor assumes this stance, it usually indicates that he or she has taken the student's misbehavior personally. Huge mistake, though human. Inspect yourself for this kind of thinking. Should you discover that you possess it, do whatever it takes to reeducate yourself. Otherwise, you could be headed for countless years of unnecessary career stress and anger. Remember with whom you're dealing. They're not the sophisticated, accomplished human beings they'd like us to believe them to be, or that they *appear* to be in some settings or instances. They have many, many rough edges to smooth and numerous lessons to learn. It's our duty to graciously assist them with these lessons. This, an educator cannot do if he or she holds grudges against particular students or believes a student's misbehavior to be a personal attack.

Chronic student misconduct generally emanates from their own pain and insecurities. They have discovered that they can dish out their own brand of torture, which for the moment lets them feel "mighty," in control, or some other emotion that seems essential to their well-being at the time. Additionally, acting out becomes a game and a way of life for some, while at the same time, the very bravado so brazenly displayed is a cover-up for misery. For sure, a student's distress, and thus, resistive behavior is sometimes caused or exacerbated by the instructor in charge. Demeaning remarks or actions can re-open old wounds, accentuate an already suffering self-image, or otherwise activate an already existing dysfunction in the student.

<u>What to Do</u>

These strategies work for students of any age, any environment.

- Maintain the **same** behavioral and academic guidelines for tough cookies as for all of your students. EXPECT them to be cooperative and good students. Demonstrate this with YOUR behavior and comments. If given the impression that you are awaiting the advent of poor behavior, they will not disappoint you.

- Smile and send a message of acceptance. It's highly likely that they are unaccustomed to acceptance of any kind.

- Exude confidence – **Do Not Avoid Them, Maintain** vigilance, being sure to tag the <u>right</u> person vs. giving the benefit of the doubt to a "good" kid.

- Make clear your boundaries and consequences at the **first** sign of trouble. Usually a private chat with individuals who test the waters with a mini disruption, to introduce yourself formally and restate your expectations, goes a long way toward prevention of further behavior problems. Be firm, fair, and pleasant.

- Seat them where they can neither hide nor be overlooked by you—a seat that places them in the midst of *academic action.*

- Call on them to participate, from the word go. Active involvement is KEY. ASSIST THEM TO SUCCEED. Their self–concepts and comfort are on the line. Your purpose is to guide them toward a *fresh view* of themselves, as serious students and good citizens.

- Expect them to have materials. Provide or help obtain materials if necessary for an <u>on-task</u> start and beyond. Assuming an "it's their responsibility" attitude will work against both you and the student. You're out to show them that they *can* achieve. Do so in a nonpatronizing or insulting manner. Be *gracious,* while holding their feet to the fire in a manner leading to positive change. They need to feel good about learning. Remember, we **are not** better than any student, no matter what.

- From day one, check their work right along with that of other students, holding them accountable in a fair, respectful manner. You're sending the message that they are valued students who *will not* be disesteemed or left behind. This is uplifting!

- Treat tough kids with regard and kindness, **no matter what they do or say**. *You* are the model. *You* bring light. Given time, it WILL begin to make a difference in their actions *and* reactions.
- Use humor when appropriate. Avoid teasing humor such as, *"I'll bet you would do this if your girlfriend/boyfriend asked."* **Remain professional at all times. Peer humor is a negative, undermining positive strategies intended to steer students toward serious scholarship and citizenship.**
- *Insist* on respect for yourself and their classmates. Neither ignore poor behavior nor overreact. Just say, "NO" to holding a grudge once you've had to administer a behavioral consequence and the incident is over. **Continue to treat the person as you would a model studen**t. Students really do live up or down to our expectations. This is imperative if you wish them to see themselves differently, giving rise to *lasting* change.
- Provide genuine support for class work without playing favorites or *waiting to be asked.* Use **effective** teaching methods. Academic frustration can bring out the worst in them.
- Activate the school's support team on their behalf, when beneficial. (social worker, psychologist, counselors, etc.) Respect confidentiality.
- Avoid assuming that they are poor or disinterested students.

  Some of the brightest students are under cover.
- Avoid labeling. Labels hurt. (e.g. At Risk, Sp. Ed., Streetwise)
- Don't allow yourself to feel threatened or intimidated by students. They'll know, and students only respect confidence. If there is a legitimate reason for feeling unsafe, **do not hesitate** for even a moment to involve the appropriate administrators and/or authorities.
- **Acknowledge** appropriate behavior or attempts to make positive change, inconspicuously.
- Make them feel **welcome** and **appreciated**, on a daily basis. You're out to alter their negative perception of *themselves*. Many truly believe that every instructor and administrator will or does dislike them.
- Involve them in extracurricular or "extension" activities. (e.g. debate

team, environmental volunteer projects, plays) Avoid suggesting stereotypical activities, *only*.

- Provide structure, structure, structure for EVERYTHING.

Assign a responsibility they've previously proven unable to handle successfully, only after first building a framework which **makes it highly unlikely that patterns of self-destructive behavior will be revisited**.

e.g. You wouldn't send a kid who routinely cuts class or disturbs other classes when he's in the corridors, on an errand. To do so, send him to the classroom *next door* to get additional textbooks, or have him accompany a paraprofessional to the storage room to help carry supplies. This will help build his self-image as a responsible person while giving him no opportunity for failure.

Follow through, devoid of anger, on all promised and appropriate consequences. They must take you seriously. Avoid giving second chances once expectations have been made perfectly clear beforehand. This would breed contempt for your authority and repetition of the offending behavior.

I observed a class in which the teacher was experiencing significant, daily disruptions from three raucous middle school boys. Though other ineffectual techniques were contributing to the problem, two of the most potent were her practices of issuing countless warnings accompanied by inaction, and writing their names with multiple checks next to them, on the chalkboard. The name was to denote ten minutes of after-school detention, with each additional check indicating some unclear amount of time. With each check added, the louder the complaints became and the greater their disruptions. Because of frustration and a desperate need to maintain order and teach the class, she began bargaining with them to decrease the time owed. Her appearance of powerlessness, coupled with their growing sense of prowess, converged to create a block of time which saw other students join in the "fun," passive or disgusted students retreat into themselves or independent activities, and chunks of class time lost or diminished in educational value. Moreover, at the conclusion of the class, the offending students hurried out without being compelled to stay for one minute of detention even though this was the last period of the day, making it simple for the teacher to follow through on the stated consequence. Needless to say, each new day became a repeat performance. The boys were merely flexing their adolescent muscles, riding high, to the detriment of their and the other students' academic success. The beleaguered instructor had chosen to permit fear to induce her to transfer authority to a group of eleven-year-olds.

The thing to remember is that students, sometimes the tough or those who appear to be nonchalant, most of all, are **fragile packages.** A choice to create disruptions in lieu of risking failure of any sort, is made—consciously or unconsciously—who knows? Teachers are wise to be aware of this possible eventuality and quickly allay their concerns. Students of all ages want to be certain that you're not going to hurt them with sarcasm, disrespect, humiliation, put-downs, or academic demands without adequate instruction. In short, deep down many are apprehensive about how they will fare in their classroom experiences. Change and/ or new situations will create anxiety in the best of us. You want to put all students at ease as soon as possible. They need to know that their academic growth will take place in a "psychological safety zone." **This knowledge and assurance will diminish discipline problems born of insecurity and fear of the unknown.**

Justice Of The Peace

Parallel with our charge to educate, parents are counting on us to care for and safeguard their little or big darlings. We are, without exception, the justices of the peace. If that means having eyes and ears on all sides of our heads, so be it. We must endeavor to conform. Why is this so crucial? It's common for some individuals to make an attempt at getting away with whatever possible. There are those in the classroom who have turned bullying and intimidation into an art form. They are the ones from whom the others must be shielded.

Intuition and vigilance play a large part in this area of classroom management. Teachers can quickly lose the respect and trust of students when perceived as being intimidated by the very same bullies rendering students' existences a terror. Furthermore, bullies gain more power when left "untamed" or are not subdued. They seem to be perceptive when it comes to discovering that a teacher is vulnerable to being pushed around. Some are actually future leaders who possess strong, unrelentingly assertive personalities which can be positively redirected, while others appear to be insensitive individuals, suffering through some kind of pain of their own in all probability, but who have made a habit of preying upon weak or passive peers and instructors. Either way the swagger is the same and the behavior must be ended without delay.

What to do? Practice vigilance and astute observance, especially of those students displaying victim characteristics. Students who are shy, timid, loners, physically or mentally challenged, homely, eccentric, goody goodies, or ones who represent a racial minority within the group, are examples of targets. Begin the school year sensitizing students to differences in people as qualities of uniqueness and beauty, openly discussing bullying behavioral characteristics, shared feelings and insecurities, ways of displaying empathy and friendliness, expectations of student to student interaction, and even consequences around this potential problem. There are times when a usually "nice" person will exhibit bullying behavior without actually recognizing it as such. If some of this destructive thinking and acting out can be forestalled early on through specific instruction, so much the better.

Packaging the information into an organized, active participatory lesson, perhaps co-presented by the school's counselor, would lend the message more potency and cohesiveness. I wouldn't suggest, however, lumping a whole grade level or team of students together. Somehow, when this is done, student focus is not as keen. Those for whom the information or forewarning is most dire seem to become lost in the crowd, netting a limited impact or less than stellar results. One wants to make sure to key on each student regardless of whether or not he or she appears to need the information. Many educators have been surprised by just who becomes involved in acts of bullying.

Beyond this initial discussion, **do not feign *naiveté or* ignorance**. Children of all ages need the adults in their environment to **take notice** and **do something** about bullies. This **includes** high school students.

Actions to Implement, for the Prevention of Bullying

1. <u>List And Explain Specific Behaviors Which Are ALWAYS Off Limits</u>
   Don't leave it up to students to *guess or assume* what is meant by any of the forbidden behaviors. e.g. name-calling, excluding others, making threats, touching another w/o permission, using another's possessions w/o permission (Enlist their help in making a classroom pamphlet.)

2. **Maintain Vigilance—Move Around the Room During Instruction**
   There are hidden acts of bullying occurring, many times, as the instructor is preoccupied with instruction, and victims who are paralyzed by fear or too embarrassed to complain.

3. Structure EVERY Activity, No Matter How Minor
   The very structure thwarts schemes of taking over. (excursions, games, parties)

4. Keep Each Student Actively Involved At All Times
   This includes times when speakers are invited into the classroom. Idleness is fertile ground for bullying and other types of shenanigans.

5. Help "Reluctant" Students, So That They Are Never Embarrassed or Humiliated, Feeling That They Must, Then, Inflict Pain On Another

6. Stop Bullying Done Openly, Right Away, Whether The Victim Says That All Is Okay or Not. Don't label it bullying unless you're speaking privately. Remain calm, and in response to *"She Doesn't Mind If I Scribble On Her Paper!"* merely state that YOU mind. (Victims are oftentimes afraid to admit being in distress, for fear of reprisal at a later time.)
   e.g. Teacher: *" Jonathan, please move your chair back about 1 foot. It's gotten a little too close to Janice, and both you and she need a tad more personal space."*
   Jonathan: *" She doesn't mind if I sit here!"*
   Teacher: *"I know, but I mind, so move now, please."*

7. Separation of Bully and Victim by Seats, Classes, Lunch Periods, Etc.
   Immediate aid needs to be provided for the victim in as discreet a manner as possible. You wouldn't want to ADD to the discomfort already being experienced, by overreacting or drawing the attention of the class to the arrangements being made for the victim's safety. Nor is it meet to humiliate the bully by "announcing" possible consequences.
   Always Move the Easier Person, For Faster Conflict Resolution

8. Peer Counseling For Bully And Victim, Handled Separately When *Trained* Peer Counselors Are Available

9. The "In Yo Face" Technique (Explained Previously)

10. Parental Contact And Involvement, When Necessary and Prudent

11. Referral To Counselor, Psychologist, Or Social Worker For Conflict Management Strategies Though both victims and bullies require help, individual counseling may work best.

Whatever you do, disallow harmful or potentially pernicious situations to fester, using the age-old premise that children have to learn to take care of themselves. It *is* the duty of the instructor to maintain a secure environment for all. There may, of course, be those students who endeavor to use conflict as an attention–getting device. However, if not initially, you will eventually discover if that is the case, prompting a provision for proper counsel or support. I believe it always more prudent to err on the side of overprotection than to neglect a student who desperately needs assistance, may not be savvy or confident enough to make the request, and without it ends up suffering torment or harm of any sort.

One of our most critical and fundamental responsibilities, as educators, is that of providing an environment highly conducive to learning from safety and stress-free standpoints. This obligation is so often overlooked or disregarded, resulting in classrooms becoming hotbeds of distress and anxiety for students. Teachers *are* the keepers of the peace, and whereas it is ideal for students to learn to resolve conflict, it's unrealistic, in most instances, to believe that they *can* do so without assistance. They just aren't equipped, as yet, with the tools required for handling the myriad of difficulties that can arise when so many personalities and needs are intertwined. Thus, when help is warranted, we are not to turn our backs. Ultimately, ***our discipline will be impaired if we allow only the strong to survive and flourish.*** The backlash created through instructor inaction, is an atmosphere of acceptance of the abuse or ravaging of the weak, spawning a need for each student to take whatever measures at his disposal to ensure his own safety. In other words, classroom warfare will have been *invited.* If this sad state of affairs is not to occur, adult intervention and meaningful consequences for compromising the mental or physical safety of *any* student, must be swift, firm, and consistent.

Dealing with Tardy Students

Student tardiness is a common challenge facing most educators. Though it can be an irritant, requiring instructors to devise plans for meeting the needs of those who arrive after important instruction has already been given, and placing habitually tardy students at a distinct disadvantage when it comes to attaining academic success, it can't always be classified as a discipline issue. As I see it, student tardies fall into one of two categories, each requiring different thinking and actions from those in charge. First and foremost, however, feelings and expressions of anger and contempt which seem to be quite widespread among educators when speaking about or dealing with tardy students, only exacerbate the behavior. Students will be tardy whether we work ourselves into a tizzy over it or not. It's a part of life from which our students and we, ourselves, are neither excluded nor granted immunity.

Category one, **tardy to school,** is an animal unto itself because there are any number of circumstances and understandable reasons which could be the cause. Elementary-aged children and even some middle and high school students are at the mercy of the adults in their lives. They have little control over the factors leading to an on-time outcome. Thus, when they arrive late to school and encounter harsh, punitive statements or consequences, the experience can be quite discouraging and alienating, leading to larger issues such as truancy and dropping out of school. With this in mind, it is essential that teachers and administrators devise an approach for handling kids who are tardy to school, which seeks to ferret out the reason for the tardiness and includes problem-solving strategies. Kind, compassionate counseling needs to be the first line of action. **Decriminalize.** Counseling needn't be a long, drawn-out process, but a private chat to <u>listen to the student,</u> offer <u>*respectful* suggestions</u>, and <u>follow up with additional help</u> or parental contact, if necessary. You'd be surprised by the number of students who haven't given thought to simple, organizational strategies that all on-time individuals take for granted. (e.g. setting an alarm clock, showering and selecting clothing the night before, preparing the backpack and making lunch before going to bed)

I once counseled a tenth grader who was on the verge of being suspended from school because of his continual tardiness. Though when in school teachers loved having him in class, he was being given the message that if he couldn't get to school on time he just as well not come at all that day. I found that message shocking. Upon speaking with him, I learned that he truly desired to succeed, but had real life and organizational issues with which he needed assistance. Further, he was not aware that he needed help, but was doing what he thought best, which obviously wasn't working! (Remember the maturity research?) His teachers and administrators kept hitting him with the "it's your responsibility" lecture, hoping that somehow he'd make a change. Nevertheless, he continued along the same path. During our chat, I discovered that he hadn't even thought about using an alarm clock. He merely went to sleep listening to his music, and inevitably awoke too late each morning to catch the bus which would have gotten him to school on time. His parents were up and off to work before he arose. The good news is that the counseling *and monitoring* worked. He appreciated the positive attention and made an effort to employ the new on-time strategies.

Building such a rapport can actually lead to a determination on the part of students to modify their own behavior, or to appeal to whomever is in control of this aspect of their lives to participate in the solution. On the other hand, spouting responsibility-of-the-student jargon, dishing out multiple detentions and other punishments, have school leaders scratching their heads trying to figure out why the same students are yet tardy. I believe that suffering negative results in the area of changing the behavior of tardy students, teaches us that an approach, even if it must eventually encompass some kind of consequence, works best to prevent undesirable behavior when it begins with regard for the individual. A successful procedure embodies a component of cooperative problem solving which *teaches* the student how to evaluate her particular set of circumstances and find reasonable solutions. Involving parents or guardians in this solution-seeking process, rather than reporting their child's tardiness as a disciplinary issue, somehow makes for a harmonious team effort, one in which each individual's self-image is elevated.

Category two, **tardy to class,** is sometimes a disciplinary matter and sometimes not. Again, prevention is the key, and lambasting, punitive comments nonproductive.

I suggest the following strategies for keeping this problem at bay.

I. Prevention

A. State guidelines, up-front—making them attainable (I consider the "in your seat" requirement for being on time, to be a bit much. But, you make the call.)

B. Communicate straightforward, reasonable consequences: no surprises

C. Begin class with an immediate, **important** assignment (It will be **timed**, **collected** *each day*, **graded**, and **counted** toward the student's overall grade.) **Do not** give a tardy student extra time to do the assignment, unless he has a note from a legitimate source.

II. Dealing Fairly With Tardy Students

A. Welcome and Inform e.g. "*Good Morning, Jay. We're discussing the map on page 54.*"

B. Avoid stating the obvious e.g. "*You're late, Jay.*" It alienates and provokes.

C. Pull the student into the lesson quickly and respectfully—no teasing, put-downs, or negative remarks of any kind.

D. Conduct a brief, *private* chat to ask the reason for the tardiness and to set up the forewarned consequence. Avoid anger, "fussing," etc.
e.g. Teacher: *"Jay, why were you tardy today?"*
Jay: " I was at my locker."
Teacher: *"I see. We've discussed this before. You may need to get all of your books for the morning, before school."*
Jay: " The books are too heavy!"
Teacher: *"I understand. Perhaps you can ask your friends what works for them. At any rate, you'll need to come in after school for 10 minutes. I'll try to help you think, then. See you at 2:35."*

E. Consistent follow-through on consequences

F. Provide solutions and encouragement

III. Sample Consequences (when tardiness is a discipline issue)

A. loss of locker privilege for a day (student must be forewarned before implemented.) e.g. Teacher: *"You've been late twice because of hanging out at your locker. If this happens again, you'll lose the use of your locker the very next day."* BE SURE THAT THE STUDENT IS NOT HAVING TROUBLE WORKING THE LOCK
Procedure:
Have the student remove and store all books and personal items in a safe place in your classroom, taking what he needs for the morning. Before lunch, he will return for afternoon items. Provide genuine, caring assistance to make this work. It is already an inconvenience. No other punitive language or measures are needed.

B. Pay back lost class time during lunch, recess, or some other student free time. Begin with 10 minutes.

Provide a quiet, pleasant atmosphere. The forfeiting of free time is the consequence, and there should be absolutely no socializing —not even with you.

C. loss of passing period (Do this only with a student who is purposely socializing with friends until it's too late to arrive in class on time.)
Forewarn of this consequence after one or two instances of this occurring. Then, follow through by asking the instructor who has the student in the class prior to yours to dismiss her a few minutes early. If you're dealing with an obstinate student, you may need a paraprofessional or other responsible adult escort the student. Again, remain pleasant. e.g. " *Thank you, Maria, for coming. Have a seat and get your materials ready. You'll have your passing period restored tomorrow."*
Maria: " I have to go to the bathroom."
Teacher: *" I'll write a pass once all students are in class and working. Please be quick, and use the bathroom on this floor."*

The consequence is the loss of her socializing time between classes, not the loss of bathroom privilege. However, if she should violate your bathroom guidelines, give an appropriate consequence.

Enough has been said about dealing with tardy students. Maintain perspective. Being tardy, though certainly an undesirable behavior, is not the grievous beast many educators make it out to be. Remain authoritative while treating students with understanding, dignity, consistency, and even empathy. When instructors run a tight academic ship, keep things interesting and hands-on, and build student self-esteem as scholars, decreasing tardiness becomes just another issue requiring a little finesse on the part of the teacher.

The Granddaddy of Them All

Bathroom privilege is a biggie. It presents a dilemma for most teachers. "*Should I or shouldn't I grant bathroom privileges to students, at will. Should I or shouldn't I trust students to be honest."* Generally, administrators advise teachers to green light student trips to the restroom in emergency situations only, in an effort to stem the tide of hall-walking and other undesirable behaviors perpetrated by a minority of students when "let out" to go to the bathroom. It is a constant source of indecision for instructors, stress for students, and a colossal headache for all involved in school discipline.

Nevertheless, for students to endure questioning upon each request to be permitted to use bathroom facilities, or have severe restrictions placed upon access, such as the once every marking period statement made by one educator, or the requirement that all bathroom needs be taken care of during recess or passing periods, <u>is not</u> humane or reasonable. Such guidelines precipitate animosity between teacher and students, classroom disharmony, and contentious student conduct. The fundamental question to consider is what you would want *your* bathroom privilege or that of your children or siblings to look like? Thought *must* be given to a plan which allows students to preserve dignity, while disallowing them the opportunity of taking advantage of the situation. That's a mouthful, I know! However, the necessity of going to the bathroom should not be a circumstance engendering anxiety and dread in our students, fearing refusal, anticipating embarrassing queries and, often, provoking explosions of untoward behavior. It's not an area in which we need seek to be boss—boss of another's bladder. It is a time, rather, when an instructor realizes that he is already in the driver's seat and can, thus, exercise trust in students, prompting them to demonstrate, through the use of proper, established guidelines, that they are up to the task of responding favorably to the consideration afforded them. No one relishes being placed in a situation of having to grovel or beg before being permitted to take care of this most basic of biological needs. Instructors may be pleasantly surprised that **most** students are extremely trustworthy, responding to confidence in them with appreciation and honesty. Of course, you will also wish to establish a fair, forewarned-of consequence for those who would assume the advantage. Nonetheless, your demonstrated faith in them to not abuse the privilege, should spur growth in maturity for those who are developmentally ready to take the next step. The opposing approach to limit, at all cost, students' bathroom exits from the classroom, creates an atmosphere of student anger, righteous indignation, and determination to MISBEHAVE.

<u>Applying Consequences</u>

It is critical that instructors engage in forethought as it pertains to establishing consequences for student misbehavior. **Reasonable** and **doable** are your two guideposts. No one desires to face repercussions from misbehavior which are over the top. Nor is it smart for an instructor to impose a consequence which cannot be adequately meted out, or one so minimal in it's effect that the student simply thumbs his nose at it. In either case, the trouble is compounded. Remembering that prevention is the real key to behavioral management, discussing with other professionals consequences successfully working for them, observing students to discover what is important and can, therefore, be used to deter adverse behavior, provide the groundwork for choosing stable consequences which hold clout in gaining student cooperation.

Further, parents need not be constantly bombarded with pleas for help involving situations that can be easily managed by the instructor alone. Many who begin with agreeable, willing spirits are worn down and worn out by a multiplicity of negative phone calls or e-mails from the teacher, eventually becoming less than gung-ho about listening or assisting. Usually, when the task of handling minute behavioral missteps by a child is shouldered by an instructor who employs effective, age-appropriate techniques, parents are appreciative, remaining extremely receptive to collaboration regarding significant student conduct issues in which their help is truly needed. Students, too, learn to acknowledge and accept the instructor's authority to make sustainable disciplinary decisions, providing an invaluable advantage to the instructor. Again, employing professional judgment, abiding by school policy as to when it is wise to inform and enlist the aid of a parent or guardian, is the way to proceed.

Heavy-duty consequences are tools at your disposal for maintaining a safe, sane classroom. However, there are precious few of them. They need to be *reserved* for times in which a student needs to feel the sting of behaving in a particularly adverse manner. Otherwise, their overuse renders them impotent, in many cases. Students begin to mimic the teacher when the same consequence is "free flowing." Some even assume a "bring it on" attitude, and are willing to *endure* whatever the instructor can dish out, while persisting in and even worsening behavior.

These heavy-hitters include extended detention, isolation from the group, not being permitted to participate in special activities or events, office referrals, getting coaches or other leaders of extracurricular or outside activities involved. They can net marvelous results when used sparingly and judiciously, but can also backfire when the opposite is the case.

Thus, behavior modification techniques are worth investigating, observing classrooms in which they are being used effectively. These techniques allow a teacher to institute a system that encourages desired student behavior, while preventing the, aforementioned, *overuse* of standard consequences so abhorred by students. The trick is to choose a program or system embodying the following:

- incentives that are turn-ons for students—
  creating enthusiastic participation
- utilizes educational rewards
- is easily managed and maintained
- discourages incentives from becoming the goal

Behavior modification is one more idea or tool to add to your chest. Then, you can step up with the big boys of consequences on rare occasions, when they are most effective and behaviorally "life changing" for students, in a positive way.

The instructor, as boss, is certainly advantageous and a vital component of managing a fun, productive classroom. Comfort and teamwork is promoted when students are aware that someone competent and confident is firmly holding the reins. Involving them in decisions in which their influence will be permitted a measure of realistic influence and is both appropriate and instructive, **forewarning of all new expectations before implementation,** and employing ***absolutely no trickery*** are techniques that work, in concert, to confront and ward off unsatisfactory behavior. Additionally, the fair and humane administering of consequences (extenuating circumstances do sometimes come into play), a dose of humor, dogged consistency, remembering that there is no such animal as the teacher's pet, are all keys to students viewing their classroom as a place of order, and their instructor as a person who will make sure that their academic and physical comfort will never be compromised or sacrificed.

Students dealt with in this manner **accept authority much better** when it's necessary for the instructor to get tough. An added bonus to this kind of respectful discipline, is that when an unpopular consequence is meted out to a fellow classmate, the others tend to side with you, making the "air" in the classroom less toxic, affording you the opportunity to move on with the lesson.

No Wimps or Pushovers Allowed

The teaching profession is one which requires courage. The faint of heart need not apply. You're probably familiar with the premise that when dogs sense fear they're more likely to attack. I believe the same to be true of children. Somehow they just seem to smell fear, prejudice, arrogance in their teachers, reacting to each via the display of disruptive behavior.

Even if you are the shy type, take charge! Reject timidity and panic. Just knowing what you desire your standards and expectations to be is a huge plus. Refuse to be wishy-washy. Students will work at getting you to vacillate or change certain expectations altogether. You must be "unmanipulatable." Don't be afraid to say that you've thought things through and have a handle on what will make the class productive and pleasant—period. Practice respectful assertiveness in front of your mirror, if you must, getting the facial expressions and voice tone just right. Whatever you do, ***resist the impulse to hem and haw in front of your students.*** One doesn't have to be an extrovert to maintain control, nor does it necessitate the use of harshness or negativity to achieve this goal. YOU are the professional. YOU are the trained one. YOU are the chosen one. YOU are the boss! Just use the strategies learned from this and other reputable sources and KNOW that what you're doing is in the best interests of your students. Be steadfast. Many a misbehaving student has "explained" her poor behavior by exclaiming, *"Well, the teacher doesn't have control of her class!"* PLEASE!

Yes, there is room for changing your mind. I particularly think it should be done after pointed thought, rather than on the spur of the moment. There are many intelligent or crafty students, capable of presenting cogent arguments favoring their own points of view, influencing instructors to doubt the wisdom of important decisions. Should this occur, pleasantly admit that they *may* have a point, allow yourself time to mull it over, confer with a respected colleague, and get back to them with your determination. It is a mistake to permit *any* student to take command. It may seem harmless at first, but inevitably backfires, concluding with the undermining of the instructor's authority and ability to maintain good discipline.

It can also be a mistake for an instructor to not be big enough to admit that a student's suggestion is a good one, one that will work just as well or better than that already put forth. By accepting a valid proposal, one can maintain essential leadership power and status, while still permitting students to exercise critical thinking within appropriate boundaries, applauding their good ideas. This kind of confident action when justifiable, actually contributes to a teacher's stature as a competent professional, usually resulting in greater respect and cooperation from students.

Roughneck or bully types also appreciate and admire an instructor who ***knows*** that he or she is top dog, one with whom they cannot get away with poor or abusive behavior. Stand your ground, aware that you are acting fairly and impartially. This courage and assertiveness need not be ill-tempered or brusque. It should be accomplished, unapologetically, through judicious actions and humanity. You are **not** the bad guy, so don't label yourself as mean or any other negative. Misbehaving students have chosen, through their misdeeds, to bring certain consequences to bear, and are now compelled to endure those consequences for the imposed period of time.

An instructor's screaming, name-calling, hurling of insults, or other such antagonistic, unpropitious disciplinary techniques do not accomplish this "no pushover" persona. Students are won over when they are treated well, just as you are won over when treated well by an administrator. Respect them by moving among them comfortably, while making them aware, in no uncertain terms, that you are the captain of the ship. This can be accomplished through tenacity, giving brief, *rational reasons* for your guidelines, and ***keeping rules humane and to a minimum.***

It was my privilege to observe a mid-career teacher take over a class of high school students whose regular teacher had chosen to leave the profession mid-semester. The students exhibited the potential for becoming terrors. Instead, because of the comfort with which their new instructor moved among them, related, and went about confidently instituting his curriculum expectations, regarding them as serious students, they immediately bought into his system, falling into a peaceful realization that there was no need to struggle against either the teacher or learning.

CHAPTER SIX
SUMMARY POINTS

1. When conducted in timely fashion, a properly formatted private chat can end or prevent untoward student behavior.

2. Creating a classroom environment devoid of mental and physical strife provides the opportunity for each student to settle in and behave.

3. Tough Cookies exist in every segment of society. There are reasons why those in the classroom have chosen to view themselves as consummate disrupters. Rather than bringing out the six-shooter, follow a prescribed plan for raising self-concepts and behavior.

4. Educators are called upon to be justices of the peace. When this job is taken seriously and handled in a proficient, caring manner, the classroom becomes a place of cooperation and comfort.

5. Bullying is a societal ill. *Naiveté* or hiding one's head in the sand merely allows it to thrive and wreak havoc in your school environment. Stay vigilant, using specific techniques to prevent or handle this misconduct.

6. There are not enough consequences to compel all students to behave well. Use prevention techniques described in prior chapters of this book, so that major consequences can be reserved for situations in which usage can bring about meaningful behavioral change.

7. The teaching profession is one in which courage and maximum self-confidence is imperative. Throw off the cloak of timidity and indecisiveness if you wish to be successful leading and managing students.

Chapter Seven

GET UP ON THAT PEDESTAL!

Professional Attire

As educators and concerned citizens, alike, peruse the maze of strategies and techniques designed to propel students in the direction of classroom deportment that facilitates and stimulates learning, the suggestion of mandating uniform student attire continually pops up. Indeed, many schools have considered such a requirement at least a partial solution for addressing undisciplined behavior, and have forged ahead to that end. Throughout the country, ordinary public schools once sanctioning the student's right to choose daily apparel based upon individual taste, have changed their minds in favor of a uniform standard of school dress. Oftentimes, this simple alteration in school or district guidelines is viewed as a panacea for the many ills suffered by schools and classrooms beleaguered by constant reprehensible student behavior. However, as much as many would like to revert to the way things were during much of twentieth century America, pertaining to strict disciplinary and clothing standards imposed on students, the same individuals and advisory groups appear to have forgotten about the clear, predominant standards addressing apparel for instructors, simultaneously in place.

In so doing, those carrying the power of change may be overlooking a distinct and dynamic strategy which contributed to the establishment of an academic environment responsible for a higher level of conduct on the part of all involved. There is truly a positive impact produced by the professional appearance of instructors, support, and ancillary school personnel. The respect level students acquire for adults who hold so much dominance and authority over their lives, tends to rise when faced by those who communicate the importance of the profession by choosing to dress in a more formal fashion. *They're* important enough for their teachers to go that extra mile to look polished and distinguished. It's a simple strategy worth exploring and seriously considering. It's a pedestal many educators have turned their backs on as being irrelevant to the way students respond to their leadership, but one proven time and again to be valued and esteemed by overall society.

What's so great about being on a pedestal? It's all so old fashioned, traditional, and maybe even a tad phony, some educators proclaim. Who needs decorum anyway? We do. We teachers who expect students to obey our rules and, in general, to follow our lead, need that little something extra—like a pedestal. A pedestal is defined as a supporting structure or piece; a base, something that will help to ground and support us as we provide grounding and stability for our students. So, what's not to like about it?

Somehow, as those trusted with reforming educational structure added innovations, the baby got thrown out with the bath water. Thrown out was the glue that kept things anchored; the foundational trappings of running educational institutions which lead to teaching and attending school each being viewed as a privilege—sought after and evoking a sense of pride in those who are able to partake of either experience. The trappings that render this everyday exposure to knowledge available to all—a prized opportunity. The trappings that actually *further* the likelihood that education will be taken seriously. Consequently, we continue to reminisce about those good ol' days, complaining about how kids just aren't as this or that as they once were, when what we don't admit is that neither are we, or society in general. Some things, however, just ought not change, not because they were begun in the good old days, making them so much more superior, but because they're noble, uplifting, or just plain work! Thus, our pedestal. Ready, set, up on that pedestal with you.

There is a popular saying, "clothes make the man." While this definitely tends to have validity in certain professions, there really *is* value to ***giving just that right impression*** to those any of us desire to influence. Have you ever pondered the reason business persons get that conservative hairdo and dress in tailored, uniform clothing, or why doctors, for whom it is vital to exude confidence, wisdom, and know-how, dress so pristine-like, carrying themselves in a particularly conservative manner? It's not because this just happens to be the way these highly skilled and knowledgeable individuals always desire to look or behave. It's because impressions <u>do</u> count, and they know it.

Educators, especially of impressionable youngsters, need to realize that dressing professionally doesn't mean that they are stiff and old fashioned. It indicates that they are aware of possessing important information to impart and, thus, desire to garner respect from their "clientele" so that there is the greatest possible chance that it will be received. Notice the reaction of your students the next time an unknown, but professionally dressed person enters your classroom. It is decidedly different from their reaction to a person entering in "dressed down" mode. How does *your* initial response to a parent in business attire, differ from that spontaneously given to one who just comes as he is? Though we may not intend to discriminate, somehow appearance just seems to indicate how seriously a person feels about something. Teachers are role models. Teachers are professionals. Like it or not, "play clothes" fail to grab the same positive attention and respect as does more formal attire. Our profession *desperately* needs to regain the prestige it once enjoyed.

You're probably thinking, "My favorite teacher wore jeans and sneakers every day." No doubt this is true for countless students, but if you stop to think about it, that person would still have been your favorite even if dressed in attire more befitting the stature of the profession. It was more than likely the teacher's manner and instructional skills which drew you in, and, perhaps, an even greater, more profound impression could have been made. Additionally, your opinion of the importance of the career of teaching, and the confidence placed in educators, would undoubtedly have been enhanced by seeing that teacher dressed differently. As aforementioned, society is increasingly demanding that even students *climb* upon the proverbial pedestal by wearing uniforms. This school of thought is predicated upon the belief that attire can influence the degree to which one holds oneself in esteem, as well as one's willingness to bestow esteem upon others, directly affecting the level of self-discipline and regard for learning displayed. Therefore, this begs the question, shouldn't we practice what we preach?

GET UP ON THAT PEDESTAL!

Communication

We owe it to ourselves as adept, competent educators, to remove the stigma of second class profession from one of the most essential, noble careers in the world. Along with this commitment to look the part, must come renewed interest in and attention paid to the quality of communication engaged in by teachers. The level of classroom discipline has a direct correlation to this aspect of an instructor's relationship with students. Correct grammar, clear diction, and a high caliber vocabulary without arrogance, are musts. We desire our students to view us as worthy role models. Worthy of their attention. Worthy of their respect. Worthy of their confidence. Worthy of their admiration for us as pedagogues. Yes, we can and should maintain a friendly rapport and conversational relationship with our students. However, this can be done without lapsing into total slang, using coarse language, or snubbing the use of appropriate vocabulary and good grammar.

GET UP ON THAT PEDESTAL!

What bearing does all of this have on the absolute necessity of and one's overall capability of maintaining a disciplined environment in the classroom? Demonstrating proficiency in successfully molding our charges into well-behaved groups of students, is directly related to how much respect an instructor manages to obtain from whomever he or she is attempting to procure discipline. ***A teacher who carries himself confidently and professionally has a leg up in mastering the techniques of good behavior management***. Further, that all-important component of effective discipline—parental support, is likely to occur more often when parents and guardians perceive teachers as both **competent** and **polished**.

Take note of your subconscious images of doctors, financial advisors, or whomever's expertise you seek and really need to trust. Most of us would feel skeptical of the credentials, or at least guarded if faced with one dressed or groomed nontraditionally. Even if you wouldn't mind transacting important business with a professional who dressed or communicated in an unconventional manner, there is still significance in doing your part as an educator in the areas of personal appearance and communication. It assists students in attaining the awareness that discipline means appropriateness in <u>all</u> areas of life. Actions *do* speak louder than words.

We have so much more than curriculum to teach students. The responsibility is mammoth, and we must be willing to discipline *ourselves* for the task at hand. The seemingly insignificant things actually enable students to better focus on why they're in school in the first place. Teachers have an obligation to give more than just lip service to preparing the "whole" child for today's society. Therefore, we need to go that extra mile, straight to the shopping mall to purchase those professional duds, and ***back to the basics*** of grammatically correct, decorous speaking. Let's get on that pedestal for our sakes as well as for our students. Respect *is* the name of the discipline game, and a little admiration wouldn't hurt either.

Character

Now that we've taken note of our clothing and conversation, one more area of professionalism warrants discussion: **character**. Practicing what we preach isn't just a nice saying. It's indispensable. Have you sat in the teachers' lounge or a staff meeting, observing from instructors and other school personnel the exact array of behaviors forbidden in their classrooms or alternate areas of student contact? Inattentiveness, complaining, aversion to change, passing the buck, chatting while another is speaking, and unwillingness to accept the democratic process are examples of common behaviors exhibited by many of the most demanding of instructors. Additionally, what about out of school activities in which educators are participants: the use of illegal recreational drugs, excessive intake of alcoholic beverages, driving under the influence, rudeness at sporting events, taunting refs at little league games, offensive language, road rage.

Though teachers are ordinary citizens, everyday people, the eyes of the world—our world, the world of children, are upon us. It matters not where we go, it is very likely that the eyes and ears of one or more of our students or someone who knows and recognizes us because we're who we are, are focused on our actions and speech. It's a mighty heavy burden for us to carry, for sure, but not one that is impossible. Let's smile and enjoy the status. Yes, status! It's sort of like being parents, only for thousands of kids. There's a question each educator must ask himself or herself. "Do I have the courage to step up to the plate and live by the same standards asked of my students, or will I rationalize and excuse my own weaknesses and poor behavior while holding students' feet to the fire?" That veneration, that admiration, that discipline, the attainment of which is oh so valuable in our pursuit of effective classroom management and potent student learning, is greatly enhanced by the "C" word—**character**.

GET UP ON THAT PEDESTAL!

"To Be, Or Not To Be..."

There are additional tough and pertinent questions to be answered. Are you sure you wish to be a teacher, one from whom so much is expected? Do you have the confidence to require and demand respect? Are you willing to reciprocate with the same level of reverence for each and every student?

Consider the following. Many educators and significant members of society who exercise influence over educational environment, seem to have become mute with regard to recommending certain elements of overall structure proven to contribute to the maintenance of an essential academic milieu—one which sustains and promotes high behavioral standards. Student and teacher dress codes, once challenged, are dropped or rendered voluntary, fundamental traditions upholding schools as institutions of pride and dignity are relaxed or rejected. Rows of desks are proclaimed rigid and old fashioned, sacrificing coveted personal space and **promoting student distractions and conflict**. New, inappropriate freedoms are thrust upon students, requiring levels of self-discipline unavailable to them at the juncture in which they find themselves. Even windows, supplying vital, energizing light and ventilation essential for depth of learning, and walls serving to aid instructors in the cultivation of student self-control, have flown the coup on some campuses, victims of *innovation*. Though openness to new, creative ideas is always a plus, who knows what else heretofore *proven* to be the embodiment of standard elements of organized, successful instructional and disciplinary blueprints, have fallen by the wayside. Who knows what continues to be tinkered and experimented with, without informed thought or attention to detail from those who are masters of pedagogy and human behavior. No wonder good discipline, in many cases, has lapsed into a coma.

You will need to invent ways of inspiring academic pride and the love of learning in your students. They are magical components assisting teachers, immeasurably, in procuring effective discipline. All kids, *bar none*, possess buttons which when pressed, turn these lights on in their lives. Relevant, age-appropriate quotes have been used by many successful teachers in the area of instilling pride and motivating students to be their best selves. The diversity and fun of this genre can prove to be quite invigorating and influential. In any case, it's one among various ideas to explore. What is known for sure, is that those students who embrace both structure and pride fare better in sustaining good behavior.

What's In A Name?

Adding to the confusion surrounding what is or is not conducive to the procurement of positive student behavior, is the question of whether or not students need to follow the age-old custom of addressing instructors and other grownups in the environment, in the traditional manner. It seems that the use of Mr., Mrs., Ms., and Miss are assumed, by some, to be too formal for learning to take place. What on earth has happened? What are we thinking? The very vestments, which when adorned can cause students to seize and accept the mantle of good discipline, have become lost in all too many school settings. Run fast, make haste to recapture the allure of good manners which gives students that healthy reverence for adults, and specifically for teachers. Refuse to relinquish your power as an adult, an authority.

Young teachers, it matters not that you are only a few years older than your high school students. Those few years and your degree make all the difference. Assuming a peer demeanor is a no-no. Require your students to address you with propriety. It prompts them to recognize that something *important* is taking place in your classroom i.e. their education! When students "feel" that importance, **good behavior occurs more naturally**. Your might as a disciplinarian comes in many different forms, and one is the use of your "title."

Society has a hierarchy, and not all hierarchies are unjust or negative. Hierarchies breed respect and, thus, restraint. Sure, it can be fun *for the students* to address you as David or Sarah, viewing you as their "bud" or equal. But make no mistake about it, your effectiveness as a teacher is being compromised, threatened, and diminished. Just keep teaching. That familiarity students feel with you just by using your first name, induces them to become casual and bold in areas you'd like to keep more orthodox—like discipline. Challenging your authority won't seem so "wrong" when one can say, "See you tomorrow, Kevin." rather than "See you tomorrow, Mr. Jones."

What's in a name? *Mucho.* Kings and other royalty knew how to keep just that little distance, vital separation from their subjects. They never suffered from a lack of love or compliance by so doing, even when no real power was present. Teachers can learn a thing or two from them.

A stress-free, well-disciplined classroom is created by attending to the little things.

GET UP ON THAT PEDESTAL!

Conversely, little things will also tear down or erode your chances of reaching that utopia of the well-disciplined classroom. No student has ever been harmed or had his opportunity for learning lessened by being asked to use the appropriate title for his teacher. This is **not** arrogance we're entertaining here. You must feel *worthy* of respect. That very posture of worthiness will permeate all that you do and say, sending a powerful nonverbal message of competence to your students. As they receive that message, their behavior will reflect the admission to themselves that you are magistrate of the classroom. Let your personality shine through, exuding *genuine* caring as you show that you value your position as teacher, professor, *sensei*. Then, begin enjoying the tranquility that comes with maintaining a disciplined and safe learning environment.

Classroom safety is derived when each student comprehends his limits, accepts instructors' guidance and authority, and becomes a willing partner in the constructive process of framing self-disciplined, cooperative learners. Of course, conflicts will still arise, but the groundwork laid affirms them as valuable human beings, deserving of a secure, enjoyable learning environment, rendering those conflicts easier to handle and resolve because the instructor has student buy-in of the disciplinary *system that* has been put into place.

Students learn to appreciate being around an adult who is masterfully in charge, one in whom they can place their trust that the classroom will be a fun, safe place to attend.

A happy teaching career is at your fingertips. Take a deep breath, roll up your sleeves, and start having fun as a teacher!

CHAPTER 7

SUMMARY POINT

MAINTAIN PROFESSIONALISM IN EVERY ASPECT
OF THE WORD.

" MANY A TEACHER,
LACKING JUDGMENT,
HINDERETH HIS OWN LESSONS."
M. Tupper

"EXCELLENCE IS NEVER AN ACCIDENT;
IT IS ALWAYS THE RESULT OF
HIGH INTENTION,
SINCERE EFFORT,
INTELLIGENT DIRECTION
SKILLFUL EXECUTION,
AND THE VISION TO SEE OBSTACLES
AS OPPORTUNITIES."

–anonymous

APPENDIX

Over the years, I've created the following in response to questions or concerns posed by instructors participating in my classroom management workshops.

Appendix Table of Contents

Appendix i

COOP GROUP GUIDELINES FOR INSTRUCTORS

I. Explain and Post Coop Group Manners

II. Display Clear Project Instructions & Timeline Via

A. Chalkboard
B. Overhead Projector
C. Typed Handout *For Each Student*
D. Chart
E. Other

III. Explain And Model Assignment/Project

IV. Have A Definite Plan For Dividing Students, Based Upon Promoting Maximum Student Productivity And Cooperation

A. Instructor Chooses Group Members
B. Count Off And *Record* Member Names (Recording prevents student switching)
C. Student Choice With Guidelines e.g. "*Choose 2 girls and 2 boys*." "*Choose a person from each table.*" "*Choose one person from each reading group.*"

V. Provide And Designate Group Work Locations Which:

A. Respect Personal Space & Minimize Socializing
B. Offer Suitable Work Space & Materials

VI. Require Each Student To Do Equal Work (Each should write whatever has to be written.)

A. Give Both Individual and Group Points For Work Accomplished, At The End Of Each Session
B. Time The Activity To Prevent Time Wasting (Use A Timer)

VII. Specify a Reasonable Session Goal (e.g. "*During this session your group should finish gathering all of the background info specified on the worksheet.)*

VIII. Move Around The Room Giving Guidance Until Groups Are Rolling Smoothly

IX. Monitor Groups Throughout

Appendix ii
UPPER AND SECONDARY GRADES

COOP GROUP

STUDENT DOs

1. Face Group Members

2. Follow Project Directions

3. On Task Discussion Only

4. Avoid Criticism, Teasing, Put-Downs

5. Listen Respectfully To One Another/Decide As A Group

6. Equal Work

7. Ask When Whole Group Is Baffled

Appendix iii
PRIMARY GRADES

COOP GROUP

STUDENT DOs

1. Sit in a circle with your group.

2. Follow the teacher's directions.

3. Be a good listener.

4. Do your share.

5. Use polite and kind words.

6. Ask the teacher for help.

Appendix iv

COOP GROUP CHECKLIST

Group Members ___________________________
Project___________________________________
Time Limit ___________
Date __________________
Points Received ______

Points Checklist Total 50 Pts.

____ immediate on task
____ on task conversation throughout
____ group cooperation
____ followed project/assignment directions
____ finished project/assignment

Appendix v

SELF-ESTEEM BOOSTERS

STUDENTS WITH GOOD SELF-ESTEEM GENERALLY DISPLAY BETTER BEHAVIOR.

1. "You're smart, creative, clever, etc."

2. "There's no dumb question. I like questions!"

3. "You're looking and sounding like scholars!"

4. "I appreciate you guys." (Communicate caring.)

5. "Talking doesn't make you a bad person. This just isn't the right time."

6. "Hang in there for 10 more minutes. I know this is the last period/ day. You're doing so well!"

7. "Thank you for not talking, and for being polite while I talked to Joe's parent." (credit when credit is due)

8 "You're wonderful kids, students, young adults." (Praise goes a long way, and works wonders when it's genuine.)

9. "You can do it! It takes time." (Show belief in them.)

10. "Nobody's perfect. I've noticed improvement."

To <u>acknowledge</u> students' feelings, even if you don't understand or agree with them, opens the opportunity for a dialogue. It creates bonds, bringing the two sides closer together.

Appendix vi

OBTAINING AND SUSTAINING GOOD CLASSROOM DISCIPLINE: 10 REMINDERS

1. Students are loyal when you treat them well. Remember and use the golden rule.
2. "Inhumane rules add to what they hate about you." (quote from a HS student)
3. Don't be an assigner, and never say this is going to be boring, too hard, etc. (setting them up for failure, then wondering why they behaved in a disinterested or defeated manner)
4. Frustration breeds anger—breeds bad behavior.
5. If everyone or most are failing, it's probably you, the teacher, and they will likely dislike you for it. (Take a look at your attitude towards them, conscious or unconscious, teaching strategies and methods, etc. Don't blame the curriculum, rethink teaching style, time frames for learning new skills, etc.— generally reevaluate)
6. Students **do care** about learning! Treat them as though they do.
7. Ridicule and putdowns only serve to destroy a student's self-esteem, and create poor behavior as a means of retaliation.
8. Provide a safe learning environment for students both mentally and physically.
9. Avoid using labels. They destroy self esteem, and kids begin to believe and become limited by them. (e.g. special ed., at risk, bully, weird, messy, loudmouth, crybaby, spoiled, lazy, wannabe, etc.)
10. Reread your child/adolescent psychology. Many infractions are simply the nature of the beast. (running, boisterous behavior, posturing, tattling, etc.) See the behavior as such, and guide toward appropriateness, instead of criticizing and judging.

Appendix vii

Nature of the Beast Solutions
Elementary Grades

Typical Behavior	**Prevention**
1. Tattling	■ pre teach guidelines for what or what not to tell (Don't Assume) ■ acknowledge, thank, ask child to repeat guidelines (help, if needed)
2. chatting	■ plan "legal" chatting (e.g.*"Turn to the person on your left and explain the rules of the game.")* ■ move around while teaching ■ direct, respectful request ■ stand near ■ diverse/hands-on activities with smooth transitions ■ immediate start ■ assigned seating ■ tight academic ship information & choice *(YOUR choices)*
3. hitting/teasing	■ direct rule/expectation ■ 0 tolerance ■ assigned seating ■ vigilance ■ lead by example ■ build community ■ private chat ■ established, organized procedures
4. toys	■ specific guideline ■ incorporate toys in lessons ■ acknowledge, offer safe place for keeping ■ be consistent

Appendix vii

Nature of the Beast Solutions
Elementary Grades cont.

Typical Behavior	**Prevention**
5. pushing/butting	■ line assignments ■ teach personal space guidelines ■ students line up singly or in pairs ■ build community
6. being first or last	■ acknowledge, decriminalize ■ devise, follow fair, organized plan for allowing each student to hold every position in line ■ build community
7. blurting/impatience/ pouting	■ pre teach guidelines ■ acknowledge, affirm, redirect ■ give info and choice
8. waving hand in teacher's face	■ pre teach guideline ■ acknowledge, affirm, redirect ■ *teache*r models correct behavior w/o putdowns or criticism
9. touching others e.g. hair, clothing, etc	■ pre teach guidelines ■ 0 tolerance ■ build community ■ assigned seating ■ vigilance

Appendix vii

Nature of the Beast Solutions
Elementary Grades cont.

Typical Behavior	**Prevention**
10. horseplay	■ "legal movement" ■ immediate start ■ tight academic ship ■ smooth transitions/ no spaces ■ disallow herding
11. quest for attention/ assurance	■ acknowledge, decriminalize ■ organized system of inclusion ■ pre teach guideline ■ timed, incremental lessons ■ *invite* questions ■ provide teacher or peer assistance
12. fidgeting	■ build in "legal" movement ■ acknowledge need for movement ■ decriminalize ■ step by step instruction with modeling ■ understand nature of beast ■ hands-on activities ■ provide reasonable breaks ■ provide personal space for each student

Appendix viii

Nature of the Beast Solutions
Secondary Grades

Typical Behavior	**Prevention**
1. music e.g. CD or MP3 players	■ specific rule ■ use low, background music when appropriate (something pleasant & calming) ■ BE CONSISTENT ■ direct request w/ "instructor" choice (*"Please put CD player in your backpack or on my desk until after class."*)
2. herding	■ begin class immediately ■ designate specific student groupings e.g. *"Only 3 people at each table, please."* ■ create areas of room for specific activities ■ stagger passing/ in class movement ■ organize student movement—singles, pairs, small groups
3. chatting	■ acknowledge, decriminalize ■ build in "legal" chatting (*"Turn to the person on your left and explain one cause of World War 1"*) ■ circulate among students during instruction ■ direct, respectful request/post-it note ■ incorporate diverse/ hands-on activities with smooth transitions ■ immediate start/ engagement ■ tight academic ship ■ stand near talkers ■ information & choice (instructor's choices) (*"There's no talking, Maria. You may stop talking and stay where you are, or move to the seat next to Carlos, now."*)

Appendix viii

Nature of the Beast Solutions
Secondary Grades cont.

Typical Behavior	**Prevention**
4. drawing	■ integrate art in some form ■ direct, respectful request ■ prevent academic frustration
5. eating	■ state specific rule/rationale ■ BE CONSISTENT ■ model the guideline ■ friendly monitoring at entrance ■ direct request w/ choice (YOURS) e.g. *"You may step outside and gobble quickly, or place it on my desk until after class."*
6. boy/girl	■ assigned seating (from day one) ■ tight academic ship ■ immediate start ■ smooth transitions ■ direct request ■ private chat ■ precise classroom procedures ■ instructor-guided groupings
7. horseplay	■ disallow herding ■ acknowledge need for movement ■ decriminalize ■ variety in lesson plans ■ built in "legal" movement ■ immediate start/opening class procedure ■ tight academic ship/smooth transition ■ ending class procedure—routine & calming

Appendix viii

Nature of the Beast Solutions
Secondary Grades cont.

Typical Behavior	**Prevention**
8. inappropriate lang.	■ pre teach direct rule/expectation ■ rewording ■ consistency ■ appropriate consequence ■ tight academic ship & academic environment ■ private chat with individual offenders ■ instructor as model
9. teasing	■ pre teach direct rule/expectation ■ 0 tolerance ■ lead by example ■ private chat ■ appropriate consequence ■ build community
10. grooming	■ decriminalize/replacemnt behavior e.g. *"Kaila, I know that you like looking your best, but you'll need to comb your hair during breaks, only."* ■ post-it note/private chat ■ humanity/understanding ■ pre teach guidelines/expectation ■ incorporate related topics into actual lessons (e.g. occupations) ■ direct request/choice (yours) ■ tight academic ship/100% active student involvement

Appendix viii

Nature of the Beast Solutions
Secondary Grades cont.

Typical Behavior	**Prevention**
11. Cell Phone Usage	■ clear guidelines stated & posted ■ decriminalize / replacement behavior ■ lead by example ■ fair, **consistent** consequences ■ information & choice e.g. *" You can't check cell messages during class, Bill. Please put your phone totally out of sight or on my desk until after class."*
12. Off Topic Conversation during group activities	■ *assigned* groups ■ written, numbered directions ■ group procedure taught ■ timeline for each part of assignment/ checkpoints ■ points tied to project segments ■ teacher movement ■ points for group dynamics
13. Off Topic Conversation during instructional lessons	■ clearly written/*communicated* curriculum-based objectives ■ redirect, give information & choice ■ creative lesson plans ■ tight academic ship/ seamless transitions ■ organized instructor ■ lead by example ■ private chat for persistent offenders ■ decriminalize/ replacement behavior e.g. *"I know that talking about our SuperBowl win is exciting, but after this last comment I'm going to ask you to continue during lunch, so that we can finish our lab."*

Appendix ix

Management Tips for Library Instructors

1. Greet and welcome students, so that they enter with a spirit of peace, viewing the environment as a place of clam and comfort.

2. Post few, essential rules—pleasantly. Explain them during students' first visit.
(Ex. Simon says always have something to read or do. He who laughs and talks too much must leave.)

3. Designate and label a specific area or tables for research book usage. This prevents students from leaving research sources all over the media center, but would not, of course, apply to a whole class coming in for research with their instructor.

4. Decide on small group size and guidelines, based upon student productivity rationale. e.g. max 4 students per table

5. Consider creating and labeling " purposeful" work areas, to prevent the congregation of large, noisy groups. This strategy also serves to prevent the disturbance or bullying of independent works. Divide and conquer!

e.g.

AREA A - COOP GROUP PROJECT WORK
AREA B - COMPUTER RESEARCH
AREA C - INDEPENDENT ASSIGNMENTS
AREA D - MAGAZINE READING

6. Treat students as serious learners and scholars. Raising self-concept raises behavior.

7. TEACH and require students to be seated upon first entering the library. From there they can fill out a **brief** "task" form, prepared by you. This serves as a statement of their objective while in the media center. It can be a simple checklist that you create, which will focus their attention on the task at hand, while preventing initial congregating and horseplay. Provide immediate and gracious help to those in need.

Name _______________ Grade___Room______
Date ________________ Teacher _____________

My Purpose for Coming to the Library
___ check out a book
____ research project
____ free reading
etc.

8. Remain Vigilant
   a. Providing help forestalls frustration & misbehavior.
   b. Disallow student bullying or disturbing of others.

Appendix x

<u>Management Ideas For Elementary School P.E. Classes</u>

- Prepare a syllabus to share with students and parents so that all know what to expect. Conveying the importance of the class helps students take it seriously, which leads to better behavior.
- Greet and welcome students as they enter **each day**. Build Rapport
- Have assigned "places" from the first day of class.
- Make the PE area inviting and comfortable. (Student stress breeds fear of failure and poor conduct.)
- Create and establish opening and ending class routines. When students enter without direction or a procedure in place, disruption is more likely to occur.
- Adhere to and enforce rules of fairness for all, from the beginning.
- Monitor fair play and locker room manners. **Don't permit abusive comments or teasing to even commence!** Victims of such learn to quickly dislike class, sometimes doing everything to sabotage both their and others' experience.
- Disallow complaining from day one. Be pleasant but firm, planning for varying abilities and putting students at ease. (e.g. *"You don't have to be perfect or like everything we do, but I want each of you to do your best during each activity.")*
- Be mindful of embarrassment, coed concerns, bully activity, and the wide range of capabilities. **VIGILANCE and kind assistance can *prevent* many disruptions!**
- Use positive, encouraging language, and beware of "innocent" joking or teasing from instructor or students. **Words DO hurt.**
- Use name tags or some other form of identification for quick name memorization. Addressing students by name can prevent nonsense.
- Give guidelines for both winning and losing behavior **before** the first game is ever played. (Be sure to use DO vs. Don't statements) e.g. *"Make positive comments when a person or team loses. Be proud of winning and remember to congratulate the other person or team for a good effort."*

Appendix xi

Management Ideas For Secondary P.E.Classes

- Prepare an instruction syllabus for the semester, based on the curriculum, to share with students and parents so that all view the class as important, and know what to expect.
- Greet and welcome students as they enter, **daily**. Build Rapport
- Issue name tags or some other form of identification, for quick name memorization.

Being able to address students by name prevents nonsense from getting underway.

- Assign "places" on the first day of class, to prevent boy/girl shenanigans and other undesired socializing. Establish opening and ending class routines.
- When middle/high schoolers do not dress for gym have an alternate **curriculum-based, written** assignment—ready! This guideline is explained to all students during the first day's procedure discussion. The assignment will require the whole period to complete, and is independent for the student. It's easier if the assignment is prepared beforehand and quickly accessed by students, so as not to interrupt the flow of the day's class. **Avoid harsh, critical remarks**, but do have the student fill out a **BRIEF form** explaining why he/she isn't dressing. Then, designate a *pleasant* place in the PE area, away from other students, but clearly seen by the instructor, for the work to be done. This prevents the student from "walking the halls" or disturbing other classes and instructors. During the procedural discussion, students should understand that this is not a "me and my friend" option, and that completion of the assignment gives a maximum passing grade of "C" rather than full credit for the period. Of course, if a student chooses this option more than once, it's time for a private chat, to ferret out the source of his/her discomfort with PE and to offer kind, respectful aid. Further, if the student chooses NOT to do the assignment, not only a failing grade is given for that day, but an appropriate consequence for not participating in the class. NOTE the importance of explaining this procedure on the first day of class. Forewarned is forearmed. (This system gives students a sense of control and fairness should they have

a legitimate reason for not dressing, and should only be utilized if the instructor is comfortable organizing such.)

- Adhere to and enforce rules of fairness for all, from the beginning. When students must fend for themselves verbal and physical disorder rules.
- Monitor fair play and locker room manners. **Disallow abusive comments and teasing from the beginning.**
- Nix complaining from day one. Be pleasant, but firm, planning for varying abilities and **sensibilities**. Express willingness to provide aid to individuals.
- Remain **vigilant** for embarrassment, coed concerns, bully activity, and the wide range of capabilities. PE class can be stressful, and stress leads to raunchy attitudes and misconduct.
- Use positive, encouraging language. Beware of "innocent" joking from teacher or students. Victims of such learn to quickly dislike class, sometimes doing everything to sabotage both their and others' experience.
- Give guidelines for both winning and losing behavior before the first game is ever played. Hurtful comments are off-limits. When the classroom becomes an unpleasant place in which to exist, fires must be constantly extinguished.

Appendix xii
Management Tips for Music, Drama, Art, Shop, Home Ec, Etc.

1. Create an instruction syllabus based upon your curriculum, to share with each student and parent. Communicating the importance and expectations of the class encourages students to take the class seriously.

2. Decorate the room appropriately and invitingly, creating a sense of importance for the class. Key in on student interests to keep projects fun.

   Environment has much to do with behavior.

3. Greet and welcome students as they enter, **daily**. Build Rapport

4. Assign seats for each class on the first day. Being able to sit with one's cronies communicates a message that the class is less significant than its academic counterparts.

5. Issue name tags or some form of student identification on day one. Calling students by name gets them connected quickly.

6. Institute a routine assignment or substantive procedure for students to follow immediately upon entering . Teach this procedure during the first session of class.

   Establish an end of class routine which prevents horseplay and chaos as class ends. BEWARE of detaining an entire group of students due to the misbehavior of individuals, causing anger and wholesale tardiness to other classes.

7. Follow effective teaching techniques . (vocabulary *instruction*, step by step process teaching, modeling, lots of student practice) **Student stress breeds fear of failure and poor behavior.** Display and communicate the daily objective(s) and agenda, sending the message that the class is not a time for "play," even though it may be less restrictive than an academic or core subject.

8. Expect and require 100% participation **from the first day**. Be pleasant and affirming, but firm in the resolve that each person stays involved.

   Provide any and all assistance to ensure reasonable student success.

   Consider using a timer when fair and appropriate, to prevent student procrastination and dawdling.

9. Speak in positive terms about your subject. Know that some students will be disinterested, but will "go with the flow" if their disinterest is not emphasized, and the instructor displays an enthusiastic, fun attitude.
10. Be aware of varying abilities, **disallowing teasing of any kind or to any degree.**
11. Run a tight ship, having high standards and giving significant points for daily work, activities, and projects. Issue weekly grade printouts just as students would receive in academic classes. When students view the class as important to their overall education, disruptions become minimal.

Appendix xiii

Tips for Student Advisors and Other School Disciplinarians

1. Devise a plan for getting to know the student body, so that a good relationship can be established *before* a problem arises.

2. Visit each class, team, grade level, once per semester or marking period.

   Maintain an upbeat, informational and respectful tone, letting them know that they are great young people even though conflicts may arise. (Communication prior to behavioral conferences nets better cooperation, and students appreciate being aware of what to expect.)

   During initial class visitations include the following:
   ■ self-introduction with a piece of fun info e.g. favorite sport
   ■ information about your duties (nonthreatening manner)
   ■ kinds of problems or student issues handled
   ■ kinds of consequences that can be given

3. Create a kinder, gentler office environment. (You want students to experience tranquility, willingness to listen and learn.)
   ■ plants, classical music, academic deco e.g. books, artwork, maps
   ■ typed procedure to be explained or handed to a student, upon entering
   ■ comfortable seating
   ■ natural light, if possible

4. Follow the typed procedure. It helps to keep the situation calm and under control. e.g.
   ■ decriminalize, genuine self-esteem booster
   ■ description of the problem and reported behavior
   ■ listening segment (if the student has a different account)
   ■ precise replacement behavior
   ■ consequences

5. End each conference on a "can do" note.

Appendix xiv

Creating A Disciplined Environment
What Is Your Plan? (A Personal Worksheet-Elementary)

Directions:
Using this form as a guide, decide how you will handle each of the following, writing your determinations on the lines provided. Remember that rules are not needed for all, but a procedure preferably decided on by you, the instructor, before school begins or before the situation arises. Devising essential procedures can be the means by which an instructor ensures the attainment of a disciplined classroom environment.

Organize everything, and structure it for your teaching assignment. **This is for instructor use only, and can be modified as needed.**

1. monitors ______________________________
2. voting/student choice ______________________________
3. lining up ______________________________
4. assigning student seating ______________________________
5. movement within classroom (i.e. rdg. groups)__________________
6. bathroom procedure ______________________________
7. opening class procedure ______________________________
8. after lunch procedure ______________________________
9. leaving class for special events ______________________________
10. asking/ answering questions ______________________________
11. coming to chalkboard, etc. ______________________________
12. assigning projects fairly ______________________________
13. disseminating materials (e.g. manipulatives, etc.) _______________
14. student presentations
    a. audience rules (e.g. cleared desks) ______________________
    b. student speaker guidelines (e.g. posture, volume, eye contact, etc.) ____________

Creating A Disciplined Environment
What Is Your Plan? (A Personal Worksheet-Elementary) cont.

15. field trip behavior (Always have and give an educational purpose.)
    a. bus seating or guidelines ______________________________
    b. assignment responsibility ______________________________
    c. on site guidelines (state in positive language—Do vs. Don't)
    ("*Each of us will look at the speaker when he is speaking.*")
16. auditorium guidelines and return to classroom (Students transition much better when an independent activity is *ready and waiting* upon their return to class.) ______________________________
17. class films (educational, curriculum-based focus works best.)
    a. student seating ______________________________
    b. student accountability ______________________________
18. class games ______________________________
    a. choosing teams, etc. ______________________________
    b. winning/losing behavior ______________________________
19. coop groups (Don't wait for student mistakes!)
    a. choosing group members ______________________________
    b. group guidelines ______________________________
20. visitors to classroom: student guidelines ____________________
21. tardy to class
    a. entering procedure ______________________________
    b. getting into the flow ______________________________
22. absences: missed assignments retrieval process ______________
23. no materials to class
    a. obtaining necessities ______________________________
    b. pencils ______________________________

Appendix xv

Creating A Disciplined Environment
What Is Your Plan? (A Personal Worksheet-Secondary)

Directions:
Using this form as a guide, decide how you will handle each of the following, writing your determinations on the lines provided. Remember that rules are not needed for all, but a procedure preferably decided on by you, the instructor, before school begins or before the situation arises. Devising essential procedures can be the means by which an instructor ensures the attainment of a disciplined classroom environment.

Organize everything, and structure it for your teaching assignment. **This is for instructor use only, and can be modified as needed.**

1. assistants ____

2. voting/student choice ____________________________________

3. entering/leaving class ____________________________________
4. assigning student seating __________________________________

5. movement within classroom (groups, circles)__________________

6. bathroom: permission procedure ______________________________

7. opening class procedure ___________________________________

8. ending class procedure ____________________________________

9. leaving class for sp. events _________________________________

10. answering classroom questions _____________________________

11. student usage of overhead projector, etc.______________________

12. assigning projects fairly __________________________________

13. disseminating materials (e.g. novels, textbooks)_______________

14. student presentations
    a. audience rules (e.g. desks)_____________________________
    b. speaker guidelines (e.g. posture, volume, eye contact, etc.) _____

What Is Your Plan? (A Personal Worksheet-Secondary) cont.

15. field trip behavior (Always have and give an educational purpose.)
    a. bus seating or guidelines ______________________________
    b. assignment responsibility ______________________________
    c. on site guidelines (remember to state in positive language, (e.g. "*You will remain with the group the entire time, taking notes from the docent.*")
16. auditorium guidelines and classroom return procedure (Remember that students do much better when an independent activity is *ready and waiting* upon their return to class.) ______________________
17. class films (educational, curriculum-based focus works best)
    a. seating ______________________________
    b. student accountability ______________________________
18. class games
    a. choosing teams, etc. ______________________________
    b. winning/losing behavior ______________________________
19. coop groups (Don't wait for student mistakes!)
    a. choosing ______________________________
    b. group guidelines ______________________________
20. visitors to classroom ______________________________
21. tardy to class
    a. entering procedure ______________________________
    b. "getting into the flow" ______________________________
22. student absences
    a. makeup work process ______________________________
    b. grading consequences ______________________________
23. food ______________________________
24. CD players, cell phones, etc. ______________________________
25. return to locker, materials to class ______________________________
26. no materials to class
    a. obtaining necessities ______________________________
    b. consequences/student accountability (remember fairness and humanity)
    c. pencils

Appendix xvi

SAMPLE CLASSROOM RULES

- Raise your hand when you wish to speak. Wait to be recognized.
- Look at and listen to whomever is speaking without speaking yourself.
- Follow all classroom procedures.
- Just say, "okay!" when an adult asks you to do something. This is a "no complaining" classroom.
- Handle all classroom materials with care.
- Ask and receive permission before touching or using another student's property. Be mindful of others' personal space at all times.
- Use appropriate language.
- Stay positive and have fun learning!

Appendix xvii

Stop The Nonsense
Techniques That Work!

- OPENING CLASS ROUTINE PROCEDURE

- IMMEDIATE START ASSIGNMENT
  (SILENT TEACHER AND SILENT STUDENTS)

- TIGHT TRANSITIONS: Pass Out/Pick Up Materials As They Work

- DAILY OBJECTIVES AND AGENDA COMMUNICATED
  TO STUDENTS

- POINTS FOR EVERYTHING: (Practice, Notes, Discussion, etc.)

- ACTIVE STUDENT INVOLVEMENT: No Idle Sitting—Just Listening

- USE OF BOOKMARKS TO FOCUS STUDENT ATTENTION
  (text, graphs, maps, textbook questions, etc.)

- ATTACH A STUDENT'S NAME TO EACH QUESTION—
  100% Participation

- ENDING CLASS ROUTINE PROCEDURE
  a. Students Actively Involved (e.g. exit question)
  b. Organized and Calming

Appendix xviii

<u>What Can I Do Now To Improve Student Behavior?</u>
Tips For Instructors Whose Classes Have Already Become Challenging

- Create an academic classroom environment.
- Arrange student seating so that focus is on the instructor. Assign seats.
- Place teacher's desk BEHIND students.
- Have an assignment for students to do immediately upon entering the classroom, at all times.
- TOTAL Organization—Know what you are going to do and have materials ready.
- Use effective and fair teaching methods.
- Over plan so that there is no time for students to goof off.
- Have a classroom procedure for EVERYTHING.
- Plan lessons so that ALL students <u>must</u> participate throughout.
- Move around the room while teaching.
- Be consistent and fair with consequences.
- MODEL respectful behavior in your dealings with students, at all times.
- Establish HUMANE rules.
- Conduct private chats with problem students, right away, to reset standards.

Appendix xix

Classroom Management Strategy Checklist

The following are strategies which, if used in a timely fashion and/or on a consistent basis, can forestall or correct student misconduct problems. Check all that you are using or have tried for a substantial period of time. Incorporate the others into your overall management system.

___ immediate on task assignment with student accountability
___ beginning of class routine procedure
___ guided step by step instruction to prevent academic frustration
___ student accountability for each assignment
___ giving specific replacement behavior
___ forewarnings, no second chances
___ logical instruction to avoid confusion
___ direct requests to students
___ instructor movement during instruction
___follow-through on fair consequences
___ students feel welcome & appreciated on DAILY basis
___ tight, thorough lesson plans
___ timed student in-class practice activities
___ teacher's desk BEHIND students for better vigilance
___ structured/ organized teaching materials
___ bell to bell instruction
___ end of class routine procedure
___ daily instruction requiring 100% student participation
___ giving information & choice
___ assigned seating focused on instructor
___ student materials ready & plentiful
___ continual checks for comprehension throughout lesson
___ private chats with individuals to reset expectations
___ issuing fair consequences
___ smooth activity transitions no down time
___ varied learning activities
___ legal chatting, legal movement
___ high academic, behavioral expectations & standards
___ audio, visual, kinesthetic instructional lessons
___ positive parental contacts
____ weekly grade reports

Appendix xx

Achieving Effective Classroom Management
What Can School Administrators Do?

OBSERVE CLASSROOMS FOR THE FOLLOWING:

- academically rich environment—regarding students as serious students
- daily instruction that includes 3 major learning styles—
  auditory, visual, kinesthetic—every lesson
- instructional objective(s) displayed and communicated to students every lesson, every day
- instructional agenda displayed and communicated—
  setting academic tone
- calming, caring classroom atmosphere for students (no putdowns, threats, confrontations, sarcasm, negative stereotyping)
- assigned seating, humane rules, established procedures
- daily hands-on student activities, for increased interest and comprehension
- teaching vs. assigning
- interactive instruction, 100% student participation
- curriculum-based warm-up assignment beginning each class
- step by step teaching, modeling, lots of student practice
- established beginning and ending class routines
- well thought-out lesson plans—bell to bell
- high expectations and support for students

Appendix xxi

Succeed As A Substitute Teacher
Tips and Tools

I. Beginning A Job

A. Know the subject or position, or just say no.

B. Dress Professionally—Promotes Respect From Students

C. Arrive Early When Possible—REFUSE to be flustered and confused.

1. Figure out the lesson plans before students enter.
2. Touch base with other teachers for school rules and guidelines.
3. Prearrange assistance in case there's a situation you can't handle solo. (adjacent classroom, administrator, etc.)
4. LOCATE whatever is needed.
5. Know the route or entry procedure for elementary students.
6. Get EVERYTHING organized into YOUR OWN system.
7. Take chairs down BEFORE students enter.
8. Be RELAXED and CONFIDENT

II. Opening Class: TAKE CHARGE PLEASANTLY AND ENTHUSIASTICALLY

A. Greet and Direct Students e.g."*Good Morning, I'm Mr. Jones. Please look at the overhead projector, sit on the floor, start the word search on your desk,* "etc.)

AVOID REMAINING BEHIND THE TEACHER'S DESK AS STUDENTS ENTER. Greet from the door, but keep your eyes also on what is happening inside of the classroom.

B. Gather elementary students in a line outside of the classroom door and have them enter as one. DO THIS PLEASANTLY, with a SMILE. (e.g. *" Hi, we're going to all line up right here and go in together. I'm glad to be here and I'm glad that you're here!")* **This can also work for middle school.**

C. Display your name, PROMINENTLY—prevents the constant asking of who you are and whether or not you're the substitute teacher

D. Start the lesson – IMMEDIATELY (You can give them information *after* the initial assignment has been done and you're discussing it.)

Have it already on their desks. NOTE: If there is no warm-up assignment, *you* give one from your tool bag. **The goal is quick on task behavior**.

1. If they're hard to settle, IMMEDIATELY start it as a *guided* group lesson to get them going and WITH YOU.

2. Take SILENT attendance, using a seating chart or by passing around an attendance sheet for them to sign. (If needed, enlist aid from a cooperative student, **inconspicuously**.)

III. Classroom Management Tips

A. Welcome students, and **communicate** in a way that lets them know that you *like* them and expect nothing but the best from them.

B. Exude confidence

C. Keep students ACTIVELY involved—every single minute (You can decide HOW you will present the lesson plans.)

D. Give points for each segment of the lesson, a meaningful checkmark, stamp imprint, etc. (* Academic and behavioral incentives work and are important to children of all ages.) Know what is appropriate and avoid going overboard or being patronizing or disingenuous.)

E. Give information and choice.

F. Provide specific replacement behavior, when needed.

G. Avoid threats, overreactions, embellishments.

H. Speak calmly and respectfully, at all times.

I. Address all noncooperative behavior. Ignoring poor behavior allows it to spread. Use respectful assertiveness, no putdowns or sarcasm, and do so privately, when possible.

(e.g. "*Jon, please turn around and do the assignment. Thank you for being cooperative.*")

J. Address students by name, and require 100% participation by calling on each student. Provide help via clues & hints, for those in need.

K. MOVE around the classroom vs. remaining in the front of the room or behind the teacher's desk.
L. Avoid Power Struggles: When students comment that their teacher doesn't do something a certain way, just say *"I know and I understand that you are accustomed to doing it that way, but just for today we'll do it this way. I appreciate you helping me out."*
M. Be willing to help students who are confused.

IV. Tool Kit:
Bring these or other items with you to each assignment, to help smooth rough edges.

A. sharpened pencils, labeled for easy recognition (Avoid insulting students by giving them putt-putt golf pencils, nubs, colored pencils, crayons, etc.) Also, avoid requesting articles of clothing or valuables. Writing names on the board under " borrowed pencils," works well.

B. Timer (for timing and signaling the end of student activities)

C. grade/subject appropriate worksheets for warm-up assignment or early finishers (Purchasing a word search or brain teaser booklet is an expense worth its weight in gold.)

D. lotion

E. tissues

D& E (above) wouldn't necessarily be displayed, but could come in handy with a student who insists he/she has a need. Models Graciousness

F. paper for attendance lists

G. Something fun: e.g. stickers for end of day or period, puppet, fun/ interesting artifact, critical thinking cards, academic bingo game, etc. (Any items used should be age appropriate, and can aid in getting students going, first thing, or refocusing them for an orderly exit.) Raid your or your children's old toy box. ☺

Appendix xxii

Avoid Judging By Labels

Following is a list of common terms many teachers, administrators, and other school personnel apply to individuals or groups of students. I submit that the use of such creates problems in the thinking of those who use and believe them, passing along negative vibes to students, subsequently propelling countless students toward disruptive behavior.

1. Wannabe
2. Lazy
3. Jock
4. Immature
5. "Don't Care"
6. Gangster/Thug
7. Spoiled
8. At Risk
9. Special Ed.
10. Inner City
11. Urban vs. Suburban
12. Slow Learner
13. Streetwise
14. Punker
15. Girl
16. Boy
17. Race
18. Religion
19. Parent's Career
20. Single Parent Home
21. Tough vs. Confident
22. Hyper vs. Enthusiastic
23. Loudmouth vs. Assertive
24. Withdrawn vs. Pensive

Appendix xxiii

Discipline Vs. Punishment

The business of guiding students toward their best selves requires that the adults in the environment employ prudent disciplinary techniques. However, there are those who would seek to punish. There is a difference. Consider.

DISCIPLINE

- INSTRUCTIVE
- GUIDANCE
- ENLIGHTEN
- PREPARE
- NOT ANGRY
- OPTIMISTIC
- REHABILITATIVE
- PERSISTENT
- CONSISTENT
- GRACIOUS/UNDERSTANDING
- DEVELOPMENTAL
- PATIENT
- BUILDS RELATIONSHIPS

PUNISHMENT

- ANGRY
- VENGEFUL
- INFLICT A PENALTY
- HARSH/HANDLE ROUGHLY
- PESSIMISTIC
- TOXIC
- DISPROPORTIONATE
- CASTIGATE/LAMBASTE
- ADVERSARIAL/ DESTROYS RELATIONSHIPS

Order Form

Classroom Discipline Made Easy: A System That Works for the Inner City or Any City, Second Edition, Revised and Expanded By Doris E. Dempsey

Fax or Phone Orders: (303)574-0785
Mail Orders: Deck Publishing, P.O. Box 390024, Denver, CO 80239

Please send_______ copies of the book, Classroom Discipline Made Easy: A System That Works for the Inner City or Any City Second Edition, Revised and Expanded at the price of $19.95 US per book, for a total of...$______

Add Shipping and Handling:..$______
(U.S. and Canada $3.95 for one, add $2.00 for each additional book)

Colorado Orders add sales tax: 7.6%.................................$______

TOTAL ....$______

Enclosed is my check or money order for $________ US
Checks made payable to Deck Publishing
NO CASH OR CREDIT CARDS PLEASE.

Shipping Address - Please Print Clearly

____

Your Name (first and last):

____

Address:

____

City, State/Province:

____

Zip Code:

____

Telephone/Fax

Notes

Notes

Notes

Notes

Notes

Notes